How We Live

Victor R. Fuchs

HOW
WE
LIVE

Harvard University Press
Cambridge, Massachusetts
and London, England

Library of Congress Cataloging in Publication Data

Fuchs, Victor Robert, 1924–
How we live.

Bibliography: p.
Includes index.
1. United States — Economic conditions — 1945 –
2. United States — Social conditions — 1945 –
3. Choice (Psychology)   4. Social choice.
5. Family — United States.   I. Title.
HC106.5.F8   1983   302′.13   82-21180
ISBN 0-674-41225-7 (cloth)
ISBN 0-674-41226-5 (paper)

To my colleagues at the National Bureau of Economic Research during the past twenty years. Their work has pointed the way toward a fuller understanding of human behavior and social institutions.

Acknowledgments

As I grow older, I become more keenly aware of the roles that others have played in determining what I know, what I am, and what I am able to do. This book is a prime example. Its completion depended upon help from many people in many different ways, and I am pleased to acknowledge their contributions.

As an economist who believes that behavior is strongly influenced by external circumstances, I think it appropriate to begin by thanking the Andrew W. Mellon Foundation and its president, John E. Sawyer, for financial support and encouragement. Their grant made it possible for me to reduce my teaching commitments in 1981–82 and to devote most of my time to writing this book. In the same vein I also want to express appreciation to the Robert Wood Johnson Foundation for their generous support of my research in health economics over many years. Out of this research came a greater appreciation of the interactions between health and other important aspects of life such as family, work, and education — interactions that are discussed extensively in this book. Grants from the Carnegie Corporation of New York and the Russell Sage Foundation in 1978–79 helped me begin work on two of the book's subjects: the problems of children and the labor force behavior of older men. A fellowship at the Center for Advanced Study in the Behavioral Sciences during that same year provided a splendid setting in which to begin thinking about the economics of the life cycle.

During the past twenty years many scholars at the National Bureau of Economic Research have had a significant influence on my approach to economic and social problems. This book in particular builds on the pioneering contributions of Gary S. Becker, whose work on human capital, the value of time, and family economics stimulated much of my own research and provided a theoretical framework for several related projects directed by our NBER colleagues. I am grateful to them for their efforts, and I also want to thank the presidents and directors of research of the NBER for encouraging my application of economics to a wide range of social problems.

Several friends and academic colleagues reviewed a preliminary draft of the entire manuscript and made many helpful suggestions concerning organization, style, and content. I am particularly grateful to Gary Becker, Andrew Cherlin, Joel Cohen, Sanford Dornbusch, Alain Enthoven, Rosemary Enthoven, Beverly Fuchs, Lawrence Fuchs, Alan Garber, Michael Grossman, John Kaplan, Marian Kessler, Richard Kessler, Frank Levy, Robert Michael, and Michael Wald for their detailed comments. For very useful advice on specific subjects or selected chapters I am happy to thank Kenneth Cone, Paula Fuchs, Nancy Fuchs-Kreimer, Seth Kreimer, Walter Oi, and John Sawyer.

Special thanks are due two people who worked very closely with me on this book from beginning to end. My secretary, Claire Gilchrist, skillfully and cheerfully typed numerous revisions of the manuscript, kept a watchful eye on the administrative details of the project, and made sure that the rest of my professional life ran smoothly. My research assistant, Leslie Goodman Perreault, did an outstanding job of preparing the data and references, as well as providing valuable editorial comments. I am also grateful to Phillip Farrell, a former research assistant, who helped with several of the statistical analyses.

Michael Aronson, general editor at Harvard University Press, worked empathically and diligently with me at all stages from first draft through publication. He provided many constructive editorial suggestions along with unflagging enthusiasm. Maria Kawecki copy-edited the manuscript with great care and insight.

Much of this book is about family, a topic that is difficult for any scholar to treat in a completely detached manner. I have tried to approach the data objectively, but my interpretations and judgments concerning the importance of family are undoubtedly influenced by my own fortunate experiences. I was blessed with loving parents who gave generously of themselves for my benefit. My brother was my closest companion throughout childhood, and a loyal friend since then. And throughout my life I have received much affection and guidance from grandparents, aunts, uncles, in-laws, and other relatives. For the past thirty-four years my wife has been at the center of my life. Capable, enthusiastic, loving — she has nurtured our family and my career while pursuing her own. "Her works praise her in the gates." Our children and their spouses have added another dimension of love and understanding and each of them has taught me a great deal, not only by sharing with me their own specialized knowledge, but also by providing windows into the next generation.

Despite the best efforts of family, colleagues, and friends, some errors and omissions probably remain; they are, of course, my responsibility. I do not expect them to be overlooked, but ask readers to note that the emphasis of this book is on synthesis and perspective. In seeking to serve the needs of a wide audience I have given greatest weight to achieving clarity, balance, and insight, and I hope that the book will be received in that spirit.

Contents

How We Live

1

The Economic

Perspective

*When the sentimentalist and the
moralist fails, he will have as a
last resource to call in the aid
of the economist.*
—*Sir Edwin Chadwick*

THIS IS A BOOK ABOUT CHOICES — the choices we make for ourselves, those that are made for us, and those that we make for
others. It examines the choices we make in our private lives and
also the ones we make collectively as citizens and voters. Through
these choices — especially those concerning family, work, health,
and education — we are constantly defining and redefining American society; that is, we are determining "how we live."

The raw statistics of recent decades suggest that Americans
have been caught up in a whirlpool of social change. For example:

In 1950 only 12 percent of married women with children under
six years of age were wage earners; by 1980 the proportion had
soared to 45 percent.

In 1960 5 percent of all births were to unmarried women,
but in 1980 the proportion was 18 percent.

In 1970 only 11 percent of women ages 25 – 29 had never been married, but in 1980 this was true of 21 percent.

The proportion of adults living alone almost tripled, from 4 percent to 11 percent, between 1950 and 1980.

Among men sixty-five and over, the proportion in the labor force fell by more than half, from 46 percent to 19 percent, between 1950 and 1980.

How are we to make sense of these radical alterations in our social fabric? How can we use the masses of data assembled by the Bureau of the Census, the Bureau of Labor Statistics, the National Center for Health Statistics, and other agencies to get some understanding of *why* things are happening, as well as what is happening? This is not purely an intellectual exercise, fascinating as that might be. We need this understanding because inevitably we all face decisions concerning these phenomena. We must make decisions as family members and breadwinners and as partici- pants in community organizations. Many of us also give advice in these areas as physicians, lawyers, teachers, social workers, clergy, and other professionals. Business executives need to be familiar with these trends in order to adapt goods and services to changing markets and to develop new personnel policies more appropriate to emerging life styles. And officials in the legislative, executive, and judicial branches of government constantly face difficult choices in these areas. Clearly, a deeper understanding of the changes that have occurred over time as well as of current intergroup differences in behavior can contribute to better private choices and more effective public policies.

The principal purpose of this book is to provide a perspective on American life — an *economic* perspective. The phenomena that it deals with are not solely economic, and economics alone cannot provide a complete explanation of them. They all have an economic dimension, however, and can be more fully understood when approached from an economic point of view. In the follow- ing chapters we will look at the significant changes that have occurred since World War II in family life, work, health, and education. The book synthesizes recent research in these areas, drawing on the results of my colleagues at the National Bureau of

Economic Research, other social scientists, and my own studies in health and labor economics. I will also identify and discuss major public policy issues that affect men and women at various stages of the life cycle from birth to death.

As we consider each stage of life, many subjects are presented in varying degrees of detail. A few themes, however, appear in almost every chapter. Probably the most central is the usefulness of viewing broad national trends as the result of choices made by individuals in response to changes in their *external circumstances.* These changes may involve a rise or fall in income or changes in the prices of goods and services; they may be technological, such as improvements in contraception; or they may be demographic, such as increases in life expectancy. Economics provides a relatively simple and broadly applicable method of analyzing the way in which circumstances affect choices. It is, therefore, a powerful tool for building an understanding of changes in human behavior and social institutions.

A second major theme emphasizes the *interrelatedness* of choices. Decisions made in one area, such as the family, frequently have significant implications for other areas, such as work or health. There are also important connections between choices at different stages of life: schooling decisions affect future earnings, choices about smoking affect future health, and work when young affects work opportunities later in life. An understanding of the interrelatedness of life's stages is particularly important in framing public policies. Policies aimed at behavior at a given stage can affect behavior not only at that stage but later in life and, if anticipated, at earlier stages as well. We will also see how programs undertaken for one purpose, such as aid to disadvantaged children, can have other consequences, such as increases in divorce and in births to unwed mothers.

Within this framework of inescapable, interrelated choices, the data examined in this book lead to three other themes: "the fading family," "demography and destiny," and "wanting and waiting." Several recent studies (such as Caplow et al. 1982) claim that the family is as strong as ever; but such claims lack credibility when, as we shall see, the birth rate has been below replacement level for a decade, when almost 25 percent of children live in one-parent or no-parent households, when two out of five marriages end in divorce, and when most of the elderly depend on the government for their daily sustenance. My reading of the data leads to a more troubled conclusion about American families. In describing the decline in importance of the conjugal family, however, I am not predicting its disappearance; neither am I denying others the right to redefine the term "family" as they wish. But there is overwhelming evidence that individuals rely less on their families today than in the past for the production of goods and services and as a source of financial and psychological support in time of need.

The "demography and destiny" theme refers to the way changes in demographic variables such as fertility and mortality transform the circumstances facing individuals, thereby altering the nation's social and economic course. Family size and life expectancy are two of the variables whose consequences we will examine in detail. The timing of birth is also important: men and women who reached adulthood during the Great Depression made decisions very different from those of youth who entered adulthood during World War II or the peacetime prosperity of the 1950s. Economist Richard Easterlin (1980) has emphasized that even variations in the *number* of young people reaching maturity can result in systematic differences in life cycle behavior.

The theme of "wanting and waiting" concerns the importance of delay of gratification, or time discount, in shaping the way we live. Almost every choice discussed in this book, whether pertaining to fertility, schooling, health, occupation, or other areas of life, involves comparisons between present and future costs and benefits. The willingness and ability of individuals to invest in the future, to forgo present wants and to wait for future benefits, have major consequences for their own lives, for the lives of their children, and for society as a whole.

The last major theme concerns the conflicts and dilemmas that face public policy makers — the impossibility of reconciling all worthwhile social goals. These conflicts arise between highly valued goals such as efficiency and justice, and between different groups such as young and old. The distinction between allocative efficiency and distributive justice receives particular attention throughout the book. Economics has a great deal to say about the former, but the justice of any particular distribution of income cannot be established by economics. All public policies, whether they concern children or the elderly, health or education, work or family life, have effects on both efficiency and justice. The economic perspective can help clarify those effects, even though it cannot provide the final answers. These must come from our *values* — from our vision of the kind of society we want to shape for ourselves and for future generations.

In developing these themes the book presents many numbers, but no more than are necessary to help the reader understand and remember the points that are being made. "The office of the scholar," said Ralph Waldo Emerson, "is . . . to guide men by showing them facts amidst appearances." Numbers serve to discipline rhetoric. Without them it is too easy for a writer — or a reader — to follow flights of fancy, to ignore the world as it is, and to "remold it nearer to the heart's desire."

This is not to say that numbers speak for themselves. Interpretations must be made, and, given the imperfections of theory and data, some scholarly disagreement about them is inevitable. For most questions about family, work, health, and education, I try to alert the reader to alternative interpretations and to indicate the degree of confidence warranted for the explanation under discussion. Thus the book offers less certainty than some would like, but does not shy away from making judgments, even when the basis for judgment is incomplete.

Despite the scope of the book, certain questions have been excluded. For instance, the causes of *economic growth* are not considered, although *it* is the basic cause of most of the phenomena under discussion. Neither does the book attempt to explain *cultural differences* in values, important though such differences may be in shaping behavior. Finally, no effort is made to explain *individual differences*. The contribution that economics makes to the understanding of human behavior is at the level of populations, not individuals. Its principal object is to explain or predict the behavior of aggregates or averages and to draw conclusions that are true in general, even though it is always possible to think of individual exceptions.

This is not a textbook in economics; but because many readers are unaccustomed to looking at problems from an economic point of view, the next section introduces the economic perspective. The six subsequent chapters develop this perspective in the context of the *life cycle,* a constant of human existence. Institutions may change, empires may rise and fall, and entire civilizations may crumble; but everyone is born, most people mature, wed, and have children, and all eventually die.

The social and economic details of the life cycle vary, however. In particular, the age at which various transitions take place has changed over time and differs among groups at any given time. Some transitions of great interest are the ages of entering and leaving the labor force, the age of parenthood, and the age of death. In this book the life cycle is divided into six stages: birth and infancy, childhood, adolescence and youth, young adulthood, middle age, and old age. Each chapter identifies major choices for persons of that age, describes long-run trends and cyclical variations, analyzes behavior, and discusses public policy issues. Although the approach is similar throughout, the substantive emphasis varies, depending upon which subjects are most salient at different ages — education for the young, for example, or health for the old.

The concluding chapter summarizes the major themes and makes explicit my own views about policy. It offers some recommendations concerning social security, health insurance, child care, births to unwed mothers, and youth unemployment, although these specific recommendations are not central to the major objectives of the book. My primary aim is not to gain agreement with my judgments and values, but to provide readers with a clearer view of the facts, a fuller understanding of relationships between behavior and external circumstances, and a deeper insight into the issues and dilemmas of public policy.

THE ECONOMIC PERSPECTIVE

Economics is the science which studies human behavior as a relationship between ends and scarce means which have alternative uses.
—*Lionel Robbins*

Life, for most people, is not so much "a bowl of cherries" as a succession of difficult decisions. Consider a typical young woman entering her senior year in high school. During the years ahead she will have to make many important choices. Stay in school, or enter the labor market? Where to live? Marriage? When and with whom? Children? When and how many? How much labor force participation? How much work at home? And there are other choices, such as those concerning smoking and alcohol, that can profoundly affect her life and the lives of those close to her.

To say that this young woman will make choices is not to say that these choices are *unconstrained*. Unless she has great mathematical aptitude, a career as a theoretical physicist is not, for all practical purposes, a choice that is open to her. Similarly, it is not realistic for her five-foot six-inch brother to aspire to be a professional basketball player. The fact that choices are constrained, however, does not mean that all choice is eliminated. Individuals still choose, but within their constraints.

A constraint of critical importance for most people is wealth, or income — two alternative ways of describing a person's command over material resources. Many choices are significantly affected by wealth, either the individual's or the family's, and there are other important resource constraints as well. Even the wealthiest person's behavior is limited by the fact that there are only twenty-four hours in a day — that is, by the constraint of time (Becker 1965; Linder 1970). The analysis of choice within a framework of constraints is what economics is all about.

The economic perspective assumes that resources are scarce relative to human wants, that these resources have alternative uses, and that people have diverse wants, not all of which can be satisfied. It follows that the basic economic problem of every society, and of every individual, is to allocate resources so as to best satisfy wants.

When thinking about questions from this perspective, there are five useful maxims to keep in mind:

1. *There is no free lunch.* This maxim does *not* deny the existence of altruism, but underscores the importance of the idea of *alternative cost.* Someone may provide a lunch that is free to *you,* but to the extent that the lunch requires labor, raw materials, and other scarce resources (and every lunch does), there is a cost to someone. A good measure of that cost is the value of the best alternative use of those resources — as the poet Robert Frost said, "the road not taken."

2. *There is more than one way to skin a cat.* This maxim reminds us that in most situations there *is* an alternative road; there is a choice. It also serves as a reminder that the "best" choice is not something to be decided only on the basis of scientific or technological data. These data are useful, indeed necessary, but they are not sufficient. A rational choice must relate the cause-and-effect information that science provides to the *values* that come from the preferences of the decision maker. For instance, science may be able to tell us how much pollution results from burning a certain quantity and quality of fuel, what the physical and biological consequences are likely to be, and what the cost will be of achieving alternative levels of pollution. What science *cannot* do is determine the optimal level of pollution; that depends on the values we assign to the consequences of alternative courses of action.

3. *Nature doesn't make leaps.* This maxim, a favorite of the great British economist Alfred Marshall, reminds us that most choices are made along a continuum — they're questions of "more" or "less." For instance, the decision about pollution will rarely be one of "yes" or "no" but rather "how much." Even questions that must be answered "yes" or "no" by the individual (to marry or not; to retire or not) can be analyzed as continuous phenomena when studying the behavior of populations (the marriage rate; the retirement rate).

4. *There can be too much of a good thing.* This warns us that there actually can be too much medical care, too much education, too much of many things that are clearly desirable and useful. We

have too much of a good thing when it is pushed to the point where the cost (the alternative forgone) is greater than the benefit it confers. The quintessential element in the economic perspective is the idea of equality at the *margin* — that is, balancing the costs and benefits of the incremental or last unit of whatever is being evaluated. When choices are made along a continuum, the optimal level will be where the benefit of a small increment (the marginal benefit) is exactly equal to its cost. Beyond that level, costs usually rise faster than benefits; short of that level, benefits increase more rapidly than costs.

5. *Time is money (or its equivalent)*. This maxim is relevant to the subjects discussed in this book in two ways. First, it reminds us that frequently an important part of the cost of some activity is the time spent doing it. For instance, the full cost of a meal prepared at home must include the value of the time spent shopping and cooking, as well as the money cost of the ingredients. Second, the maxim reminds us that when the cost or benefit of some activity will be realized in the *future,* a rate of time discount (or rate of return or interest rate) must be applied to obtain the *present value* of that cost or benefit. For instance, if two alternative occupations yield the same total earnings over a lifetime, but one of them pays more earlier in life, it will have a greater present value than the one that pays later because it affords an opportunity to earn interest on the differential earnings in hand. When alternative courses of action involve costs and benefits that occur at different times, rational decision making requires comparison of the present value of those costs and benefits. Sometimes both applications of the maxim will be relevant in analyzing a single activity, as in deciding whether to go to school now in order to increase earnings later in life. The current cost includes not only tuition, but also the value of the time spent in study. Because the benefits will be realized only in the future, a rate of time discount must be applied so that they can be compared to costs in terms of present value.

The economic way of thinking about problems stands in sharp contrast to two other points of view, which I have labeled the romantic and the monotechnic (Fuchs 1974a). The romantic point of view denies the existence of scarcity or blames it on some convenient scapegoat such as communism, capitalism, unions, advertising, or defense spending. Unfortunately, the problem of scarcity cannot be solved by denying its existence. For all our affluence, we still live in a world where our wants exceed our ability to fulfill them, and, so far as anyone can see, we always will. The necessity for choice is part of what it means to be human. The monotechnic point of view acknowledges scarcity, but seeks an optimal solution as defined by a particular technology. This approach denies a role for the values of those who must bear the costs. For instance, a specialist in medicine (or in education) might understandably want to provide as much medical care (or schooling) as is technically possible, even though the resources required would be more valuable in some other use.

Helpful as it is, the economic perspective is only a partial one because people face problems other than scarcity. For instance, there is the problem of peace and order, both in the community and in relations with other countries. There are problems of learning, of socialization, and of human relations. Finally, there are problems of meaning, ethics, and aesthetics. The diversity of human problems makes clear the importance of many ap-proaches — political, sociological, psychological, philosophical, religious, and others. To avoid falling into a monotechnic fallacy of economics, we must remember that scarcity is only one aspect of the human condition. Economists are trained to deal with questions of scarcity, but we must not assume that scarcity is the only problem and that the most efficient use of resources is the only goal.

In applying the economic perspective to behavior over the life cycle, it is usually appropriate to adopt a *universalist* view of humanity — a view that emphasizes the similarity of human experience across eras, continents, and individuals. Birth and death, the beginning and the end of each human life, are the same regardless of how varied are the years in between. From biology and psychology come many insights about developmental pro-cesses that are experienced by all or nearly all individuals. Moreover, every society needs a system for the mating of adults of childbearing age, a system for caring for helpless infants, a system for educating and socializing the young, and a system for producing and distributing goods and services.

Opposed to universalism is the *particularist* view, which emphasizes the uniqueness of every human being and the features of life cycle development special to each cohort — that is, each set of people born in a given period within the same society. There is much to be said for such a view. No two human beings are exactly alike; even twins have different fingerprints. Not only do individuals vary, but there are differences among societies and among cohorts in the same society.

Preoccupation with the particularist view, however, limits analysis of the questions pursued in this book because it is relatively devoid of theoretical content. It warns us that each individual is different, but awareness of differences alone does not provide a general guide to understanding behavior. The economic point of view attempts to provide such understanding. It assumes that people are basically alike in the sense that they share similar drives and goals. If we observe different cohorts, or different groups within the same cohort behaving differently, economic theory suggests where to look for explanations. Such suggestions are not always helpful because economic theory is far from perfect, but it does provide a systematic *framework* for analyzing behavior.

To say that economic theory provides a framework rather than precise predictions is not to damn it with faint praise. Darwin's theory of natural selection, long regarded as one of the great scientific insights of all time, does not provide precise theoretical predictions either. It, too, is a loose theory, a framework that helps us think about and describe important phenomena. Finally, it should be emphasized that our focus here is on American society in the second half of the twentieth century. We do not need to face the question of how well the universalist assumption would hold if we were simultaneously trying to explain behavior in classical Athens, medieval England, and the contemporary Kalihari desert.

With these qualifications in mind, we can return to the economic perspective and look at its most important application — the market paradigm.

THE MARKET PARADIGM

The combined assumptions of maximizing behavior, market equilibrium, and stable preferences, used relentlessly and unflinchingly, form the heart of the economic approach. —Gary S. Becker

Ever since Adam Smith, economists have devoted a great deal of thought and effort to gaining a better understanding of how markets work. Much of the power of economics is rooted in the fact that a single set of assumptions and a single set of analytical concepts (demand, supply, price, quantity) have proven useful in explaining behavior in such diverse settings as commodity markets, labor markets, foreign exchange markets, and so on. In recent years, economists led by Gary Becker (1964, 1976, 1981) have been using the market paradigm to obtain new insights about many so-called nonmarket phenomena such as marriage, divorce, fertility, health, education, and crime. The central features of this paradigm are as follows.

1. People are constantly confronted with the necessity of making choices — as consumers, workers, investors, parents, and in many other roles.

2. In making these choices, they try to do the best they can, given the constraints they face — constraints of money, time, energy, and information.

3. Their choices are influenced by relative "prices" — using this term in its broadest sense to include not only money costs but time costs, psychic costs, alternative costs, and others.

4. Their choices may also be influenced by a host of other factors, such as religion, social class, physical and psychological needs, and external pressures. When we observe large-scale, systematic changes in behavior, however, a sensible research strategy is to look first to see if there have been changes in the constraints or in relative prices.

The applicability of this paradigm to consumer behavior in

supermarkets is readily evident. Shoppers are influenced by many taste factors that have their origins in culture, climate, biology, and so on. If these factors are held constant, however (by abstracting from them or assuming that they have not changed), we can see that consumer choices are determined by *income* and by the *prices* of the commodities themselves. A rise in income (prices and other things remaining the same) will sharply increase the demand for filet mignon and other luxuries; a decline in income will have the reverse effect. How large the change will be for each commodity depends upon its *income elasticity* of demand — the percent change in the quantity demanded divided by the percent change in income.

Now let's keep income the same and vary prices. Suppose that a frost in Brazil cuts the coffee crop in half and sends the price of coffee up in the supermarket. Again, we will see a response, though not necessarily by every consumer. The quantity of coffee put into shopping carts is likely to decline, while the quantity of tea, cocoa, and other substitutes is likely to rise. Purchases of some other goods, such as cream, that are used with coffee — called complementary goods — might decline. How much effect a price change will have depends upon the *price elasticity* of demand — that is, the percent change in the quantity demanded divided by the percent change in price.

These concepts are usually used by economists to analyze market choices, but in this book they are mostly used to analyze behavior outside conventional markets. What role has income played in increasing the proportion of adults who live alone? How has the birth rate been affected by a decrease in the cost (primarily psychic) of birth control through the introduction of the pill and intrauterine devices? Why do men now retire from work at a much younger age than they did thirty years ago? As constraints change, or as prices change, it is not surprising that people's nonmarket behavior changes, much as their behavior in the supermarket does.

It would be foolish to claim that income and price are the only things that ever affect social behavior. Decisions about fertility, marriage, living arrangements, health, and the like are affected by other factors, just as the amount of coffee demanded also depends upon one's taste for coffee, the weather, one's sleeping habits, and so on. Moreover, there may be irrational, subconscious forces at work that conflict with the model of a rational decision maker who is trying to maximize his or her well-being. The economic perspective does not assert that these other factors and forces are never present. It simply says that it is useful to analyze the effects of changes in constraints and prices under the assumption that the other factors are constant. Sometimes this is a reasonable assumption; sometimes it is not. To the extent that we know about changes in the other variables, we can try to control for them. For instance, in studying the influence of income and price on the demand for medical care, it is possible to take into account changes in health which we know also affect this demand.

Without an economic perspective, changes in household living arrangements, fertility, and other social phenomena are often automatically attributed to changing "norms" (or "preferences" or "attitudes"). A more careful examination, however, might reveal that the changes are the result of shifts in income or prices within a stable set of preferences. The distinction is more than a semantic one; a clearer description of what is happening facilitates clearer thinking about causes and consequences. After all, when we observe people buying more filet mignon in response to rising income, or when we see a decrease in the quantity of coffee demanded as a result of an increase in its price, it is neither accurate nor helpful to say that people's "preferences" for filet mignon or coffee have changed.

One further point helps clarify the economic approach to understanding behavior. Economists, as a rule, are not concerned with the internal thought processes of the decision maker or in the rationalizations that the decision maker offers to explain his or her behavior. Economists believe that what people *do* is more relevant than what they say. The novelist I. B. Singer epitomizes this point of view in a story he tells about a boy who came to the *cheder* (Hebrew school) where Singer studied. The boy said, "My father wanted to box my ears." The teacher said, "How do you know that?" The boy replied, "He did it."

2

Every Night and Every Morn

Birth and Infancy

Every night and every morn
Some to misery are born;
Every morn and every night
Some are born to sweet delight.
— *William Blake*

OF ALL THE LIFE CHOICES men and women make, none is more important for society, none has more far-reaching consequences, none represents a more complete blending of economic, social, biological, and emotional forces than the decision to bring another life into the world. For an individual, the timing and circumstances of birth significantly affect the character, quality, and duration of life. For a society, the birth rate is a major determinant of its economic, political, and social development. Let the rate exceed society's capacity to provide the necessities of life, and the outcome will be the poverty and misery so graphically described by Thomas Malthus. Let the rate fall below the replacement ratio, and the society is on its way to extinction.

U.S. fertility is now only one-fourth of what it was in 1800 and has been below replacement level since 1973. We will examine the long-term downward trend in the light of changes in the costs and benefits of children and changes in the cost of preventing births. The economic perspective will also help us understand why the number of births per thousand women of childbearing age rose by 67 percent from 1936 to 1957 and then fell by 55 percent during the following two decades.

Once a baby is born, the paramount question has traditionally been "Will it survive?" For most of human history the life cycle for many has been extremely brief—birth, followed quickly by death. Under primitive conditions it is not unusual for half of all newborns to die before the age of one, and prior to the Industrial Revolution even so favored a group as Europe's royalty experienced infant mortality of over 200 per thousand live births. Now the U.S. rate is approaching 10 per thousand and even in families designated as living in poverty the rate is probably under 20. Widespread interest in infant mortality arises not only from its emotional impact but also because it is an indicator of economic and social conditions. The decline in the *average* rate has been accompanied by a considerable reduction in *inequality* of infant survival probabilities across groups, except for the black-white differential. The major proximate cause of the race differential and of infant mortality in general is low birth weight—that is, birth weight less than 2,500 grams (five pounds eight ounces), the standard set by the World Health Organization. Many observers ascribe differences in birth weight to income, education, and prenatal care, but as we will see, there are several reasons for doubting these explanations.

In addition to describing and analyzing variations in fertility and infant mortality, this chapter addresses the causes and consequences of major changes in the circumstances of birth, especially those relating to cohort size and birth order, and the age, education, and marital status of the mother. It concludes with a discussion of public policy issues concerning fertility and infant mortality that may become important in the next decade.

FERTILITY

The birth rates of nonhuman species are determined by biological drives and capacities. Humans are different. In most societies there are systematic attempts to influence fertility through formal or informal controls over sexual practices and age of marriage. In modern society the decision to have a baby is frequently as deliberate and as calculated as the decision to attend graduate school, buy a house, or move to a new state. Differences in fertility among nations, among groups within the same nation, and over time within groups have broad implications for education, health care, labor markets, standards of living — indeed the entire society. The ability to predict changes in fertility would be extremely valuable, but neither economics nor any other discipline has been able to do so consistently in the past. The economic perspective, however, does provide some helpful insights into this crucial aspect of how we live.

The Long-term Trend

Over the long term the general fertility rate (the number of births per thousand women ages 15 – 44) has moved sharply downward.* Between 1800 and 1910 the rate fell by more than half, and between 1910 and 1980 it again fell by half. Most economists believe that this long-term downward trend, which has its counterpart in all economically developed countries, can be explained by three types of changes: a decrease in the benefits to parents from having children, an increase in the costs of having children, and a decrease in the costs of avoiding having children — that is, the costs of birth control (Willis 1973).

The benefits of children are many and varied. For most parents children are a source of pride and delight, a link with the future, an object and a source of love and affection. In agricultural societies children are often valued for their contribution to production; in that sense the demand for them is analogous to the demand for

---

* The general fertility rate is a more useful measure of fertility than the better known crude birth rate (number of births per one thousand population) because it allows for changes in the number of women of childbearing age as a proportion of the population.

farm machinery.* Moreover, in societies that lack banks, insurance companies, and other financial institutions, investment in children is a principal method of providing for the future (Willis 1980).

Industrialization substantially reduced the economic benefits of children. Economic development shifted the locus of work from the farm to the city and raised the age at which children began work, thus making them less valuable to parents as a source of production and income. Growing opportunities for accumulating savings in banks, securities, and annuities virtually eliminated the need for children as a method of saving. And the expanding role of government in providing retirement benefits, health insurance, unemployment insurance, and other social programs diminished the importance of having *one's own* children as a source of insurance later in life, even though society as a whole depends upon future generations to pay the retirement benefits of the preceding ones.

While the economic benefits of children have been decreasing, the costs of raising them have been increasing. Some of this increase is associated with the shift from rural to urban life, a shift that caused more than proportionate increases in the prices of housing and food. However, the prices of some services (adjusted for quality), such as education and medical care, are probably lower in urban than in rural settings. Thus, as the period of child-rearing has lengthened and expenditures for human services have become more important relative to bare necessities, rural birth rates have followed urban rates in their downward course.

Traditionally, one of the largest costs of child-rearing has been the time spent by the mother. A good measure of the alternative cost of this time is what the mother could earn if she held a paying job. Thus, the long-term rise in women's earnings has increased the "price" of children, and at any given time the price is higher for better-educated women because they have higher potential

---

* In traditional agricultural societies infant and child death rates are usually higher for females than for males, probably because males are viewed as more productive assets and are given better care.

earnings. Better-educated women tend to have fewer children, and, if husband's schooling is held constant, the negative effect of wife's education on fertility is even more pronounced (Sanderson and Willis 1971).

In cross-sectional studies at a given point in time, fertility tends to be higher the higher the husband's education (holding wife's education constant) because of the positive relation between his education and family income. Over time, however, rising income also raises the "price" of children because expenditures per child are closely tied to the income and living standards of the parents. This rise in "price" may result in a decrease in the *number* of children demanded, even though *total expenditures* on children (number times expenditures per child) usually rise as income rises (Becker and Lewis 1973).

The effect on the demand for children of falling benefits and rising costs has been augmented by a third set of factors: changes in the costs of birth control. Not every couple have exactly the number of children that they ideally would want if that number could be controlled at zero cost. Some parents have fewer than they would like (because of infertility), but historically there have been many more children born than would have been if birth control were costless and perfect. As a result of technological improvements in contraception, weakening or changing religious views that affect the psychic costs of averting birth, and the legalization of abortion, the costs of averting birth have declined substantially in recent years. Most women come closer now than in the past to having the number of children they ideally would want.

The experience of Romania in the 1960s and 1970s provides a dramatic example of how fertility is affected by changes in the cost of averting births. During the first half of the 1960s the Romanian fertility rate was only about 60 per thousand women ages 15–44, and reached a low of 56 per thousand in 1966. The Romanian authorities became alarmed because the rate was far below that which would sustain a stationary population in the long run (about 70 per thousand). Inasmuch as a high abortion rate seemed to be contributing to the low fertility, they suddenly made abortion illegal.

The immediate effect was astounding. In 1967 the fertility rate almost doubled, to 106 per thousand. In subsequent years, however, the rate began to fall as other ways of averting births were implemented. Within a relatively few years the fertility rate moved back to the 70–80 range — still higher than it had been when legal abortion was freely available. Raising the "price" of averting births did have a long-run effect on fertility. That it was the abortion ban which made the difference is substantiated by the fact that fertility in the U.S.S.R., where no such change in abortion occurred, showed relative stability during the very period in which the Romanian rate was undergoing drastic change.

Cyclical Variations

In the nineteenth century U.S. fertility declined steadily at approximately 0.8 percent per annum; there was no twenty-year span when the rate of change departed markedly from this long-term trend. During the twentieth century the average rate of decline has been similar, about 0.9 percent per annum, but the rate of change has been extremely unstable (see Figure 2.1). Between 1925 and 1935 fertility plummeted at the rate of 3.2 percent per annum. From 1935 to 1955 fertility actually rose by 2.1 percent per annum; then between 1955 and 1975 it fell at 2.9 percent per annum. Economic factors appear to have been significant in all these cyclical swings.

The role of the Great Depression in causing a sharp drop in fertility is so well understood and widely accepted as to require little additional discussion. Between 1929 and 1933 real income per capita in the U.S. declined by almost one-third. Widespread unemployment, a disastrous fall in stock prices, and numerous financial failures led many young men and women to postpone marriage and induced those who were married to delay having children or to abandon the idea entirely. The effect of the Depression on many was permanent, as evidenced by the fact that the cohort of women who were born around 1910 (and who entered the major child-bearing ages at the time of the Great Depression) had, on average, fewer children over their lifetimes than did the cohorts that preceded and followed them.

Figure 2.1. Fertility rate and number of live births, United States, 1910–1980.

(*Sources:* U.S. Bureau of the Census, *Historical Statistics of the United States, Colonial Times to 1970,* series B-1 and B-8; idem, *Statistical Abstract of the United States, 1981,* table 85, and Statistical Abstracts for 1975 and 1980; National Center for Health Statistics, *Monthly Vital Statistics Report* March 18, 1982.)

The relationship between economic factors and the "baby boom" of the 1950s is not as obvious as is the case of the decline of the 1930s, but I believe it is just as strong. The fullest discussion of this relation can be found in the work of Richard Easterlin (1968, 1980), who emphasized the importance of the relative economic position of young men and women. According to Easterlin, the low birth rates of the 1930s meant that relatively few men and women entered the labor market in the 1950s. Those who did found good jobs, had good incomes, and were therefore disposed to marry early and to have many children. Apparently, higher incomes more than offset the fact that the "price" of time (as measured by hourly wages) was also rising.

In 1956 I presented a simple version of a *relative-income* hypothesis in order to explain why fertility was high in the 1950s and why I expected it to decline (Fuchs 1956). I suggested that in countries where income is well above subsistence, "the absolute level of income is of little consequence [in explaining fertility], while the direction and rate of change of income is by far the more important factor" (p. 3). Not only were young people enjoying considerable prosperity in the 1950s, but, having grown up in the thirties and forties, they were more prosperous than they had ever *expected* to be. This relative-income view also helps us understand the decline of the 1930s. After all, even during the Depression the level of living in the United States was much higher than it had been fifty years before, and much higher than in most other countries. In terms of absolute income it doesn't make much sense to say that people couldn't afford to have children. But in relative terms it does. Measured against aspirational levels formed earlier, many young people in the 1930s felt that their incomes were too low.

This same line of reasoning could help explain why fertility dropped sharply in the 1970s even though real hourly earnings were 35 percent higher than in the 1950s. Earnings were high in an absolute sense, but many young people who grew up and formed their expectations in the 1950s and 1960s perceived economic conditions in the 1970s as unsatisfactory. The unemployment rate averaged 6.2 percent of the labor force during the seventies, compared with 4.8 percent in the sixties and 4.5 percent in the fifties. The deterioration in the rate of growth of real hourly earnings was even more striking. During the 1950s this basic indicator of earning power grew at 2.4 percent per annum. In the 1960s the rate of increase was 1.8 percent per annum, but during the 1970s real hourly earnings rose a scant 0.2 percent per annum. Not only did the overall economic situation worsen, but employment and earnings prospects were particularly poor for *young* men and women — the very ones who had grown up during two of the most prosperous decades in our country's history. The failure of the 1970s to meet the rising tide of expectations undoubtedly contributed to the increase in the age of marriage and the low fertility rate in that decade.

THE CIRCUMSTANCES OF BIRTH

Every man was not born with a silver spoon in his mouth.
— Miguel de Cervantes

Henry Adams, son of a distinguished American diplomat, grandson of the sixth president of the United States, and great-grandson of the second president, began his famous autobiography by noting the extraordinary circumstances of his birth. He wrote: "Had he [Adams] been born in Jerusalem under the shadow of the Temple and circumcised in the Synagogue by his uncle the high priest, under the name of Israel Cohen, he would scarcely have been more distinctly branded" (Adams 1918). The Declaration of Independence states that "all men are created equal," but it is obvious that men (and women) are born into unequal circumstances. It is also obvious that these circumstances, while not all-determining, strongly affect future development. How we live depends a great deal on when and to whom we are born. This section considers some of the principal factors that, *on average,* have important implications for an infant's prospects in life.

Cohort Size

The fertility rate multiplied by the number of women of child-bearing age determines the number of babies born in any time period — that is, the cohort size. Cohort size and fertility normally change together, but the echo effects of previous shifts in fertility can produce divergent trends such as those that emerged in the late 1970s (see Figure 2.1). At that time the large cohorts born in the 1950s reached child-bearing age; thus, the number of births rose even though the fertility rate did not.

Does it matter to children whether they are born as part of a small or a large cohort? On average, the answer is certainly yes. Economic theory suggests that the demand for goods and services (such as schooling) that are cohort-specific will, other things equal, increase as cohort size increases. If the supply of those goods and services is not completely elastic — will not increase without limit unless the price rises — this increase in demand will result in a higher price, or poorer quality. Similarly, when a large cohort enters the labor market, the increase in supply will depress the relative wages of entry-level jobs, unless the demand for such labor is completely elastic.

These theoretical conclusions seem to have been confirmed by the experiences of the small cohorts that were born in the 1930s and of the large ones that were born in the 1950s. The former group appears to have had a relatively smooth journey over the life cycle, in part because they were few in number. Schools and colleges had ample room for them, and as young adults they found employers competing strenuously to hire them. By contrast, the unusually large cohorts of the 1950s have had to contend with crowded classrooms from kindergarten on, and when they reached maturity in the late 1970s and early 1980s their large numbers depressed the market for entry-level jobs and inflated the demand for apartments and houses. Such large swings in fertility create special problems for women born during years in which cohort size is increasing rapidly. Women in these cohorts have a smaller supply of eligible husbands because most women marry men from cohorts a few years ahead of theirs. The same reasoning suggests that men who are born when cohort size is decreasing rapidly (in the 1960s, for example) will face a similar problem, sometimes referred to as a "marriage squeeze."

Birth Order and Number of Siblings

Two phenomena that are closely related to cohort size and that have important consequences for children are birth order and number of siblings. Birth order is important because many studies have indicated that first-born children enjoy a small advantage with respect to achievement in school and in later life (Belmont and Marolla 1973; Zajonc and Markus 1975). According to one theory, this advantage results from their receiving more parental attention than their siblings do.

The probability of being a first-born has fluctuated considerably since 1940 (see Figure 2.2). During the 1940s almost 40 percent of all white births were first-borns; the proportion for nonwhites was between 25 percent and 30 percent. Subsequently, first-order births declined in relative importance for both races,

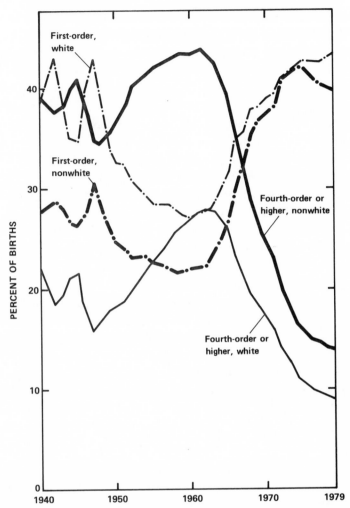

Figure 2.2.   First-order births and fourth-order or higher births as a percent of total births, by race, 1940–1979.

(*Sources:* U.S. Bureau of the Census, *Historical Statistics of the United States, Colonial Times to 1970,* series B20–B27; idem, *Statistical Abstract of the United States, 1980,* table 88, and Statistical Abstracts for 1979 and 1981; National Center for Health Statistics, *Vital Statistics of the United States, 1976,* vol. 1.)

reaching a low point in the late 1950s and early 1960s. Thereafter the proportion rose rapidly, especially for nonwhites; by 1975 it was well over 40 percent for both races. At the opposite end of the birth-order distribution the reverse pattern prevailed. The proportion of births that were fourth-order or above rose in the 1950s and then declined very sharply in the 1960s and 1970s.

The rapid decline in higher-order births is consistent with the economic explanations for the overall decline in fertility: decreasing benefits and increasing costs of large families, plus lower costs of birth control through improved contraception and legalized abortion. The demand for one or two children to satisfy the psychic desires of parents is undoubtedly stronger than the demand for higher-order births, and women now find it much easier to control the number of children they bear. It is not just a coincidence that the decrease in the relative importance of higher-order births during the 1960s and early 1970s coincided with the diffusion of birth-control pills and intrauterine devices, two highly effective methods of contraception. When fertility dropped rapidly in the 1930s, the decline was not so heavily concentrated in the higher-order births.

One consequence of the decline in the relative importance of higher-order births is that fewer children will have to share parental resources with large numbers of siblings. If, as many observers believe, such sharing contributes to physical and intellectual deficits in some children, the next generation should in this respect be much better off. Dennis DeTray, for instance, studied the relationship between number of children and amount of schooling that the children received and concluded that, on average, children in large families receive less education than children in small families, even after controlling for family income, the value of the mother's time, and the education of parents (1978, p. 36).

The decline in the relative importance of higher-order births (and in the number of large families) has been more marked for nonwhites than for whites. During the 1940s and 1950s a nonwhite infant was much more likely to be the fourth, fifth, or even higher-order birth than to be a first-born. By the late 1970s the situation was completely reversed. The consequences of this large change for the educational attainment, health, and labor market success of nonwhite children may be particularly favorable.

Marital Status of the Mother

The decrease in the proportion of infants born into large families has tended to increase equality of opportunity among children. Concomitantly, a tendency toward *less* equality has resulted from an extraordinary increase in the proportion of children born to unmarried women (see Figure 2.3). Between 1960 and 1978 the fertility rate of married women fell from 156.3 to 96.8 per thousand, while the rate for unmarried women rose from 21.6 to 26.2 per thousand. The trends by marital status have been so divergent that the illegitimacy *ratio* (births to unmarried mothers as a percentage of all births) in 1979 was 17 percent—up from 5 percent in 1960. In 1979 the ratio was almost 10 percent for white births and almost 50 percent for nonwhite births.

Some unmarried mothers are mature, well educated, and self-supporting; they are eager to have a child, but not necessarily

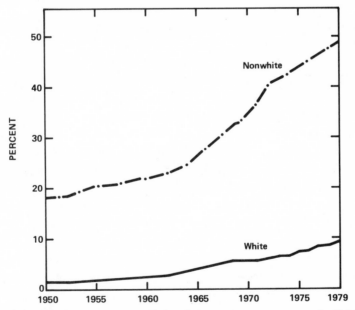

Figure 2.3. Births to unmarried mothers as a percentage of all births, 1950–1979.

(*Sources:* National Center for Health Statistics, *Vital Statistics of the United States, 1976*, vol. 1; U.S. Bureau of the Census, *Statistical Abstract of the United States, 1981*, tables 85 and 98.)

a husband. The great majority of unwed mothers, however, are young and poorly educated, and many depend on meager government welfare programs to feed their children and themselves. Although there has been considerable reduction in the stigma attached to births out of wedlock, the infant who begins life under such circumstances still faces many disadvantages. The probability of being of low birth weight is appreciably higher for babies born to unmarried women, even after controlling for race and age of mother. Low birth weight is the most important precursor of infant mortality and low-weight babies are more likely to have subsequent mental and physical handicaps, especially in low-income families. Most of the women who bear children out of wedlock eventually marry, but most of these marriages end in divorce. The infant, although usually wanted by the mother at the time of birth, may eventually be regarded as a burden, and probably faces a greater likelihood than other children of becoming a victim of neglect or abuse (Gil 1970; American Humane Association 1979).

A fuller discussion of the causes and consequences of the increase in the illegitimacy ratio is reserved for the chapter dealing with adolescence and youth. At this point it should be noted that economic considerations probably play some role. The ratio (adjusted for birth order and age of mother) rose particularly rapidly during the 1960s — the same decade during which the average monthly payment per AFDC (Aid to Families with Dependent Children) recipient grew fastest. Several observers have suggested that higher AFDC payments have contributed to the rise in the illegitimacy ratio.

Education and Age of Mother

Education is one of the most important correlates of health, income, and many other things that people regard as part of a good life. For several reasons, the years of schooling of the mother is a good indicator of an infant's circumstances of birth. First, greater schooling may enhance the mother's ability to raise a bright, healthy child by increasing her knowledge and skill in activities such as preventive health care. Second, the mother's education is frequently a good proxy for the long-run economic well-being of the family (and the resources available for children) because women with more schooling earn more themselves and, on average, are married to better-educated, higher-income men.

Between 1950 and 1979 there were large changes in the distribution of children by the education of mother (Table 2.1). In the earlier year, half of the children of women ages 35–44 had mothers with eight years of schooling or less, and only one in ten had a mother with more than a high school diploma. By 1979 only one child in ten had a mother with no high school education, and one in four had a mother who had attended college. The average level of education of mothers rose, while relative inequality fell by almost one-third. Virtually all of this decline in inequality was the result of greater equality in the educational distribution of women regardless of their fertility. On average, the children's mothers had slightly less education than the average of all women 35–44 in both years: there was a tendency for number of children to be negatively related to the education of mother.

The fact that the average child today has a much better-educated mother than the average child did in 1950 should have favorable consequences when these children mature. Unless there are offsetting factors, the children of recent cohorts should be healthier and do better in school. The additional fact that there is less inequality in the education of mothers should lead to more equality in the achievements of their children.

These favorable effects of trends in mothers' education may be offset, in the short run, by changes in the distribution of births by age of mother. While most infants do well regardless of the age of mother, the birth weight and infant mortality data suggest that infants born to mothers ages 25–29 face the best prospects, at least in the first year of life. The probability of being underweight at birth and of dying in the first year are appreciably higher for infants born to mothers under 20 or over 40 years of age.

Unfortunately, the percentage of babies born to teenagers jumped from 11.7 in 1950 to 18.9 in 1975. Most of this increase was the result of a disproportionate increase in the *number* of teenagers; the teenage fertility *rate* has dropped almost as rapidly as the rate for all women of childbearing age. In 1950 women 15–19 represented 15.5 percent of all women 15–44. In 1975 they represented 21.8 percent, but by 1985 the proportion will fall back to 17 percent and by 1990 to 14 percent. Thus, as the number of teenagers declines in the 1980s, it is highly likely that the proportion of infants born to women under 20 will also decline. At the other end of the age spectrum the proportion of births accounted for by women 40 and over was small in 1950 (2.2 percent), and became even smaller (less than 1 percent) in the late 1970s. The proportion of babies delivered by women 35–39 has also dropped, partly because the baby boom cohorts have not yet reached that age, but also because the fertility rate at ages 35–39 is only 35 percent of what it was in 1950.

INFANT MORTALITY

The infant mortality rate — the number of deaths before the age of one, divided by the number of live births — has long been regarded as an excellent indicator of the level of economic development and of the quantity and quality of medical and social care available to a population. In a broad sense this is certainly true: a few socioeconomic variables explain many of the differences in infant mortality over time and between groups at a point in time. There are, however, several puzzling aspects about infant mortality in the United States that remain unexplained.

During the past two hundred years the economic and technological advances that were set in motion by the Industrial Revolution have reduced infant mortality to a tiny fraction of its historical level. Philosophers can endlessly debate whether economic development has increased or decreased human happiness, but one fact is indisputable: only in modern times has the average parent been spared the grief of having to bury one or more children. Only in modern times has the average infant had a good chance of reaching adulthood. One effect of the large decrease in infant and child mortality has been the long-term decline in fertility. Even as recently as 1900 a woman who wanted to have three children reach adulthood would have needed, on average, to have four children. Indeed, since there is always the possibility of worse than average survival, she would have needed to have five children if she wanted to be 90 percent certain that three would survive to adulthood.

At the beginning of the nineteenth century the infant death rate in Western Europe and the United States varied from 200 to 300 deaths per thousand live births; at the end of the century the rate ranged from 100 to 200, depending primarily upon income levels and sanitary conditions. The U.S. rate, which was 100 in 1915, fell to 12 per thousand live births by 1981, a rate of decrease of more than 3 percent per annum. The only sustained interruption in this downward trend occurred in the late 1950s and early 1960s when, for reasons not understood, the U.S. rate was relatively stable. The period coincided with the peak of the baby boom, but standardization for birth order, age of mother, and other demographic variables does not eliminate the mystery.*

The median rate for the countries of northwestern Europe, North America, Australasia, and Japan is now below 13, and in some countries there are fewer than 10 deaths per thousand live births. Not long ago such low rates were regarded as biologically unattainable. The principal factors responsible for the decline have been rising living standards, improvements in public and private health practices, control of infectious disease through vaccinations and antibiotics, improved contraceptive techniques, legalization of abortion, and, most recently, significant advances in techniques for caring for babies of low birth weight.

Income and Public Health

Over the long term, rising income and advances in public health practices have been the most important reasons for the fall in infant mortality. When per capita income is very low, even a modest gain raises resistance to disease because there is more food, cleaner water, better shelter, and improved sanitation.

---

* Ernest Sternglass (1969) attributed the retardation to radioactive fallout from nuclear weapons tests, but a systematic review of interstate differences in levels and trends of infant mortality showed no relationship to variations in the amount of radioactivity experienced by different states (Fuchs 1981b).

Rising income in the industrialized nations has been accompanied by greater knowledge about the causes and nature of disease, knowledge that has now been put to use in other parts of the world.

Currently, even in the poorest areas of the world such as Africa and Southeast Asia, the infant mortality rate is generally below 100 per thousand live births. Real income per capita in these areas is still much lower than it was in the United States in 1900, but the diffusion of public health and medical knowledge from the developed countries has resulted in declining infant death rates even in the face of low income levels. More generally, it can be shown that the decline in infant mortality throughout the world is attributable partly to rising real income and partly to advances in medicine and public health that raise health levels at any given level of income. In studies of interstate and international differences in infant mortality in 1937 and 1965, I found that approximately one-third of the improvement between those dates could be attributed to higher real income, and two-thirds to factors that lowered infant mortality, holding income constant (Fuchs 1974c).

Not only has there been a large decline in the average rate of infant mortality, but *differences* in rates across regions and socioeconomic groups have also decreased substantially. In 1940 the ten states with highest infant mortality (for whites) had a median rate that was 58 percent higher than the median of the ten most favored states (54.2 versus 34.4 deaths per thousand live births). By 1977 the ten states with the worst rates exceeded the ten with the best by only 25 percent (13.5 versus 10.8). This narrowing of differentials is partly attributable to a decline in income inequality across states. Even if income inequality remains constant, however, we should expect some narrowing of infant mortality differentials as the average level of income rises because the effect of income differentials on infant mortality diminishes as income rises.

In an analysis of interstate differentials in 1940, I found that on average a 10 percent increase in income was associated with a decrease of 3.6 percent in infant mortality. A similar analysis for 1970 showed a decrease of only 2.2 percent for a 10 percent increase in income. The primary reason for the change is that income has a smaller effect on neonatal deaths (those that occur within twenty-eight days after birth) than on postneonatal deaths (those that occur during the next eleven months). As income rises, postneonatal deaths, which are more responsive to income, drop more rapidly, thus increasing the relative importance of the neonatal category. Postneonatal rates are more sensitive to income differences because the causes of death are predominantly infections, accidents, and other environment-related factors. Neonatal deaths are often the result of congenital problems, injuries at birth, and other causes that are less closely related to income. Also, care given in hospitals (where most neonatal deaths occur) is probably less closely related to income than is care given at home.

Black-White Differential

Although the gap between rich and poor with respect to infant mortality has been considerably reduced, a major continuing concern to health policy makers and an unyielding problem to health analysts is the large differential in infant mortality between nonwhites and whites — or, more accurately, between blacks and whites. (Most other nonwhites such as Chinese and Japanese in the United States have infant death rates as low as or lower than those of whites.) In 1978 the nonwhite rate was 76 percent above the white. Since 1940 the differential has varied between 60 percent and 90 percent, with no clear trend. This differential is far greater than can be explained by racial differences in income, education, age of mother, or birth order. Marital status of the mother (almost 50 percent of nonwhite babies are born out of wedlock) explains some of the gap, but a substantial race differential in infant mortality within each marital status remains.

Birth Weight

Analysts agree that the most important proximate "explanation" for the race differential in infant mortality is the difference in distribution of births by birth weight. Within each race mortality rises as birth weight falls. For the United States as a whole, babies weighing under 2,500 grams account for only about 7 percent of all births, but account for more than half of all infant deaths and three-fourths of all neonatal deaths. Approximately 6 percent of white babies are of low birth weight, compared to a startling 13 percent of black babies. Standardization for differences in birth weight between blacks and whites eliminates about two-thirds of the race differential in infant mortality.

Identification of low birth weight as the proximate cause of the relatively high rate of black infant mortality is not a satisfactory explanation, however, because it is not known why there are so many low-weight babies born to black mothers. Some of the factors associated with low birth weight — age, education, and marital status of the mother, and the timing and amount of prenatal care — do differ by race, but the differences are not large enough to explain the difference in birth weight distributions (Table 2.2). For instance, among mothers with exactly twelve years of schooling, low-weight babies are still twice as likely for blacks as for whites. A detailed study of the risk of low birth weight concluded that "Black mothers were more likely than White mothers to have low birth weight babies at every level of every factor studied" (Eisner et al. 1979).

Two recent econometric studies have attempted to look at socioeconomic determinants of fetal development with more sophisticated theoretical and statistical models than have previously been applied (Harris 1982; Rosenzweig and Schultz 1982). They do not explain the black-white differential, but they do illuminate the difficulty of analyzing fetal development. Harris tries to take into account the complex mutual causality between the progress of a pregnancy and the initiation of prenatal care. For instance, some mothers may seek care early in their pregnancy because they are experiencing physical difficulty. In such cases it would usually be inappropriate to blame the care for the subsequent bad outcome. An opposite bias may be introduced when women deliver prematurely prior to seeking care. It is not necessarily correct to blame the low weight of the premature baby on the absence of care.

Jeffrey Harris analyzed the pregnancy outcomes of 6,800 black women in Massachusetts in 1975–76 who were pregnant for at least twenty weeks. Controlling for variables such as mother's age, schooling, marital status, and birth order, he found that prenatal care tended to reduce the risk of premature births; but holding gestation constant, prenatal care had very little effect on birth weight. Although the conventional wisdom is that prenatal care, by changing the mother's behavior with respect to smoking, nutrition, and weight gain, contributes to favorable pregnancy outcomes, Harris speculated that prenatal care may be serving as a proxy for a more complex set of phenomena associated with access to a wide range of social support services. Moreover, if prenatal care truly has a causal role in reducing infant mortality, it may be because it permits early identification of those pregnancies which will benefit most from intensive *perinatal* care — that is, care immediately preceding and following birth.

Mark R. Rosenzweig and T. Paul Schultz (1982) analyzed the birth weight and length of gestation of a national probability sample of over nine thousand births to married mothers in 1967, 1968, and 1969. In their study they emphasized the importance of jointly estimating the parents' demand for the various factors that influence the production of a healthy baby and the effect of those factors on fetal development.

Their most significant finding is that cigarette smoking by the mother has a large negative effect on birth weight, both unadjusted and adjusted for gestation. Controlling for other variables, one pack of cigarettes per day during pregnancy lowers average birth weight by one pound, thus approximately doubling the probability of having a low-weight baby. Delay in seeking prenatal care is also associated with lower birth weight, but the effect is relatively small — an average loss of 1.5 ounces as a result of a delay of six months.

According to Rosenzweig and Schultz, the strong impact of smoking on birth weight helps explain some other puzzling relationships. For instance, mothers with *some* high school education have a higher proportion of low-weight babies than do mothers with *no* high school; also, residence in large metropolitan areas tends to be associated with lower birth weight, despite the greater availability of medical care. The authors suggested that in both instances, differences in smoking behavior may explain the unexpected relation. Differences in smoking could not, however, help explain the lower birth weight of babies born to black mothers. Indeed, standardization for differences in smoking tended to increase the black-white differential in birth weight because in their sample black women smoked less than white women.

A Tale of Two Cultures

Although there is a large black-white differential in the proportion of babies born at low weight, it is difficult to identify one or two conclusive explanations because blacks and whites differ in so many respects, including income, education, access to medical care, and family living arrangements. There are, however, two other groups of women who also differ greatly from each other in the likelihood of delivering low-weight babies, even though they are similar in most other respects: they are women of Puerto Rican origin and women of Mexican origin who give birth while living in the continental United States. Fully 9 percent of Puerto Rican babies are born weighing less than 2,500 grams, while only 5 percent of the Mexican babies are in this high-risk category. As might be expected, this difference in birth weight results in a large difference in infant mortality. In Texas, for instance, the Spanish-surname population (predominantly of Mexican origin) enjoys the same low infant mortality as the white Anglo population (Griner et al. 1982). By contrast, in New York, where there is a large population of Puerto Rican origin, infant mortality among Hispanics is much higher than that of other whites.

What can explain the huge difference between two groups that speak the same language, have the same religion, and appear to be similar in many other respects as well? The answer surely cannot be differences in income or education: women of Mexican origin are just as disadvantaged as are those of Puerto Rican origin (Table 2.3). Access to medical care? It is highly unlikely that Mexican women in Texas have better access to care than do Puerto Rican women in New York City.

The groups do differ in one important respect: women of Puerto Rican origin are much less likely to have grown up in a stable family and much less likely to be married at the time they give birth. In Puerto Rico the divorce rate is as high as the average for all groups in the United States (about 20 per thousand married couples per year), whereas in Mexico it is less than 4 per thousand. In the continental United States at ages 25–44, 25 percent of Puerto Rican families are headed by a woman; this is true of only 12 percent of Mexican-American families. Perhaps fetal development depends upon strong social support from family and community. The absence of such support may result in poor diet or other detrimental behaviors, or could create stress and other psychological problems that affect length of gestation and weight gain by the fetus.

This tale of two cultures thus reinforces other reasons for doubting that the most popular explanations for low birth weight — income, education, and access to medical care — are to be taken at face value. Over the past thirty years all groups in the U.S. population have experienced large increases in real income, years of schooling, and access to medical care, but the incidence of low-weight babies is not much lower now than in 1950. It is also difficult to reconcile these explanations with the fact that foreign-born mothers in the United States are slightly *less* likely to deliver babies of low birth weight than are native-born white mothers.

Nutrition

Poor pregnancy outcomes are frequently attributed to nutritional deficiencies, but a recent effort to provide nutritional supplements to a group of disadvantaged pregnant women had negative results. In a randomized controlled study, the mothers who received concentrated protein supplements actually had slightly worse pregnancy outcomes than did the mothers in the control group (Rush, Stein, and Susser 1980). Several explanations have been offered for this negative finding. It is possible that nutritional supplements during pregnancy cannot remedy a lifetime of nutritional deprivation. One critic suggested that the women receiving the supplements may have cut down on their other food intake in order to provide more food or other goods to their families (Jacobson 1980). If this criticism is correct, it should serve as a warning to policy makers that the impact of any policy aimed at improving the welfare of a particular family member (a pregnant mother, a school child) may be blunted by offsetting redistributions undertaken within the family. Becker's economic model of the family predicts that such redistributions *will* take place as long as there is a head of household who is concerned about the welfare of the various members of the family and who is in a position to reallocate resources (Becker 1981, ch. 8). The point is not that the family does not benefit from the intervention (say, free food for school children), but that the benefit — and the allocation — will be the same as if the family were given more income rather than a subsidy tied to a particular good or service.

Social Programs and Scientific Advances

Since the mid-1960s infant mortality has fallen at an unusually rapid rate. Between 1964 and 1981, for instance, the average annual rate of decline was 4.5 percent; this was greater than the rate of improvement in earlier decades when per capita income was rising more rapidly and many new wonder drugs were introduced. Because "success has many fathers," there has been no shortage of explanations for the recent decline, including improved contraception, legalized abortion, better access to health care in poverty areas, and scientific advances in obstetrics and neonatology. In my judgment, we do not really understand why the gains have been so rapid, but one aspect is clear. More than 80 percent of the reduction is attributable to improved survival probabilities at given birth weights, not to a change in the distribution of births by birth weight (Williams and Chen 1982). Those programs that allegedly work through reducing the probability of low birth weight cannot logically claim credit for the gains made in the 1960s and 1970s.

One study attempted to assess the contribution of Medicaid, maternal and infant care projects, family-planning clinics, and legalized abortion through an analysis of differences in neonatal mortality among U.S. counties in 1970–72; it concluded that legalized abortion had the greatest favorable impact (Grossman

and Jacobowitz 1981). The hypothesis that a reduction in unwanted births improves the survival probabilities of those infants
that are born seems reasonable, but needs further study. If
abortion is a major explanation for the fall in infant mortality, it is
difficult to understand why the infant death rate in Utah, where
there is very little abortion, has declined even more rapidly than
in the country as a whole. Indeed, the experience in Utah con-
founds all explanations that relate the fall in infant mortality to
the decline in the birth rate, because the birth rate in that state
has remained quite high.

The past two decades have not only been marked by the
introduction of major new social programs, but they have also
been a period of significant scientific advance and large-scale
change in obstetrical and neonatal practice. Routine monitoring
of fetal heart rate has been adopted in many hospitals, delivery by
Caesarean section has become much more common (the proportion of such deliveries tripled in California between 1960 and
1977), and intensive neonatal care of high-risk infants has become a major activity at most university medical centers. Numerous observers have been quick to attribute the rapid decline in
infant mortality to these technological changes, but some analysts have questioned the relative costs and benefits (Banta and
Thacker 1979; Wood et al. 1981).

Questions of cost aside, the increased effectiveness of intensive care for low-weight babies seems to be beyond doubt. At the
University Hospitals of Cleveland, for instance, the neonatal
mortality for infants born weighing 1,000–1,500 grams was 190
per thousand in 1976–78 (Hack et al. 1979), whereas the national
rate for such babies in 1960 was over 500. Comparable progress
was recorded at other neonatal intensive care units throughout
the country as a result of significant technological advances
(mechanical ventilators, exchange transfusions, phototherapy),
improved scientific understanding of thermal, fluid, and caloric
requirements for infant development, and better cooperation
between obstetricians and pediatricians.

A comprehensive study of births in California in 1960 and 1977
confirms the belief that neonatal mortality has fallen rapidly for
low-weight babies (except those weighing less than 1,000 grams).

Surprisingly, this study shows an equally rapid rate of mortality decline for babies weighing *more* than 2,500 grams. In absolute terms, however, the improved survival probabilities for low-weight babies explains most of the overall decline because so much of neonatal mortality occurs in that group (Williams and Chen 1982).

The increased survival of very low-weight babies is achieved at considerable cost. One study of seventy-five infants with birth weights under 1,000 grams who were cared for at the Cedars-Sinai Medical Center in Los Angeles revealed that the average hospital charges for the thirty infants who survived was $40,000 per baby. The average for the forty-five infants who did *not* survive — and had much shorter average stays — was $14,000 per infant (Pomerance et al. 1978). These estimates do not include physicians' fees and are based on 1976 hospital rates. The current full costs are probably higher, except for those who die soon after admission to an intensive care unit.

With costs running so high, it is the rare parent who can afford to pay for intensive care out of current income or even past savings. Clearly private insurance or public funds must bear the burden. Regardless of who pays, the aggregate costs are considerable. Approximately one out of every hundred babies is likely to be born weighing less than 1,250 grams. Thus, an expenditure of $40,000 for such babies, shared equally by all expectant families, would add $400 to the cost of each pregnancy. Another way of looking at the problem is to note that there are over 3.5 million babies born each year in the United States — which means over 35,000 babies born weighing less than 1,250 grams. A cost of $40,000 for each very low-weight baby implies a total cost of over $1.4 billion per year. The development of appropriate public policies to deal with problems of low birth weight is a formidable challenge.

PUBLIC POLICY ISSUES

Of the many issues discussed in this chapter, which ones are likely to be of great public concern in the 1980s and 1990s? I believe that low fertility, inequality in the circumstances of birth, and the high cost of further reductions in infant mortality will receive increasing attention and debate.

Fertility

As mentioned earlier, the fertility rate in 1980 was 40 percent lower than in 1950, and since 1973 it has been below the replacement level. (The population continues to grow in the short run primarily because an unusually large proportion of women are of child-bearing age, and secondarily as a result of immigration.) Opinions concerning future trends in fertility differ widely. A leading mathematical demographer, Nathan Keyfitz, believes that there is virtually no chance for a substantial upturn:

> Without knowing precisely why the birth rate is falling, we know that its fall is tied to a number of specific social changes. These changes together are a cluster that will not easily be reversed, and one can say with some confidence that the birth rate will remain low for the foreseeable future, both in the United States and in all other industrialized countries . . . For the birth rate to rise substantially, women would have to go back to housework — some would say to being domestics in their own homes; they would give up the satisfactions of work and independent incomes in favor of the satisfactions of having many children; they would put up with unsatisfactory marriages rather than undergo divorces. All this is hard to imagine. (Keyfitz 1980, p. 53)

Richard Easterlin, an economic historian and demographer, disagrees. He believes that as the size of the cohort entering adulthood gets smaller, young men and women will encounter better job prospects, will marry earlier, and will have more children (Easterlin 1980). A test of his hypothesis will come in the 1990s, when the number reaching the age of 20 will be 17 percent less than in the 1970s. According to Easterlin, young people in the 1990s will enjoy a relatively strong demand for their services in the labor market.

Changes in relative cohort size and relative income probably do affect fertility, but will these effects be large enough to offset the economic and technological factors that tend to reduce fertility in the long run? For instance, further improvements in contraception seem likely, and these improvements will decrease fertility. According to a 1976 survey, 12 percent of all births in that year were reported by mothers as "not wanted" or "probably not wanted" at the time of pregnancy (U.S. Bureau of the Census, *Statistical Abstract, 1980,* p. 68). Moreover, there were a substantial number of "wanted" births to unmarried teenagers, and society would like to reduce the number of infants born in those circumstances. Changes in age distribution will also tend to lower the fertility rate. During the 1970s approximately 38 percent of women of child-bearing ages were between 20 and 29, the ages of highest fertility. (These women accounted for 65 percent of all births.) By 1990, however, only 34 percent of women of child-bearing ages will be in this group.

A leveling off of U.S. population, or even a small decline, might not occasion much concern, but a prolonged period of low fertility would lead to such low projections of future population as to stimulate some attention to pronatalist policies. In Europe this has already occurred. A recent survey of population policy in European countries noted that "low population growth has reached the political agenda in virtually all the advanced industrialized nations" (McIntosh 1981, p. 182). Many of the low-fertility communist countries of Eastern Europe have moved decisively to implement pronatalist policies, including sharply restricted access to legalized abortion. The countries of Western Europe have debated the issues, but have not yet introduced comprehensive, vigorous policies because "the sense of urgency over population decline is still far from acute in the liberal democracies of Western Europe" (ibid., p. 201).

If policy makers begin to ask, "How can fertility be increased?" the answers are likely to range from repeal of legalized abortion to child subsidies to preachments about the joys of family life. The discussion of fertility decline earlier in this chapter suggests that pronatalist policies could take three forms: increase the cost and difficulty of averting births, increase the benefit of having children, and decrease the cost of raising them.

The most direct way to increase the cost of averting births

would be to make abortions illegal. Because there are already significant groups supporting antiabortion policies on other grounds, the prospects for such a policy change are not as far-fetched as they might have seemed a decade ago. In considering antiabortion legislation as a pronatalist policy, several points deserve mention. First, the long-run impact on fertility is not likely to be large because couples will find other ways of averting births, including sterilization, better contraceptive methods, more careful use of existing methods, and illegal abortions. Second, while there will probably be some increase in fertility, it will be obtained at considerable cost. The cost will not appear in the federal budget, but it will be a real cost nevertheless, as men and women are forced to adopt what they regard as less satisfactory methods of averting births. In addition to psychic costs, there are likely to be adverse health effects resulting from illegal abortions and a higher infant mortality rate. A third consideration is that these costs are likely to be borne most heavily by individuals with low education and low income because they will be, on average, least able to find satisfactory alternatives to legal abortion. Finally, three out of four abortions are obtained by unmarried women, and one out of three by a teenager. Thus, any profertility impact is likely to take the form of an increase in those births that public policy in general seeks to reduce.

A second pronatalist strategy would be to try to restore the conditions that make children an economic benefit to families. For instance, a cut in taxes matched by reductions in federal retirement benefits, Medicare, disability and unemployment insurance, and other social welfare legislation would increase the importance of children as a source of insurance and care in time of need. As in the case of abortion, there are individuals and groups who favor such changes independently of their pronatalist implications, but in my judgment the prospects for a large reversal of social welfare legislation are small. The Reagan administration's policy regarding social welfare is probably only a pause in the long-term trend rather than the beginning of a major trend in the opposite direction. The pressure to redistribute income is the basic driving force behind social legislation in all the developed countries. The family achieves redistribution among its own members, but only government programs can compel redistribution among families.

The third and probably most promising strategy to increase fertility is to reduce the family's cost of raising children. This reduction could be achieved in many ways, such as direct child allowances, increased tax deductions for children, or subsidized child care. The rationale for such expenditures is that children now provide significant external benefits for society as a whole. Adult children may no longer contribute to the support of their *own* parents, but as workers contributing to Social Security they fund the transfers being made to the previous generation. Because the fertility decisions of parents, based on the private costs and benefits of children, tend to ignore such external effects, there may be an economic case for child subsidies. The pros and cons of this argument and the relative merits of particular types of subsidies will be discussed in more detail in the next chapter.

Even if low fertility makes a pronatalist policy desirable, the policy may not be implemented because its costs will come quickly, but the benefits will appear only many years later. The costs of pronatalism begin as soon as the birth rate rises, in the form of transfer payments from those who do not increase their fertility to those who do and in the real costs to society of caring for and educating the additional children. The social benefits will not be realized until the children mature, enter the labor force, and contribute to national output. In democratic countries where political office holders must seek popular support every few years, they are usually reluctant to propose a policy that raises costs in the short run even if it yields large benefits over the long term.

Inequality in the Circumstances of Birth

Infants who start life with two strikes against them have virtually no chance of hitting a home run, and usually have trouble even getting on base. Not only may their own lives be blighted, but society as a whole pays a large price through the costs of crime, illness, and dependency that are often the consequences of a bleak beginning. Thus, gross inequalities in the circumstances of birth are of serious concern to thoughtful people regardless of their political ideology or philosophical belief.*

This shared concern does not translate into a consensus on public policy, however, because proposed solutions to the problem of inequality of birth conflict with other goals and values, and some solutions seem to create as many problems as they solve. For instance, if one wanted to reduce inequality of opportunity at all costs, the most effective approach would be to take children away from parents at birth and raise them in a uniform environment. Even such a draconian measure would leave much mental and physical inequality as the result of differences in hereditary factors and in the prenatal environment (for example, the disadvantages of an infant whose mother smokes during pregnancy). Moreover, the conflict between such a policy and other values of U.S. society makes even dedicated egalitarians reluctant to advocate such an extreme action.

A very different but equally radical approach would be to prohibit births to women in circumstances that suggest a high probability of problems — unmarried, below a certain age, below a certain level of education. Although a reduction in such births may be widely and strongly desired, there is little likelihood that such a policy would be introduced because it requires an unacceptable degree of interference with personal freedom.

As we move from these extremes, we can see the logical development of possible policies and can also see the conflicts that they create. Short of taking infants away from their parents, public policy could try to make circumstances more uniform by transfers of income to disadvantaged mothers or by the provision of services such as those offered by Project Headstart. If these transfers or services had no effect on the number of children born into disadvantaged circumstances, they would clearly reduce inequality of opportunity. If, however, the existence of even a meager AFDC program encouraged young, unmarried women to

---

* It is inequality per se that is the problem, not failure to reach some fixed, arbitrary standard. Even those families designated as living in "poverty" in the United States in 1980 commanded far more resources than did the average U.S. family in 1880, and more than do most families in the world today.

have children (as some observers believe), a favorable effect on inequality would not be certain.

To approach the problem from the other end, instead of *prohibiting* births under certain circumstances, public policy could try to *discourage* these births by making life more difficult for such women if they have children. However, even if such a policy had some success in reducing the number of infants born in disadvantaged circumstances, the net result might be unfavorable because of the worsened prospects for those infants who are born.

This tension over inequality is a pervasive problem of modern society. At every stage of the life cycle we will note the acuity of Raymond Aron's observation: "The contradictions within the egalitarian ideal, together with the contradictions between that ideal and the other goals of the collectivity — productivity and the mastery of nature — have precluded any effective stabilization of modern societies" (1968, p. 4). These contradictions will never be resolved, but I believe that the long-term trend in the United States will be toward reducing gross differences in the circumstances of birth, coming ever closer but never reaching the American ideal of equality of opportunity.

Infant Mortality

A lower average rate of infant mortality and a reduction in differences in infant mortality among groups have been major goals of public health policy for many decades. To an unusual extent these goals have been achieved. The average rate is now one-tenth of what it was at the beginning of the twentieth century, and differences across regions and income groups have been sharply reduced. One unresolved problem is the high proportion of low-weight babies born to black mothers. A reduction in births to unmarried teenagers would help narrow the race differential, but the biggest portion would remain, for reasons not currently understood. Inasmuch as standardization for all the variables thought to be important in low birth weight does not eliminate the racial differential, it is difficult to formulate a public policy that has a good chance of success.

Regardless of race, infant mortality is heavily concentrated among low-weight babies. Prospects for survival for such babies when treated in well-equipped intensive care units have increased greatly, and the percentage of survivors without severe handicaps has also been increasing. Nevertheless, among babies born weighing 751 – 1,000 grams, about one out of every four survivors will have at least one major handicap such as very low IQ, hearing loss, or spastic disorders (Kumar et al. 1980; Cohen et al. 1982). It is possible that the high cost of intensive neonatal care and possible subsequent costs if the survivors are handicapped will lead to a reexamination of public policy in this area.

Pediatricians throughout the country are understandably pleased by the progress they have made. However, the pressure for health care resources to be used in other ways — for the elderly, the chronically ill, the mentally disturbed — and the competition between health and other social goals indicates that society will have to make some hard choices about how far it is prepared to go to keep high-risk babies alive. The choices concern not only low-weight babies, but also those born with congenital anomalies or malformations (Down's syndrome, spina bifida) as well as other genetic defects that will result in severe morbidity and premature mortality. It has been estimated that three out of every hundred liveborn infants need very intensive neonatal care and that another six need somewhat less intensive special care (Sinclair et al. 1981).

Many genetic abnormalities can now be detected during pregnancy through amniocentesis or ultrasound. When the probability of giving birth to a severely handicapped child is high, some parents may prefer a selective abortion; some may not. The rate of progress in understanding and controlling human genetics is extremely rapid, and each breakthrough will offer new opportunities to improve the health of the population at the same time that it will pose significant economic, political, and moral problems. Who should benefit from these new advances? Who should pay for them? What criteria should be used in deciding whether or not to implement a new technology, such as genetic repair? Should free choice always prevail, or are there circumstances when the government is justified in regulating behavior? This book is too general in scope to attempt to supply specific answers for specific situations, but a restatement of some general considerations is in order.

First, it must be recognized that the assertion "Costs and benefits are irrelevant where human life is concerned" reflects an irresponsible approach to health policy. Such an attitude lacks merit in the real world because choices *must* be made and every choice necessarily reflects a set of values. These values underlie all implicit and explicit weighing of costs and benefits. Because resources are scarce relative to wants, we do not have the option of evaluating or not evaluating. The only option is whether to evaluate explicitly, systematically, and openly, as economics forces us to do, or whether to evaluate implicitly, haphazardly, and secretly, as has been done so often in the past. Moreover, we must recognize that neither scientific data nor economic analyses are sufficient for resolving these policy dilemmas. Science tells us about cause-and-effect relationships: "If we do X, the result will be Y." Whether we *should* do X or not will depend on the values attached to Y and to the alternative consequences of not doing X. Economics can help identify the relevant consequences (often called costs and benefits) and develop their quantitative importance. It can make explicit the distributional implications of any policy and trace their relationship to general questions of distributional justice. It can help the policy maker deal with the intertemporal dimension of decisions that involve costs and benefits occurring at different times in the future. What economics *cannot* do, any more than science can, is to say what the policy *should* be.

Parents naturally want their infants to receive all the care that modern technology makes possible, especially when the cost of that care is being borne by an insurance company or by the government. And it is reasonable to expect practicing physicians, driven as they are by a commitment to the welfare of patients and a desire to expand the frontier of their specialty, to ignore costs and see only the potential benefits. The best time, therefore, for making evaluations and tradeoffs is usually when decisions are made about construction of facilities, development and diffusion of new technologies, training of personnel, and setting of standards and procedures. By making the hard decisions "upstream," it may be possible to insulate individual practitioners and parents from some of the most painful choices regarding birth and infancy (Schelling 1968).

Faced with a newborn infant struggling for life, a conscientious physician will usually try to do everything possible to save it. What is possible, however, will in large part have been previously determined by the facilities, equipment, and personnel available, and by the physician's own training. If society believes that some of the resources going to intensive neonatal care could be more fruitfully used, say, to prevent high-risk births or to vaccinate preschool children, society must make the difficult choice. If it is left to the individual physician or parent at the time of crisis, further escalation of costs is inevitable.

3

As Morning Shows the Day

Childhood

The childhood shows the man, as morning shows the day.
—*John Milton*

ARE AMERICAN CHILDREN being shortchanged? If so, by whom? Every source of information, from scholarly treatises to the nightly newscast, reinforces the impression that many kids are in trouble — physically, mentally, and emotionally — but there is far less agreement as to why. Some criticize taxpayers for their unwillingness to provide enough funds for children, even though government expenditures per child for education and medical care have grown much more rapidly than per capita income. Others blame television, noting that the average child spends more hours in front of the television set than in the classroom. Still others ask whether the large increase in one-parent homes and the growing propensity of married mothers of small children to work outside the home have adversely affected children.

In considering how children live, we must recognize that certain features of the human condition are determined by biology, not by culture or society. The unusually long dependence of young humans on their elders makes it imperative that there be an economic and social structure to provide physical and psychological support for many years after birth. At least since the Industrial Revolution, if not earlier, the conjugal family has been the prevalent form of organization to provide that support, although other forms such as extended families, kibbutzim, and orphan asylums have played a role in particular times and places. Not only have parents traditionally borne major responsibility for the physical welfare of their children, but as sociologist William J. Goode has written, "The family is the only social institution charged with transforming a biological organism into a human being" (1964, p. 8).

In this chapter the themes of the fading family and wanting and waiting receive particular attention because the well-being of children depends so much on the care provided in families and on the willingness and ability of parents to invest in the future of their children. Two economic concepts, human capital and home production, are particularly useful for discussing these themes. *Human capital* refers to the development in the child of a healthy body and mind, general and specific skills, and other qualities that will help determine how well the child will fare later in life. The development of these traits typically requires *investment* by parents and society — that is, an expenditure of resources when the child is young in the expectation of a return to the child, parents, and society when the child matures.

Home production refers to productive activities that take place in the home and contribute to the economic well-being of the household members, just as income earned in market production does. Some of this home production primarily increases current consumption (for example, preparation of meals), while some is primarily devoted to investment in human capital (for example, a parent teaching a child how to read). The value of home production is *not* included in measures of gross national product (GNP) or family income, but failure to take account of it can seriously distort measures of the services provided to children and analyses of children's well-being.

In order to answer the questions posed at the opening of this chapter, we need to examine trends in the services provided to children through the market and in the home. We also need to consider changes in child well-being and review what is known about their causes. The public policy section of this chapter considers the arguments for a substantial increase in child care subsidies and discusses their probable consequences.

THE CARE OF CHILDREN

Train up a child in the way he should go, and when he is old he will not depart from it. — *Proverbs 22:6*

The care of children and the creation of human capital in them depends on market-produced services such as schooling and health care, and on home-produced services that are provided by parents. Changes in the value of parents' time, especially the time of the mother, directly affect the "price" of home-produced services and indirectly affect the demand for market-produced services. Other things constant, a rise in the wage rate that parents earn or could earn increases the demand for services such as nursery schools that are substitutes for home production. On the other hand, the same rise decreases the demand for market services that require the parents' time as a complementary input (visits to the pediatrician for preventive checkups, for example). In this section we will look at changes over time and variations at a given point in time in some market-produced services for children and in parental inputs to home production.

Market-Produced Services

According to some writers, American society is definitely short-changing its children (Keniston 1977; de Lone 1979; Grubb and Lazerson 1982). Their books tell a frightening and convincing story of declining performance in school, rising juvenile delinquency and crime, drug abuse, neglected children, and more. What is less convincing are the attempts to absolve parents of any responsibility for these problems — it is the schools, or the medical profession, or society that is to blame. A close look at some relevant data, however, suggests a different view of the matter.

Consider schooling. The rhetoric about how American society has been neglecting its schools is not supported by the data on inputs to public education. On the contrary, there has been a sharp rise in teacher/pupil ratios and an even sharper rise in real expenditures per child. Between 1960 and 1978 the number of teachers per thousand pupils in public elementary schools rose from 35 to 47. After taking account of inflation, expenditures per pupil in the public schools increased by almost 5 percent per annum between 1965–66 and 1977–78.* This was double the rate of growth of real GNP per capita, and more rapid than the growth of real expenditures per pupil between 1950 and 1965 (Table 3.1). Teachers' salaries since 1965 have grown at about the same rate as the average hourly earnings of all employed persons, and the educational attainment of teachers has increased. Perhaps society expects too much from schools, or expects the wrong things, but if the schools have been "failing our children," it is not because they have been denied an ever-increasing share of resources.

Expenditures for the health care of children have also grown at a rapid pace (Table 3.1). The increase has been particularly strong for tax-supported expenditures per child; after adjustment for inflation, they grew at the extraordinary rate of 8.8 percent per annum between 1965 and 1978.

Not only have real expenditures for public schools and medical care grown rapidly, but nursery school enrollments have soared. In 1968 only 10 percent of 3- and 4-year-olds were in school (either half-day or full-day), but by 1981 the proportion was close to 40 percent. The use of nursery schools varies greatly from state to state, and analysis of this variation can help us understand the increase in enrollment over time. I studied interstate differences in the percent enrolled in 1970 and found that four factors explained 87 percent of the variation: the level of female educa-

---

* A small part of the increase, about 0.2 percent or 0.3 percent per annum, is associated with an increase in the proportion of pupils in secondary schools, which have higher per pupil expenditures than do elementary schools.

tion, the proportion of children in female-headed families, the labor force participation rate of married mothers of small children, and the percent of the population living in standard metropolitan statistical areas. The higher the level of each of these variables, the higher was enrollment, holding constant the levels of the others. Three other variables — income per capita, percent of the population that was black, and a variable distinguishing the South from other regions — were not significantly related to the percent enrolled after controlling for the other variables.

Between 1965 and 1978 there was a large increase nationally in the proportion of children in female-headed families, as well as significant increases in female education levels and the labor force participation rate of mothers of small children. There was also a slight increase in the percent of the population living in standard metropolitan statistical areas. If the changes in these variables over time had the same effect on nursery school enrollment as they have in the cross-state analysis, they would explain about 85 percent of the national increase from 1965 to 1977, with the rise of *female-headed families* contributing almost half of the total amount explained.

A strong relationship between nursery school enrollment and mother's education is apparent in national data classified by years of schooling of the mother. Among 3-year-olds whose mothers have not completed high school, about 10 percent were enrolled in 1975, but almost 50 percent of those children whose mothers had completed college were in school at least part of the day (Table 3.2). The differential enrollment by schooling of mother is also very large for children 4 years of age. This relation between nursery school enrollment and education cannot be attributed to an income effect because enrollment is only weakly related to income (Table 3.2).

The growth of schooling and health services for children has been substantial, but in many respects it pales into insignificance when compared with the time and money now devoted to television. According to the Nielson Survey (1981), the average child aged 2–5 spends about 30 hours per week watching TV. Moreover, once children are in school there is little decline in viewing. Nielson reports an average of over 25 hours per week at ages 6–11 and only slightly less TV watching by teenagers. A 1981 survey of sixth-grade students in California discovered that one-half watch TV until 11 P.M. or later, and one-third watch TV in their own or a sibling's bedroom (California Assessment Program 1982). The amount of TV viewing falls as the family's socioeconomic status rises. The average (median) child in a professional family watched 2.5 hours each weekday, whereas the average child of an unskilled worker watched 3.6 hours. Children of semiprofessional and skilled workers were intermediate in their TV viewing at 3.1 and 3.4 hours per weekday, respectively.

Home Production

Among the many recent economic and social changes, three are potentially of great significance to children. They are the rise of one-parent households, the increased propensity of mothers of small children to work outside the home, and the decline in family size.

One-parent households. When life expectancy was low, the loss of a parent through death was not uncommon and often deprived the surviving children of income and care. As adult mortality declined, the proportion of children raised by two parents rose. In the past thirty years, however, a startling change has occurred with respect to children in the United States — namely, a dramatic increase in the proportion who do *not* live with two parents. In 1950 about one child (under age 18) in ten was in that situation; by 1980 the proportion was almost one in four. The percentage rose continuously throughout the three decades, but the greatest increase occurred after 1970. The most important proximate causes of the increase are a rise in divorce rates (discussed in some detail in Chapter 5), and a rise in births to unmarried mothers (discussed in the previous chapter and in Chapter 4).

The divorce rate was steady from 1950 to 1965 at about 10 per year per thousand married women, but between 1965 and 1975 the rate doubled, and has remained above 20 per thousand ever since. This increase has resulted in many more children living with a divorced parent (usually the mother); the average number of children involved per divorce has remained relatively stable at about one per divorce. The statistics on one-parent families may overstate the adverse impact of divorce on children, because in many cases the other parent is alive and providing physical and psychological support to the child. On the other hand, these statistics also understate the impact of marital dissolution on children because they exclude an additional 10 percent of children who are living with one biological parent who has remarried.

The percentage of children living with a never-married mother more than tripled between 1970 and 1980 (from 0.8 percent to 2.8 percent), but it is still small relative to the 10 percent of children *born* to unmarried mothers in the eighteen years preceding 1980. This suggests that most unmarried mothers eventually marry, although women who marry after becoming a mother or when pregnant have considerably higher than average probability of divorce (Becker, Landes, and Michael 1977). Some babies of *unmarried* mothers are born to women who were previously married — and therefore are excluded from the *never married* category — but they probably account for only a small part of the total since most unmarried mothers are quite young.

The proportion of children not living with two parents and the relative importance of alternative arrangements vary considerably by race; a black child is more than three times as likely as a white child not to be in a two-parent family (Table 3.3). The largest relative differences between the races are in the categories "living with a never-married mother," "with a mother whose spouse is absent," and "other." The last category probably indicates the greater importance of extended family ties for blacks, including grandparents and other close relatives. These ties undoubtedly help black children, but the absence of a father must add to the disadvantages that black children otherwise face as a result of racial prejudice and lower income. There is no simple explanation for the fact that only 45 percent of black children live with two parents, nor is there any obvious public policy that would quickly change that situation.

The large black-white differential in family living arrangements is thought by some to be a result of the race difference in income (Bane 1976), and to a certain extent it is, but a closer look at variations over time and by region indicates that much remains unexplained. If low income were the main determinant of unwed motherhood, separation, and divorce, these behaviors should have *diminished* instead of rising rapidly between 1950 and 1980, because real income per capita for blacks as well as whites almost doubled over the three decades. Even more damaging to the income hypothesis is the fact that the black-white difference in income is much greater in the South than in the Northeast, but the race differential in the percentage of children not living with both parents is greater in the Northeast than in the South. The large differences in living arrangements between families of Mexican origin and those of Puerto Rican origin (noted in Chapter 2) also indicate that income is not the decisive determinant. Indeed, when we examine the behavior of young adults, we will note some reasons for believing that an increase in income to the woman could lead to an *increase* in the percentage of children not living with two parents by making it possible for the divorced or unmarried mother to maintain a separate household.

Although the rise in the illegitimacy *ratio* and the divorce rate has not been fully explained by any discipline, the economic perspective sheds some light on this matter. First, it suggests that many of the considerations that lead to an increase in unwed motherhood also lead to an increase in divorce; these are not independent phenomena. Both reflect an increase in the desire of women to raise their children alone or an increase in their ability to do so. These changes in adult behavior are discussed in detail in Chapters 4 and 5, but a few comments about possible reasons are appropriate here.

What happened between 1950 and 1980 that might have made women more willing and able to raise children without a spouse present? One explanation is the expansion of employment opportunities for women, especially in the rapidly growing service industries. Also, the ability of women to raise children without a husband has been aided by the growth of the AFDC program, poverty health programs, subsidized housing, food stamps, day care centers, and other subsidies. Finally, better control over fertility through improvements in contraception and legalization of abortion also have an effect because women can now have an active sex life without a high probability of becoming pregnant. They are, therefore, less dependent on the security of marriage and less willing to suffer physical and mental abuse from husbands or to accept the subordinate role that characterized many traditional marriages.

Changes in the labor market, new government programs, and better fertility control give women greater independence, and make them less tolerant of the unwillingness of most men to assume an equal share of responsibility for housework and child care. Several studies of time budgets and family behavior show that even when the wife works full time in the labor market, the husband's contribution to work in the home is small (Hill and Stafford 1980; Inkeles 1980). Many working women with children have decided that the disadvantages of marriage outweigh the advantages.

Working mothers. Not only are more and more children being raised by one parent (predominantly the mother), but more and more children in two-parent homes find that both parents are away from the home in paid employment. Mothers of young children are currently participating in the labor force to an extent unprecedented in the history of industrialized nations. This trend has three proximate causes: first, an increase in the proportion of mothers who are divorced, separated, or never married — all of whom have traditionally had high labor force participation rates; second, a small increase in participation rates of these nonmarried mothers; and, third, a large increase in participation by mothers who are married, with spouse present. The last has been by far the most important phenomenon, accounting for the bulk of the increase in the participation rate of mothers of young children.

Who takes care of small children when the mother works for pay? According to a special report based on the *Current Population Survey,* a surprisingly large number are said to be cared for by "child's parent in own home." When the mother works part time, 77 percent of white and 63 percent of black children ages 3–6 are reported as being cared for by "own parent in own home" (Table 3.4). Even when the mothers work full time, over 40 percent of the children are reported as being cared for in this way. The other major categories of care are in "own home by a nonparent" or in some other home either by a relative or nonrelative. White full-time working mothers tend to make more use of nonrelatives than relatives, but blacks are more likely to use relatives. The percentage of children ages 3–6 cared for in day care centers is very low for all categories — reaching a high of only 7 percent for white mothers employed full time.

The large percentage reported as cared for by "own parent" is difficult to explain. In some families, the father may be at home while the mother is at work, but time-budget studies show very little child care by fathers, even when the mother is employed full time. Some mothers work at home and take care of the child at the same time, but the proportion is small. A more plausible explanation is that the child is in nursery school or kindergarten while the mother is at work, and is cared for by the mother after school. In addition, many children are left alone or with another child. A 1979 survey of families who had previously been involved in New York City's public day care program revealed that 19 percent leave their children alone at some time during working hours (Community Service Society of New York 1982). Almost 30 percent of the respondents indicated that they left children in the care of a sibling who was under 14 years of age (p. 41). The study concluded: "There are large numbers of 'latch key' children coming home after school either to sit by the television or to roam the streets" (p. 44).

Family size. In most families the absence of one parent or the participation of both parents in the labor force tends to reduce the amount of home production that children receive. From the perspective of the average child, however, these trends may be offset to some extent by the decrease in fertility and family size. Between 1970 and 1979 the average number of children per household (in households that had at least one child) decreased from 2.4 to 2.0. Moreover, because the decrease occurred primarily in very large families, the change in the average number of other children in the household from the point of view of each child is even more striking. In 1970 the average child had 2.4 siblings under 18 years of age, but in 1979 had only 1.6.*

The reduction in large families has been particularly great among blacks. In 1970 the average black child had 3.4 siblings under 18 years of age. By 1979 he or she had only 2.1 siblings — fewer than the 2.3 siblings the average *white* child had in 1970. Does this reduction in number of children per household matter? Several studies of birth order and number of siblings suggest that the reduction may matter a great deal. Most of these studies indicate that first-borns and children from small families have numerous advantages throughout life. These advantages are usually ascribed to the greater amount of investment in human capital that these children receive.

A negative relation between number of children and mother's education is one of the most systematic and consistent features of American families (see Figure 3.1). Numerous reasons have been advanced to explain this relationship; most of them assume that the causality runs from education to fertility. For instance, on average, educated women can earn higher wages, and the higher value of their time leads them to want fewer children. Some observers argue that better-educated women want to make more human capital investments in each child; therefore, holding husband's income constant, they want fewer children. Another possibility is that better-educated women are more effective contraceptors, and therefore have fewer unwanted children. These explanations all seem reasonable, but it is also plausible that some of the causality runs from fertility to education. The clearest example of this is the case of the teenage mother who must stop her schooling because she has started a family. More generally, young women who do not want to have children, or who

---

* The average number of children per family is simply the number of children divided by the number of families, but the average number of children in a family from the point of view of the children is a weighted average where the number of families of each size is weighted by the number of children in that size family. This number minus one equals the number of siblings of the average child. For example, if one family has two children, and one family has four, the average number of children per family is three. But there are four children living in a four-child family and only two in a two-child family, so from the child's point of view the average number is three and a third, and the average number of siblings per child is two and a third.

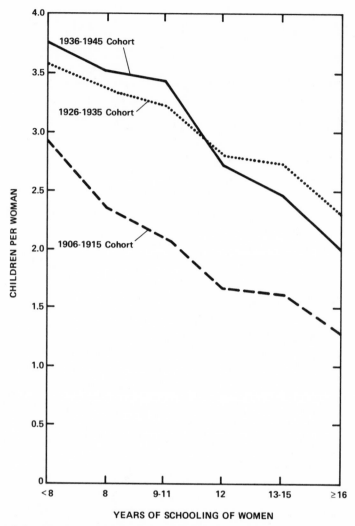

Figure 3.1. Number of children ever born to women ages 35 – 44, by birth cohort and years of schooling completed.

(*Sources:* U.S. Bureau of the Census, *Census of Population, 1960,* vol. 1, Characteristics of the Population, pt. 1, United States Summary, table 178; idem, *Statistical Abstract of the United States, 1977;* idem, *Census of Population, 1970,* Detailed Characteristics, United States Summary, tables 199 and 213; idem, *Current Population Reports,* series P-20, no. 358, table 8.)

know that they will want only one or two, are more likely to continue their education in order to prepare for a higher-paying career in the labor market.

Although family size falls as education rises, other factors are also important, as evidenced by variation in the number of children born to women of different races and ethnic groups after controlling for level of education. The following figures, giving number of children ever born to women ages 35–44, show that part of the higher fertility of Hispanic and black women can be explained by their lower education. But even after adjustment for years of schooling, their fertility is still substantially above the white level; Japanese-American women, by contrast, have 23 percent fewer children than do white women, after adjusting for education (U.S. Bureau of the Census 1973a, table 213).

	Children ever born to women ages 35–44, 1970	
	Actual	*Adjusted for education*
Hispanic	3.65	3.37
Black	3.49	3.32
White (except Hispanic)	2.85	2.90
Chinese	2.83	2.81
Japanese	2.15	2.22

To summarize the data on services to children, in recent decades there has been an increase in the quantity provided outside the home, but there has probably been a substantial decline in home-produced services. Many women have been seeking to escape from their traditional, highly specialized, subordinate role, and most men have not made compensating changes in their behavior except to acquiesce in the trend toward smaller families.

THE WELL-BEING OF CHILDREN

Is it well with the child? — II Kings 4:26

Describing trends and group differences in market-produced services and in family living arrangements is not easy, but the task of assessing their consequences for the well-being of children is far more difficult. We don't fully understand why there have been such dramatic changes in family size, structure, and function, and we know even less about their effects on children. One problem is inadequate data, particularly the absence of good measures of children's well-being. Another problem arises in trying to separate the effects of changes in family living arrangements from the effects of other contemporary changes such as the growth of real income or the advent of television. One of the biggest problems with public policy research on children is a failure to look at the effects of working mothers or one-parent homes in a dynamic context. For example, most studies conclude that there is no effect on children of the mother's going to work when marital status is held constant and no effect of being in a one-parent home when family income is held constant. But if the mother's going to work increases the probability of divorce and if being in a one-parent home increases the probability of lower income, it is misleading to say that these changes have had no effect on children.

The health of children and their performance in school provide some information about their development and well-being. We will look at changes in these two areas and consider how children are affected by what has been happening outside and within their homes.

Child Health

Measured by the crude but thoroughly objective indicator of mortality, the health of American children has continued to improve in recent decades, albeit at a slower pace than during the first half of this century. From 1900 to 1950 the number of deaths per one thousand children ages 1–4 plummeted from 19.8 to 1.4, a rate of decrease of over 5 percent per annum, while the death rate for children 5–14 fell at 3.7 percent per annum, from 3.9 to 0.6 per thousand. In absolute terms, the largest declines were achieved prior to the discovery of anti-infectious drugs and were due to rising standards of living and improved public health practices. The relative rate of decrease, however, accelerated with the introduction of penicillin, sulfa, and other effective drugs in the 1930s and 1940s.

Between 1950 and 1980 the decline in child mortality continued, but at a much slower rate than in the first half of the century. The grim toll previously taken by infectious diseases has been virtually eliminated, and great progress has been made in treating other fatal childhood diseases such as acute leukemia. Motor vehicle accidents and other trauma now account for more than half of all child deaths. Mortality in childhood is still appreciably higher for blacks than whites, but there has been some narrowing of the race differential since 1965. The average annual rate of decline at ages 1–4 was 4.3 percent for blacks compared with 2.4 percent for whites, and the rates of change at ages 5–9 were 3.1 percent and 2.0 percent, respectively. This narrowing is not simply an artifact attributable to the higher initial levels for blacks: they also had higher levels in 1960, but between 1960 and 1965 the rates of decline were more rapid for whites than for blacks.

With mortality in childhood now quite low (except for accidents), public health specialists have shifted their emphasis toward other aspects of health such as illness and disability, and to child health practices that may result in problems later in life. One of the chief objects of concern has been nutrition. The mass media frequently dramatize a relation between poverty and hunger, but an analysis of diet and development of young children by economists Dov Chernichovsky and Douglas Coate (1980) found no evidence that low income contributed to insufficient intake of calories or proteins. Although their observations (the Ten-State Nutrition Survey, 1968–1970) were predominantly of children from low-income families, the average intake of calories and proteins was equal to or above recommended dietary allowances, and the average height, weight, and head size of these children were approximately equal to national norms. Furthermore, statistical analysis of differences among these families failed to identify any significant relation between income and intake of calories and proteins. Holding income constant, poor diet was more frequently found in large families, leading the authors to conclude that in their sample it was family size *per se,* and not the effect of family size on per capita income, that was associated with poor nutrition (p. 226). Their conclusion that poor diet was not the result of low income was reaffirmed in a report issued by the Department of Health, Education, and Welfare, *The Status of Children, 1977,* which stated: "Adequacy of nutrition in the United States is not primarily a problem of low income; true malnutrition is virtually nonexistent in this country. However, poor nutrition and poor nutritional habits are found in all income groups and over the years have become perhaps typical for most segments of our society" (p. 89; Administration for Children, Youth, and Families 1978).

Many health experts allege that children consume too many calories in the form of sugar and fat, and not enough in the form of complex carbohydrates such as those obtained from fruits, vegetables, and whole grains; they recommend a reduction in the consumption of sugar-coated cereals, soft drinks, cookies, and candy. The deterioration of children's eating habits is often attributed to television advertising, but we might also ask what role parents are playing or should play with respect to their children's nutrition. Superficially, it appears easier to control "outside" influences such as television than to expect parents to act more responsibly, but there are other costs to regulation and other benefits from greater parental involvement in children's eating habits. Some experts have suggested that children in families that eat together at regular times benefit from the support and discipline associated with such regularity.

The parental role also needs to be examined with respect to preventive health care for children. For instance, in 1979 a shocking 40 percent of children 1–4 years of age had not been adequately immunized against poliomyelitis, and 35 percent had not received the recommended doses of the DTP (diphtheria, tetanus, and pertussis) vaccines. By contrast, in 1965, when real per capita income was 30 percent below 1979 levels and there were 27 percent fewer physicians per capita, only 26 percent of children were without adequate protection against polio and DTP. To be sure, a few parents find it difficult to immunize their children because of inadequate access to medical care or their own poor health, but it is unlikely that these problems were *greater* in 1979 than in 1965. Furthermore, more than three-fourths of the children who have not been adequately immunized live in families with income *above* the poverty level.

In a detailed economic analysis of the utilization of pediatric care by children ages 1–5, Ann Colle and Michael Grossman (1978) found that the most important variables are mother's schooling and the number of children in the family. Holding constant a large number of other socioeconomic and health-related variables, they found that the probability of a preventive visit during 1970 increased by 4 percentage points for each additional year of mother's schooling, and decreased by 3 percentage points for each additional child in the family. (The average probability for this national sample, disproportionately weighted with low income and black families, was 32 percent.) An increase in family income had a small positive effect on the demand for preventive visits, especially as income rose from low to medium levels. Receipt of welfare income (which the authors treated as a proxy for Medicaid eligibility) also had a positive effect on utilization.

These results concerning preventive health services for young children are similar in some respects to the findings regarding the utilization of nursery schools. In particular, a strong relation between mother's education and investment in children is one of the most consistent and widespread findings of social science research in this field. Why do better-educated mothers (holding income and other relevant variables constant) spend more time with their young children, send them to nursery school, and take them for preventive health visits at a higher rate than do their less educated peers? The answers to this question fall into two main categories, and within each there are several possible variants.

One category of answers assumes that the additional schooling *causes* the difference in behavior. Noneconomists tend to emphasize the effect of schooling on *preferences,* whereas economists, especially those working within the Beckerian framework of stable preferences and maximizing behavior, believe that the additional schooling makes women more efficient in their role as mothers just as it enhances their productivity in paid employment. According to this view, the differences in behavior reflect the different (and presumably superior) judgments that well-educated mothers make about what is good for their children.

The other category of explanations for the relation between

mother's schooling and investment in young children holds that both are the result of one or more "third" variables. For instance, women who have obtained more schooling may have come from homes with different values (as evidenced by the greater investment that their own parents made in *them*), and they in turn place a higher value on investment in their children. One promising hypothesis is that the mothers with more schooling have lower rates of *time discount:* they are more willing to incur a *current* cost, in money, time, or energy, for some *future* benefit. The fact that they have acquired more schooling themselves suggests that they (or their parents) were more willing and able to invest in the future. Or it may be that the additional schooling lowered their rate of time discount. My research has convinced me that time discount tends to be lower, the higher the level of schooling. I suspect that the causality runs primarily from time discount to schooling, but definitive answers are not presently available (Fuchs 1982b).

Differences in rates of time discount probably have an important effect on decisions about health, schooling, fertility, occupation — in short, most of the major choices that determine how long people will live and how well they will live. A political scientist, Edward Banfield (1968), described variation in time discount at the aggregate level as a pervasive phenomenon associated with differences in social class. Walter Mischel, a leader in psychological studies of delay of gratification in children, wrote: "It is difficult to conceive of socialization (or, indeed, of civilization) without such self-imposed delays. Learning to wait for desired outcomes and to act in the light of anticipated future consequences is fundamental for planning and for the foresight and future-orientation on which complex goal-directed behavior depends" (Mischel 1974, p. 250). He found that the ability to delay gratification during childhood is positively related to the presence of a father in the home as well as to intelligence and achievement orientation.

School Performance

The increasing commitment of resources to public education suggests that the 1970s might have been a golden age for schools, but measures of children's performance in school lead to an opposite conclusion. For instance, declining scores on college entrance examinations have been difficult to explain and have made the schools a handy target for a variety of social critics. Defenders of the public schools say that the increase in enrollment of minority students from disadvantaged backgrounds has made the school's task more difficult, and there is probably some validity to this point, especially for schools in those large cities that have experienced a major influx of minority families. For the country as a whole, however, the proportion of black and Hispanic students in the public schools increased by about 7 percentage points between 1965 and 1980, hardly a staggering change. Furthermore, the decline in performance on college entrance tests and the increase in disciplinary problems seem to be widespread, including schools that have had no change in minority enrollments.

Some education experts note that the 1960s and 1970s were marked by an emphasis on "leveling up" — that is, improving the educational experiences of those children who were most in need rather than catering to those with above-average performance. According to this view, the increased resources in most school districts were devoted to special-education classes, remedial programs, bilingual classes, school desegregation, and similar efforts to aid disadvantaged children. Whether as a result of such efforts or for other reasons, white-black differentials in test scores at age 9 did decline appreciably during the 1970s. A difference of 17.8 percentage points in mathematics in 1972–73 was cut to 12.8 by 1977–78, and the race differential in reading fell from 16.7 percentage points in 1971–72 to 13.2 in 1974–75 (National Center for Education Statistics 1980, pp. 30, 32).

Television. The diffusion of television into almost every home in the United States and the enormous amount of time committed to it by most children and adults make it one of the great changes of the post–World War II era. This universality, however, hampers efforts to measure its role in the declining performance and increasing violence in the schools. There is some variation in the amount of TV viewing among families, but this variation is often associated with socioeconomic differences, thus confounding attempts to study the effects of TV alone. As an example, a survey of fifteen thousand sixth-grade students in California in 1981 found that test scores in reading, writing, and mathematics were lower among children who watched more TV (California Assessment Program 1982). The report could not conclude that TV was the cause, however, because students with high scores tended to come from better-educated, higher-income families where there may have been more emphasis on learning. When students were grouped by parents' occupation, there was little relation between achievement and time spent watching TV within each group, except for a noticeable decline in test scores among children who watched six hours or more per day.

One reason for uncertainty about the effect of TV is that it probably varies, depending upon the alternatives available to the child. If the child's home is devoid of books, magazines, newspapers, or the opportunity to participate in or at least hear stimulating conversation, TV watching could make a positive contribution to intellectual development. On the other hand, in a family that offers many positive alternatives to TV, achievement in school probably suffers from overviewing.

Another barrier to generalizing about the effects of TV on school performance is the likelihood that the effect varies with the age of the child. TV viewing at ages 2–5 could increase a child's readiness for school because some of the most popular programs watched by that age group have a clear educational thrust and the time spent in viewing is probably not at the expense of other educational activities. By contrast, TV watching by older children falls into a different pattern. The programs rarely have much educational content and the time spent in front of the set is time that could be spent reading or doing homework.

With respect to the effect of TV on aggressive behavior, a recent summary report concluded that televised violence is definitely a cause of aggression in children (National Institute of Mental Health, *Television and Behavior: Ten Years of Scientific Progress and Implications for the Eighties,* vol. 1, Summary Report, 1982). The report was silent, however, on the question of how much of the increase in violence and crime by youngsters is the result of TV and how much is due to other causes. The strongest evidence that TV has an adverse effect comes from laboratory studies in which children are shown films or video-tapes that contain violent scenes. These children become more aggressive than controls who have not been shown such films. Some researchers, however, have questioned whether it is reasonable to extrapolate from these laboratory experiments to real-world TV viewing and real-world behavior. Those studies that have attempted to assess the impact of TV on children through survey-type research also conclude that there is an effect, but the evidence is weak. For instance, one study reported that children ages 6–10 who view TV shows that include considerable violence are rated as more aggressive by their classmates, but the study did not adequately control for related variables such as socioeconomic status and school achievement; neither did it test whether the causality is from TV viewing to aggressive behavior or the reverse (Eron 1982).

Working mothers. If TV is not the culprit, can the poorer performance of children in schools result from their mothers' going to work? Definitive answers to this question are not available, partly for the same reasons that make it so difficult to determine the effects of TV — the presence of numerous interrelated variables. A study of kindergarten children in North Carolina that examined ten different measures of achievement and development (Farel 1980) found that, on average, all ten were lower for children of working mothers — seven at high levels of statistical significance. This relationship disappeared, however, when mother's education, family income, and race were held constant. After controlling for these other variables, only six of the ten measures were lower, and only one was significantly so.

Economist Arleen Leibowitz (1977) analyzed the results of the Peabody Picture Vocabulary Test given to 3-, 4-, and 5-year-olds. After controlling for socioeconomic differences, she found that children of mothers who spent time reading (either alone or with the child) scored about 5 percent higher than did the children of mothers who watched television (with or without the child), but there was no difference in achievement between children of working and nonworking mothers. A study by Hill and Stafford sheds some light on this last result. Their analysis of time-budget data reveals that working mothers, especially those with higher education, devote a great deal of time to child care "at the expense of sleep and personal free time" (1980, p. 229). A question that Hill and Stafford did not investigate is the extent to which working mothers who devote a great deal of time to child care do so at the expense of time spent doing things with or for their husbands. Conflicting demands for time and attention between children and husband must be a strain for many working mothers and may contribute to the high divorce rate.

The effect of working mothers on children is sometimes studied indirectly by analyzing the effects of day care, but the results are inconclusive. Although there has been considerable research on day care, most reviewers of this literature agree with Urie Bronfenbrenner that "no firm conclusions can be drawn about the impact of day versus home care on the cognitive development of children" (1976, p. 121). Moreover, even if the day care studies were more definitive, they would still leave great uncertainty about the effects of both parents' working. As Belsky and Steinberg (1978) emphasize, only a small fraction of the children of working mothers are cared for in day care centers, and even within that setting most of the research has been limited to university-connected centers with high staff/child ratios and well designed programs. Their reading of the literature suggests that for *disadvantaged* children, such centers "may have an enduring positive effect, for it appears that such day care experience may attenuate the declines in test scores typically associated with high risk populations after 18 months of age" (p. 931). They also perceptively note and criticize the failure of most researchers to study anything beyond the immediate and direct effects on the child. They urge consideration of the interrelationships between day care, maternal employment, marital relationships, family income, and even broader issues of culture and ideology.

One-parent homes. Failure to consider all the pathways through which adult behaviors affect the well-being of children is particularly serious in appraisals of the one-parent homes that usually result from divorce and unwed motherhood. Comparison within schools of children from one-parent and two-parent homes usually shows the former as performing worse by almost every criterion (*Principal* 1980). However, researchers who have re-

viewed the available evidence typically conclude that the differences tend to disappear after controlling for family income, race,
education of mother, and other socioeconomic variables (Ross
and Sawhill 1975). Assuming that the differences do disappear,
what inference should be drawn about the effects of divorce or
unwed motherhood on the child? Is it helpful to say that there are
no effects "controlling for income" when 51 percent of the children in female-headed families are living in poverty compared
with only 8 percent in husband-wife families? (See Hofferth 1982,
p. 1.) Isn't this a little like saying that cigarette smoking has no
adverse consequences on health, "holding constant the condition
of the lungs and the heart"? (From the standpoint of a behavioral
scientist seeking to discover the relationship between child care
settings and development, the emphasis on controls is appropriate. From a policy perspective, however, it is important to draw
a distinction between those control variables that are unaffected
by the phenomena under study — for example, race — and those
that are likely to be affected — for example, family income.)

What is the impact of divorce on children? A breakdown in the
relationship between parents is likely to be emotionally harmful
to their children regardless of whether it leads to divorce or not. As
Judith Wallerstein and Joan Kelly note, "Neither unhappy marriage nor divorce are especially congenial for children; each
imposes its own set of stresses" (1980, p. 307). The negative effect
of divorce on children's *economic* well-being, however, is much
more certain.

Prior to divorce, two parents and their children share one
household, thus benefiting from economies of scale in the use of
space, equipment, and supplies, and from the cooperative en-
deavors of the partnership. After divorce, there are typically two
households to maintain, the economies of scale are lost, and
cooperative efforts at best become more difficult. The material
well-being of the child is thus likely to suffer, even if there is no
change in the *proportion* of the parents' resources (money, time,
energy) devoted to the child. Moreover, frequently there is a
decrease in the proportion as well. The father, who is usually the
primary source of money income, often reduces or eliminates
child support when the mother has custody. He may do this in part

because he no longer cares as much about the well-being of the child or because he can no longer exert as much control over how the money is spent. If, as is often the case, the mother begins or increases paid employment following divorce, the child loses some of the mother's home production. In short, it is highly likely that divorce will make children worse off economically, no matter what divorce settlement is reached or what kind of adjustments parents make.

Given the economic straits facing children in one-parent homes, many child advocates think the obvious solution is for the government to give these families more money. Such transfers may be warranted, but it should be recognized that they may adversely affect children in two ways. First, the additional taxes needed to fund such transfers will reduce the resources available to children in two-parent homes. Second, by making divorce and unwed motherhood less burdensome, the transfers will probably lead to an increase in the number of children living in one-parent homes. The following example helps to bring to the surface the complex issues of justice and efficiency that are inherent in the problem.

Consider the case of two married couples who are equal with respect to family income, number of children, and other socioeconomic variables. In both marriages the husband and wife have their differences, but one couple divorces and sets up two households and the other does not. The children of the divorced couple are almost certainly worse off *economically* than the children of the couple that stayed together. If we consider only the children, a transfer of income from the intact to the fragmented family might seem justified, but if we consider the adults it is difficult to see the justice of such redistribution. One might as well argue that married couples should redistribute income to single persons at comparable income levels because single individuals face higher costs of living if they maintain separate households.

Who should bear the principal responsibility for children — their parents or society? If a man starts to manufacture plastics and in the process dumps chemicals into the water, current public opinion holds that he should be responsible for the external costs imposed on society. But if that man fathers one or more children and then dumps them and their mother on society by divorce or desertion, many so-called progressive writers argue that society, rather than the father, should be responsible for their care.

One of the principal reasons given for this position is that the man is likely to remarry and father other children, and therefore will have difficulty supporting the first set. In the words of the otherwise usually sensible *Economist,* "One salary can rarely support two households. The logical conclusion is that no man should be legally obliged to maintain more than one wife and one set of children. The former wife and children should receive a full state allowance without the automatic deduction now made for the maintenance payments wrung out of the hard-pressed ex-husband" (*The Economist,* April 24–30, 1982, p. 84).

What nonsense. To be sure, a humane society will not want to let children starve, regardless of the behavior of their fathers. But it is one thing to say that the state will provide support as a last resort, and another to guarantee to men in advance that they can father and abandon children with impunity, knowing that society will pick up the check.

There is no perfect solution to the problem of ensuring greater equality of opportunity for children while pursuing justice and efficiency with respect to adult behavior, but greater understanding of the dilemma might lead to a more constructive discussion of the issues.

Family values. Although the rise of one-parent homes probably does contribute to the problems of children, it seems highly unlikely that this is the only, or even the major, factor affecting the performance of children in school. Most households still have two parents, and the investments these parents make in their children and the values they instill in them are major determinants of how the children will fare in school and in later life. School districts are usually quite sensitive to the demands of their communities (sometimes distressingly so, as in their willingness to remove books from school libraries). If most parents wanted more homework and were willing to spend the time making sure that it was done, and if most parents wanted higher standards and firmer discipline and were willing to accept the consequences, it is unlikely that school superintendents, principals, and teachers would not cooperate. As the president of Rutgers University, Edward J. Bloustein, recently said, "If discipline does not begin in the home, it can hardly succeed in the school" (1982, p. 5).

The success of children of Asian background in U.S. public schools indicates that study, hard work, respect for teachers, and heavy parental involvement in the educational progress of children still pay off. Many of these children come from low-income families and many from families in which English is the second language or not spoken at all, but their educational achievements are extraordinary. On standardized tests, students of Asian background score higher than any other group, including native-born whites. Asian students are winning top honors at high schools across the country and are being admitted to the leading universities at rates far out of proportion to their presence in the population. In Harvard's class of 1985, for instance, 9 percent of the students are Asian-Americans — six times their representation in the U.S. population; and at the University of California, Berkeley, 20 percent of the undergraduates are of Asian origin — four times their proportion in the California population.

Social scientists who have studied this phenomenon agree with the students themselves that this extraordinary success story is related to the high value placed on scholarship in Asian societies and to a strong family structure that transmits this value. The Japanese *kyoiku-mama* (the "education-mama") is now taking her place alongside the stereotypical "Jewish mother" because of the time and attention she devotes to her children and the extent to which she encourages and helps them to do well in school (Feinberg 1981). There is probably a significant relation between their scholastic success and the small size of the Japanese-American family, but caution must be exercised in inferring causality. Children of Japanese origin may do well in school because they come from small families, or their parents may have small families because they want to invest a great deal in each child. Most likely, both forces are at work.

Cohort size. The example of the Japanese family suggests that the nationwide decline in school performance in the 1970s could be partly related to the changes in fertility and cohort size. As we have seen, the proportion of children who were first-borns reached a low point and the proportion of births of fourth-order or higher reached a peak in the years around 1960. These are the cohorts that were moving through the high schools in the 1970s. Psychologists, sociologists, and economists all report that first-borns and children in small families have higher IQ's and achieve more in school and as adults than do other children. It is probably more than just a coincidence that twenty of the first twenty-nine astronauts were first-borns.

In one of the most interesting studies of the effect of sibling position, Peter Lindert (1977) focused on *intra*family differences in order to obtain better control of unmeasured differences among families that might have explained results based on cross-sectional studies. He found that first-borns do have an advantage over their later-born siblings, and he provided some evidence indicating that "the simple reason is that sharing family time and money with siblings is a drag on achievement" (p. 203). The reduction in family size that occurred in the 1970s implies that each child could obtain more parental input.

In cross-sectional studies that control for other socioeconomic variables, children in large families are less likely to go to nursery school and more likely to suffer malnutrition. Also, on average they complete fewer years of schooling and receive less preventive health care. Although the correlation is beyond doubt, there are several possible explanations, and conclusions about causality are difficult to reach. If the number of children were predetermined in the sense of being beyond the control of the parents, one could reasonably argue that the causality runs from the number of children to the investment behavior. It is clear, however, that family size is itself a consequence of parental decisions. If the number of children is completely and costlessly determined by the parents, one could argue that the causality runs from the amount of investment parents want to make in each child to the number of children they actually have. According to the French historian Philippe Ariès, this was the force behind the decline in birth rates in Western Europe after the French and Industrial Revolutions. He writes, "The parents' chief psychological and material investment consisted of helping the children to get ahead . . . The number of these children . . . could not be left to chance. Wise management required reducing their number to the minimum that corresponded to the family's financial outlook. The fewer the children, the more time and care could be devoted to each and the better the results" (1980, pp. 646–647).

It seems to me likely that both the number of children *and* the investment in them are jointly determined by parents as a result of differences in their objective circumstances and subjective values. Furthermore, the number of children actually born may differ from the number the parents prefer, depending upon their choice of contraceptive technique and their effectiveness in using it. Delay of gratification — their rate of time discount — may enter as an explanatory variable, affecting family size through contraceptive behavior and affecting investment per child directly and through family size.

According to Ariès, the recent decline in fertility in Western countries is *not* for the most part motivated by the earlier desire to invest more in each child: "The days of the child king are over . . . Couples — and individuals — no longer plan life in terms of the child and his personal future, as was the case during the 19th and early 20th centuries. This does not mean that the child has disappeared from such plans, but that he fits into them as one of the various components that make it possible for adults to blossom as individuals" (ibid., pp. 649, 650). If Ariès is correct, the trend toward small families will not have as favorable an impact on children as would be predicted from the size-of-family effects observed in cross-sectional studies. On the other hand, to the extent that the decline in fertility reflects improvement in the ability of parents to avoid unwanted births or their desire to invest more in each child, the small cohorts born in the 1970s should perform much better in school than did the huge cohorts born between 1955 and 1965.

PUBLIC POLICY ISSUES

The list of public policy issues that involve children is long and varied; birth control, abortion, divorce, day care, and Medicaid are just some of the areas in which decisions by the legislative, executive, and judicial branches of government have considerable potential impact on children. Because it is not feasible to discuss each issue in detail, this section is devoted to a systematic review of one issue that may leap to the forefront of public concern in the next decade — the question of large-scale federal subsidies for children. What are the principal arguments in favor of subsidies and what policy objectives might subsidies serve? What forms could these subsidies take and how would particular forms relate to particular objectives? The economic perspective is useful in posing and answering these questions.

Why Child Subsidies?

Although the proponents of increased federal support for children do not marshal their arguments in neat, conceptually distinct categories, these arguments can usually be reduced to four principal types: (1) greater human capital investment in each child would be socially beneficial; (2) child subsidies would contribute to greater equality of opportunity, and equality of outcomes; (3) subsidies for children would help women; and (4) subsidies are needed to raise fertility to a level that would prevent population decline in the long run.

Human capital investment. The essence of this argument is that the average family "underinvests" in its children — that is, does not spend as much time and money on children as would be socially desirable — and that child subsidies would correct this misallocation of resources. This is an argument about *efficiency,* not *justice.* An easy way to keep the distinction clear is to think in terms of the "average" family, one that would pay in taxes (or higher prices, if the taxes are levied on firms) an amount exactly equal to the value of the subsidy (assuming for the moment no administrative or incentive costs associated with the additional taxes).

For such families, two principal questions need to be answered. First, why aren't they investing more in their children? Second, would child subsidies induce them to increase their investment? Economic theory answers the first question by pointing out that parents will invest less in their children's health or education than would be socially optimal if some of the benefits of such investment will be realized by others, but the costs must be borne by the parents. The existence of such external effects has long been assumed with respect to elementary and secondary education and is the main reason why schooling is publicly subsidized and made compulsory. Whether such underinvestment takes place at preschool age is difficult to say. The failure of many parents to have their children immunized against communicable diseases is one bit of evidence suggesting some underinvestment. Reports of child neglect provide a more alarming example, but the data necessary for a precise quantitative assessment are not available.

It is also difficult to determine the extent to which child subsidies would induce the average family to alter its level of investment. Suppose, for instance, that the family had to pay an additional $1,000 in taxes and received $1,000 back in the form of a "family allowance." In such a case, there is no reason to expect the family to make any change in its investment in children — the amount that seemed best to it before will seem best after, as well. (The case where the amount of the subsidy is tied to the *number* of children is discussed below, under the pronatalist argument.)

What if the subsidy does not come as a monetary grant but takes the form of free nursery schools or free pediatric care? The chances that such programs will raise the overall level of investment in children by the average family are greater than for the monetary grant, but even such "tied" subsidies may not induce much change in behavior. For instance, suppose that the average family is investing $2,000 a year in services for their children. If the government imposes a tax of $1,000 and provides $1,000 worth of free services, isn't it reasonable for the family to cut its own investment in services by $1,000, leaving the total investment in children unaffected by the program? Economic theory predicts such a no-change outcome as long as the amount of the subsidized service provided does not exceed the amount that was being purchased prior to the new taxes and subsidies. If it *does* exceed that amount, the price of the subsidized service at the margin (the last unit purchased) is reduced, and then it is reasonable to expect an increase in the quantity purchased by the parents.

Equality of opportunity. Nowhere is the conflict between equality and other social goals more evident than in the formulation of policies that affect children. That this country is very far from offering equal opportunity to all children is painfully obvious. Some children are blessed with kind, loving, intelligent parents who are willing and able to devote ample resources to their development. Others grow up in situations characterized by deficits of one kind or another — low income, one parent missing, or perhaps parental indifference. Still other children are the victims of criminal neglect and abuse.

Not only is the inequality of opportunity obvious, but numerous studies confirm the common-sense judgment that an unequal start contributes substantially to inequality later in life in education, health, work, and other indicators of achievement and well-being. If we seek to reduce inequality of opportunity, several questions need to be addressed. How can equality for children be reconciled with fair treatment of adults? What policies would lead to greater equality? What are some of the obstacles to more egalitarian policies? In considering these questions let us assume that there are no external effects, in order to focus on issues of justice per se. It will become readily apparent that the resolution of such issues depends a great deal on value judgments, not economic analysis; but analysis does help to illuminate the discussion.

Consider two couples who are identical with respect to income and education, but one couple has one child and the other has three. The goal of equality of opportunity for children would probably require some transfer of resources from the first to the second couple, but is that equitable to the parents? What if the first couple had only one child because they wanted to invest a great deal in it? If there is no transfer, however, children in the larger families will, on average, receive less investment.

Inequality of opportunity among children arises not only as a result of inequality in family size and family income, but for other reasons. Genetic endowments affecting IQ, appearance, health, and other characteristics differ widely. Furthermore, parents are not alike in their child-rearing abilities and interests, and some children suffer from parental fighting or marital dissolution.

Discrimination on racial, religious, or ethnic grounds might also contribute to inequality. Should a policy aimed at increasing equality of opportunity try to take these nonmonetary differences into account, or should it concentrate solely on money income? The latter may be all that is feasible, but we should be aware that it addresses only one source of inequality.

What about families that have the same income and the same number of children but differ greatly in the amount they invest in their children? Should the state seek to ensure greater uniformity? Are there policy instruments available to accomplish such an objective? An attempt to limit the amount of investment undertaken by families who opt for a high level would probably be rejected as beyond the legitimate scope of government. Publicly established *minimums* would no doubt be more acceptable, but if they were much above the levels that families would voluntarily choose, they would be difficult to enforce. Such problems are likely to be particularly great in the case of young children because many significant sources of inequality are related to subtle, qualitative differences in parental warmth and attention rather than to quantifiable inputs of food, clothing, or similar commodities. It was a Brookings Institution political scientist, not a right-wing economist, who wrote, "Government has no mechanism to enforce love, affection, and concern between husband and wife, between parent and child, or between one sibling and another" (Steiner 1981).

Some of the questions raised about tied subsidies in our discussion of human capital apply to issues of justice as well. Can government force parents to be nicer to their children than they would otherwise want to be? Probably only to a very limited extent. Moreover, when inequality per se is the issue rather than failure to meet some minimum level, another problem arises. Some parents place a value on giving their children a *better than average* start in life. If a widespread subsidy program raises the average level, those parents would respond by increasing *their* investments, thus partially negating the effort to reduce inequality.

In short, a good deal of inequality is inherent in any system that does not remove children from their homes at birth and place them in a uniform institutional setting. Even then, genetically determined differences in IQ, appearance, health, and other characteristics would remain. The above arguments notwithstanding, more equality of opportunity could be introduced into our society by redistributing income. What the analytical studies warn is that even in a world of complete equality of income, children would still experience a great deal of inequality from other sources.

Profeminist policy. Both in this country and abroad, the question of subsidies for children is frequently seen as a feminist issue. This theme dominates the discussion of child care subsidies in Sweden and Denmark — two countries whose social trends and programs have frequently been leading indicators for subsequent developments in the United States (Steiner 1981). According to U.S. social policy analysts Sheila Kamerman and Alfred Kahn, "we are beginning to experience the push of employed women for the right to marry and bear and rear children" (1979, p. 86). Some feminists argue that the failure of society to subsidize child care deprives women of their "right" to have both a job and children. Child subsidies are thus seen as contributing to equity between women and men. Although not stated explicitly, the equity argument must be based on the assumption that women have a greater demand for children and feel a greater obligation to them than do men. Differential demand may be related to age because the years when reproduction is possible are more limited for women than for men. Whatever the reason, the greater obligation is a liability that mothers bear when they strike an explicit or implicit contract with the fathers of their children. If fathers felt an equal obligation, child subsidies would not be any more relevant to women than to men.

To understand this reasoning, consider again an average family that pays in taxes an amount equal to what it receives as a child subsidy. Is the family any better off from such a program? The answer is clearly no. Has the wife gained relative to the husband? The answer to that is not as clear. Many women believe that a subsidy for child care would make them better off, in which case the husband would be worse off because the overall position of the family is unchanged.

Subsidization of child care will help the mother at the expense of the father in the average family if the mother cares more about the children than the father does; if they care equally, the subsidy will have no effect on the distribution of resources within the family. The logic of this result can be seen most clearly in the case where the father has abandoned the mother and child and she provides all the support. The taxes for the child's subsidy will be borne both by the father and the mother, but the mother will get the benefit of the subsidy.

Even when the family is intact, the net effect of the taxes and subsidy will differentially favor the mother if she cares more than the father does about the child. To understand why this is so, we can consider an analogous situation: a business partnership between two men. First, let's suppose that the partners are brothers and that they feel equal responsibility for their elderly mother. Let's also suppose that one brother actually provides the care because he is better at it, lives nearer the mother, or for some similar reason. Because both brothers care equally about their mother, the cost of the time spent by the caregiver will be taken account of in the partnership agreement. If the government imposes a tax on the partnership and uses the money to provide care for elderly mothers, the effect on the two brothers will be approximately the same. With the new program in place, neither brother will have to spend time caring for the mother; the responsibilities and rights within the partnership will be rearranged so that the relative welfare of the brothers will be unaltered. If the value of the subsidy is equal to the value of the tax, their absolute welfare will likewise be unaltered. The fact that one brother has been physically providing the care prior to the subsidy is irrelevant as long as both feel equally responsible.

Now let's change one of the assumptions. Let's again assume that the men are brothers, but only one feels responsible for his mother while the other does not. The time spent by the caregiver will not be taken into account in their partnership agreement. In this case if the government imposes a tax on the partnership and uses the money to provide care for elderly mothers, the one who feels responsible will benefit and the one who does not will lose.

These examples help us see that the wife will gain from child subsidy at the expense of her husband if she cares more about the children than he does. If they care equally, there will be no redistribution of well-being within the family regardless of who was actually providing the care prior to the subsidy.

Pronatalist policy. Probably the most controversial, but in the long run possibly most important, argument for child subsidies is their contribution to a national policy to maintain or increase fertility. Increase fertility? In a country where echoes of the Zero Population Growth and abortion-on-demand crusades still reverberate, is it reasonable to contemplate a time when national policy will be pronatal? I believe the answer is yes, and some of the child subsidy proponents have already begun to make this point, albeit circumspectly. An example is Kamerman and Kahn's discussion of children as "the future labor force and citizenry, the producers of the goods that pay the pensions of the elderly, and the parents of the next generation" (1979, p. 88). They implicitly view children as in part a public good and seem concerned that parents, left to make unsubsidized choices on the basis of private benefit/cost calculations, may choose to have fewer children than would be socially desirable. A review of fertility policy in Europe notes that "the effect of age-structural change on the financial bases of social security systems . . . [is] the justification for a pro-natalist policy most commonly articulated by officials and scholars" (McIntosh 1981, p. 186).

That there is some basis for concern is evident in the data on U.S. fertility presented in Chapter 2. One useful measure of fertility behavior is the *total fertility rate* (TFR), which shows the number of births that one thousand women would have in their lifetime if, at each year of age, they experienced the birth rate occurring in a specified year. The TFR, which averaged 3,500 per year over the period from 1950 to 1964, has been under 2,100 (the replacement level) since 1972. In other words, the *intrinsic rate of natural increase*—the rate that would eventually prevail if a population were to experience at each year of age the birth rate and death rate of the specified year and if these rates remained unchanged over a long period of time — has been *negative* since

1972. To be sure, the "birth dearth" of the 1970s may be partly a cyclical reaction to the baby boom of the fifties. However, with the conspicuous exception of the post–World War II decade (which was marked by the confluence of several exceptional circumstances), U.S. fertility has declined throughout the past two centuries.

Will the birth rate ever rise without any special pronatalist programs? Of course it might, but probably only temporarily. If one lists the major factors associated with the long-term downward trend—urbanization, greater female labor force participation, improved contraception, nationalized retirement benefits, rising costs of child-rearing—it is difficult to see what will cause a major, sustained reversal. According to economists William Butz and Michael Ward (1979) the low birth rates of the past decade are consistent with women's stated expectations about completed fertility, and any large-scale catching up is unlikely. They predict that fertility will continue to decline in the long run, with some fluctuations in the short run based on labor market conditions. When unemployment is low and job prospects for women are good, they expect birth rates to fall because the cost to women of dropping out of the labor market will be high. This is the opposite of Richard Easterlin's prediction that buoyant labor markets will stimulate fertility because marriage rates will rise and women will not have to work to supplement their husbands' earnings.

Assuming that public policy does shift to a pronatalist stance, would child subsidies have any effect on fertility? The available evidence is inconclusive. Several writers have noted that birth rates in Europe are low despite child subsidy programs, but this does not answer the question satisfactorily. Perhaps the rates would be even lower in the absence of such programs. Economic theory suggests that a reduction in the "price" of children will increase the quantity demanded. The size of the response, however, will vary, depending in part on the size of the subsidy relative to the total cost of children. McIntosh notes that in France the economic magnitude of pronatalist incentives has been steadily eroded (1981, p. 189). Small subsidies are likely to have small effects. Furthermore, the response might be different, depending upon how the subsidy is allocated. For instance, the effect on fertility will be greater if all of the subsidy is given for a third child rather than spread evenly over the first, second, and third children.

What Kind of Subsidies?

A general decision to provide subsidies for children can only be implemented by choosing one or more specific types of subsidy; the consequences for efficiency and for justice are likely to vary considerably, depending on what form the subsidy takes. The two principal possibilities are general monetary subsidies (such as cash grants and tax deductions) and restricted subsidies tied to a particular good or service (such as food stamps or free nursery schools).

Most economists believe that general monetary subsidies are preferable if the goal is to help the poor as much as possible. The reasons are fairly straightforward, some of them harking back to John Stuart Mill's famous essay, "On Liberty," if not earlier. First, it is reasonable to presume that individual families will consider their own interests, whereas the advocates of tied subsidies, be they in health care, education, law, or other fields, have a potential conflict of interest between the needs of families and their own desire to expand demand for their services. Second, even when those advocating tied subsidies are acting with only the best interests of poor families in mind, they are not likely to know and understand those interests as well as the families themselves. Moreover, families differ. The more general the subsidy, the more likely it is that the individual families can use it in ways that seem best for them.

Advocates of tied subsidies sometimes argue that their concern is for the children rather than for the parents, and that subsidization of particular services does more for children than a grant of a comparable amount of money to the parents. Perhaps. Becker and Tomes (1976) pointed out that as long as parents control other expenditures on behalf of their children, they can reallocate these expenditures to achieve whatever balance they deem appropriate. To the extent that reallocation is possible, the tied subsidy will have no more effect on the family's investment in their children than would a comparable grant of money.

If a decision is made to tie the child subsidy to a particular service (say, out-of-home care for preschool youngsters), parents should be given as wide a choice as possible of how to use the subsidy (for example, through a voucher system rather than having the subsidy restricted to a particular setting such as government-run day care centers). Advocates of a highly restricted subsidy argue that there "aren't enough good settings available," but this ignores the responsiveness of supply to the increase in *effective* demand that a large-scale voucher system would create. Child care is, for the most part, an atomistic, highly competitive industry with relatively easy entry (except when inhibited by overly protective government regulations). There is little reason to believe that supply would not expand along with the growth of effective demand.

Moreover, recent experience with government-run day care centers in the United States does not provide much support for the idea of granting them a monopoly or even preferential treatment. Many observers believe that the cost of such centers (relative to the quality of care) is high compared with the cost of private centers under either nonprofit or for-profit auspices. Furthermore, the current choices of parents, including parents with high income and high education, suggest that informal arrangements, such as family day care, are often preferable to institutional care regardless of sponsorship.

Some other efficiency and equity considerations need to be mentioned. Should the government tax childless adults in order to provide subsidies to other adults (with children) at comparable levels of income? If children create large benefits for society, such transfers may be efficient, but are they just? The theory of progressive taxation says that transfers should go from those who are "better off" to those who are "worse off." When some adults have children, and others at comparable levels of income do not, which group is better off?

Even worse problems arise if the child subsidy is made available conditional on the marital status and/or labor force status of the mother. The diversity of arguments heard on this issue highlights the confusion that surrounds child subsidies and brings into sharp relief the different and often conflicting objectives of the proponents. For instance, some of our present subsidies (such as the tax deductibility of child care expenditures, and some day care centers) are available only if the mother works. Other proposals would provide subsidies only if the mother does *not* work; indeed, the main thrust of our welfare programs is in that direction. Some subsidies are conditional on there being no father in the home, enforcing this either explicitly as an administrative requirement, or implicitly because the father's income would make the family ineligible for assistance.

To make progress out of this tangled mess of confusing and conflicting incentives and constraints will not be easy. What we need to do first is eschew any grandiose notions of an overall "family policy." As Gilbert Steiner so cogently argued, "A collection of ideas and initiatives that would define a coherent pro-family policy eludes formulation because the meaning of *pro-family* cannot be agreed upon" (1981, p. 26). In order to formulate a more coherent, efficient, and equitable set of policies about *children,* we must reach some agreement concerning the *objectives* of such policy and then take advantage of theory and experience to think through the most appropriate *means* to reach those objectives. At present, public policy toward children provides a quintessential example of the ancient Talmudic dictum, "If you don't know where you're going, any road will take you there."

4

Reason in a State of Fever

Adolescence and Youth

What is youth? A perpetual intoxication;
reason in a state of fever.
— *La Rochefoucauld*

"YOUTH," said Goethe, "is a disease that time cures"; Samuel Butler likened it to spring, "an over-praised season." Whether these remarks represent the wisdom of maturity or the envy of old age is not certain. It is obvious, however, that youth (generally synonymous with adolescence; see Elder 1975) is a "difficult" age — difficult to define, difficult to experience, and difficult to analyze. Much of the difficulty arises because of its transitory character.

More than any other stage of life, adolescence is viewed as a time of transition. The duration of this transition varies considerably among societies; in some the stage is virtually nonexistent and individuals move directly from childhood to adult status. Even within a single society (the United States today, for instance) adolescence may last a few years or more than ten. Differences in the length of adolescence among and within societies are largely determined by economic factors. The onset of the stage is triggered by actual or expected biological changes, but the end is usually marked by some socioeconomic event such as obtaining full-time employment or getting married or having a baby. The age at which these events occur depends primarily upon the general level of economic development of the society, on the circumstances and values of the adolescent's parents, and on the adolescent's own prospects and aspirations for the future.

In adolescence the individual begins to make significant choices independently, but these choices are heavily influenced by the circumstances of birth and by the investments made by parents during the childhood years, as well as by the support they provide at this stage. In like manner, the choices adolescents make about schooling, work, parenthood, cigarette smoking, and other behaviors will have major consequences later in their lives and in the lives of their children. Willingness and ability to invest in the future — wanting and waiting — play a critical role in many of these choices. Demography and destiny is another theme that integrates several of the subjects in this chapter, especially through cohort size. The large swings in fertility described in Chapter 2 resulted in equally large changes in the number of youth two decades later, with impacts on schooling, work, marriage, and health.

This chapter begins with an examination of trends in the most important variable of adolescence, the length of formal education. An analysis of youth employment follows, with special attention to differences between blacks and whites in levels and trends. The third section considers motherhood within or outside marriage as a significant factor in the lives of adolescent women, and the fourth section discusses two major health problems of youth: suicide and cigarette smoking. A review of public policy issues concerning unwed motherhood and teenage unemployment concludes the chapter.

EDUCATION

Education is an ornament in prosperity and a refuge in adversity.
— *Attributed to Aristotle*

What most distinguishes modern adolescents from their counterparts in previous eras (and what makes adolescence today a more clearly identifiable stage of life) is the extension of the period of formal education. Every civilization worthy of the name has had its academies and scholars, but it is only in industrial and especially postindustrial societies that schools play a major role in preparing most of the population for adult life. This is particularly true in the United States where, more than in any other country, school attendance continues into the late teens and early twenties for a substantial proportion of the population.

In 1980 approximately 42 percent of the population between the ages of 16 and 24 was enrolled in school, a substantial increase over the 27 percent enrolled in 1950.* The pace of change, however, has not been smooth either for the total population or for the sexes and races. Partly as a result of the Vietnam War, school enrollment of men ages 18–19 soared from 48 percent in 1960 to over 60 percent in 1968, only to fall back to 47 percent by 1980. Enrollment of women at this age also rose rapidly in the 1960s, from 30 percent in 1960 to 41 percent in 1968, but then continued to rise to 43 percent in 1980. Black enrollment rates were substantially below white rates in 1960, but were almost equal by 1980. The patterns of change in enrollment rates at ages 20–21 were similar to those at 18 and 19.

Why Stay in School?

Why are enrollments so high at these ages? Compulsion is obviously not the answer, inasmuch as most states require attendance at school only until age 16. If almost one out of every two 18–19-year-olds, and one out of every three 20–21-year-olds are enrolled in school, it must be because they and their parents

---

* Percentages were calculated on a standardized age distribution to remove any influence of changes in age distributions within the 16–24 range.

believe that this use of their time is better than any available alternative. Economists find that additional schooling has been a worthwhile form of *investment* for the average young person, at least until recently. The *cost* of this investment to the individual consists of direct outlays for tuition, books, and other special expenses attributable to being in school, plus the indirect cost of the value of the time spent in school. The latter is usually measured by what could have been earned if the young man or woman had not been in school. The material *benefits* of investment in schooling to the individual are primarily enhanced earnings (Schultz 1963) and increased productivity in home production, such as managing the family budget, child care, or health care (Michael 1972; Grossman 1972). Numerous estimates of the benefits and the costs of investment in schooling have been calculated, and they usually indicate a rate of return at least as favorable as alternative investment opportunities.

Critics of this "human capital" view of investment in schooling have argued that schooling doesn't raise productivity — all it does is screen and sort each cohort (Spence 1973). According to this view, people with more ability obtain more schooling, but the fact that they are admitted to, and graduated from, higher-level schools simply serves as a signal to employers that they are more able. They obtain better jobs, earn more money, and *are* more productive, but not because of anything they learned in school. The screening theory implies that investment in schooling could be socially wasteful even when it pays off for the individual.

Schools undoubtedly play a screening role in society, but I doubt that this is a sufficient explanation for the high enrollment. One reason for skepticism is the large cost of such screening, initially to the individual who goes to school and subsequently to the firms that must pay higher salaries when they hire those who are credentialed. If screening were the only function of schools, it seems likely that business firms would have developed lower-cost methods such as comprehensive tests, extensive interviews, and probationary work periods. A second reason for skepticism is that young men and women who intend to enter a family business or start one of their own have much less need for screening, but they also seem to value additional education.

While conceding that a college education was a good investment in the past, some economists have argued that the rate of
return fell dramatically in the 1970s (Freeman 1976, 1980). They
point to the large increase in the supply of college-trained
workers, and to a decrease in the relative earnings of recent
college graduates. The increase in the number of college-educated
young men and women has been enormous. Approximately one
million earned a bachelor's (or first professional) degree in 1978;
only 400,000 earned such a degree in 1960. About two-thirds of the
increase is attributable to the increase in cohort size and about
one-third to an increase in the proportion of the cohort that
earned a degree. Over the same period the number of jobs in the
economy increased by only about 50 percent; thus, the combination of larger cohort size and rising proportion of well-educated
young persons has had a depressing effect on their labor market
prospects.

James Smith and Finis Welch contend that the increase in
cohort size in the 1970s depressed earnings for *all* new entrants to
the labor force, regardless of education, and that "attending
college continues to be a lucrative investment" (1981). They claim
that the adverse effects of being in a large cohort are much greater
at the time of entering the labor force than at older ages because
there is not much substitution between entry-level jobs and other
jobs. For example, let us assume that there are 10 million entry-
level jobs that can be filled by inexperienced workers and 90
million that require more seasoned, experienced workers. Let us
further assume that there is no substitution between these categories. If an unusually large cohort, say an extra two million, enters
the job market, this implies an increase of 20 percent in the supply
of entry-level workers; this increase will depress wages and increase unemployment among the new entrants. When that same
increase in supply of two million gets older and moves into the
experienced job market, it will represent only a 2.2 percent (2
million divided by 90 million) increase in supply; the effect on
wages and unemployment is likely to be much smaller.

Richard Easterlin, the economist who has done the most to
focus attention on cohort size as a major force in U.S. society,
believes that there will be large effects at all stages of life. This

issue will not be fully resolved until the large cohorts move through the life cycle and we see the extent to which cohort size continues to depress earnings.

Who Stays in School?

Tuition-free education through high school is available to nearly all Americans, and most states provide opportunities for higher education at low tuition; but there is still considerable variation in the number of years of schooling completed. In 1980, for instance, almost 25 percent of Americans ages 25–34 had completed four years or more of college, 20 percent had finished one to three years of college, about 40 percent were high school graduates, and 15 percent had not completed high school. From a policy perspective it is very important to understand the causes and the consequences of differences in years of schooling completed. Almost every subject touched on in this book, from fertility to mortality, from cigarette smoking to unemployment, from migration to earnings, is strongly related to years of schooling. Does the additional schooling play a causal role in these behaviors? Why does schooling vary among individuals and groups? If we knew the answers to these questions we would be in a much better position to devise appropriate public policies to deal with such diverse problems as poverty, illness, and teenage pregnancy.

Social scientists differ in the weight they give to the causes of variation in education, but there is a reasonably good consensus that parental wealth and education, family size and structure, and the aptitude and performance of the adolescent all play a role. The relative importance of these causes varies, depending upon whether one is interested in explaining dropping out of high school or the completion of college and postgraduate education. For instance, family background (especially income) appears to be more important in schooling decisions at the lower than at the higher levels of education (Mare 1980). The relative importance of some variables may depend upon the family's general circumstances: the presence in the home of newspapers, magazines, and a library card is more strongly related to youngsters' staying in school in disadvantaged families than in two-parent, high-income households (Rumberger, forthcoming).

College enrollment tends to rise with family income, although the relationship was stronger in 1967 than in 1977. Even in the latter year, however, the proportion enrolled in school at ages 18–24 was 60 percent in families with income over $27,000 but only 23 percent in families with income under $9,000. This relationship could be consistent with the investment model of education because high-income families are more able to undertake investment, even at equal or lower rates of return. It is also possible that young men and women from higher-income families have superior academic ability or better family connections which would enable them to use the additional schooling to obtain higher incomes.

Although it is easy to discover a large number of variables that are related to schooling, it is often difficult to determine the direction of causality or to measure the size of the effect because of complex interrelationships among the variables. For instance, performance in school is probably the best single predictor of continuation in school, but performance is influenced by preschool investments as well as by initial genetic endowment. Furthermore, students who expect to attend college will frequently perform better in high school *because* of their intentions. Similar problems of analysis pervade efforts to understand exactly the relationship between schooling and number of siblings, absence of a father, and other background variables. One conclusion is beyond doubt. There is considerable variability in the amount of schooling individuals complete, and a substantial portion of that variability is related to the circumstances into which the individual is born. It is also clear that inequality in educational attainment has diminished in recent decades (Table 2.1). This reduction, along with the reduction in the number of very large families, contributes to equality of opportunity for the cohorts born in the 1970s. On the other hand, the increase in the proportion of births to unwed teenagers works in the opposite direction.

Test Scores

No discussion of the education of American youth would be complete without at least a brief reference to the declining scores on the Scholastic Aptitude Test (SAT). Mean scores on both the verbal and mathematical parts were remarkably stable from the early 1950s until about 1964, but then the mean verbal score dropped from 473 (800 is the highest score attainable) to 428 (average of 1977–1979) and the mean mathematics score declined from 496 to 468. In the early 1980s scores stopped falling. Numerous attempts to explain the decline have been relatively unsuccessful. There is substantial agreement, however, that the decline is real, not simply an artifact of changes in test questions or grading scales. It is also agreed that the decline since 1970 cannot be attributed to changes in the socioeconomic background of those taking the test, although such changes may explain the decrease that occurred in the second half of the 1960s (College Entrance Examination Board 1977).

Two other findings from this research are of special interest. First, scores in highly regarded schools in affluent suburban areas have declined as much as scores in other schools. Second, declines have occurred in all types of schools — traditional as well as experimental, private as well as public. Two differences in the pattern of decline are worth noting. First, the decline has been much greater for the verbal than for the mathematical part, suggesting that the substitution of television viewing for reading (and concomitant change in the amount and difficulty of reading and writing assignments at school) has played a role. Second, in the 1970s the rate of decline was greater for women than for men. (Between 1967–69 and 1977–79 verbal scores declined from 462 to 432 for men and from 467 to 425 for women. The change in the mathematics scores was from 513 to 495 for men and from 469 to 444 for women.) This difference is probably related to the large increase in the proportion of female high school graduates going on to college. As this percentage increases, it seems likely that the college-bound group includes a larger proportion of women who are of average or below average academic ability.

A final, speculative point about the decline in scholastic achievement is that its timing coincided with the surge in cohort size. As discussed previously, the children of the baby boom may have received less parental input per child than did earlier cohorts, and they certainly forced American schools to expand at an extremely rapid rate, possibly adversely affecting the quality of education. The SAT scores may, therefore, level off or even rise as the smaller cohorts born in the late 1960s and the 1970s reach college age. According to Census Bureau projections, the proportion of the population ages 14–17 will be only 5.2 percent in 1990, down sharply from 7.9 percent in 1975 and even below the 5.5 percent level of 1950.

EMPLOYMENT

The 1940 census was the first one in which questions about work were limited to persons 14 years of age or older. Prior to that time the count of the "gainfully employed" could include anyone 10 years of age and over. The official cutoff at age 14 lasted until 1966 when it was raised to the present level of 16 years. These simple facts, more eloquently than elaborate statistics, tell us that one of the principal concomitants of long-run economic development has been an increase in the age at which youngsters begin to work for pay, a natural corollary of the trend toward longer schooling.

In recent decades, however, young people have shown an increasing desire to seek paid employment. Labor force participation rates were higher in 1979 than in 1960 for men and women ages 16–19 and much higher for women 20–24. Among youth (those ages 16–24), only men 20–24 showed a slight decline. The labor force is defined to include both employed and unemployed, and a great deal of attention has been focused on youth unemployment, especially the problems of young nonwhites in large Northern cities. Because of the extensive media coverage of unemployment, most readers will probably be as surprised as I was to learn that in recent decades (1) youth *employment* rates (civilian employment divided by civilian population) have *increased;* (2) the proportion of nonwhite youth who are out of school and out of work has *decreased* slightly; (3) youth employment rates of nonwhites relative to whites worsened appreciably in the South, but did not change much outside the South. We will see that the falling employment rate of nonwhite youth is partly a consequence of a sharp increase in school enrollment, and we will also note the adverse impacts of mechanization in Southern agriculture and of minimum wage legislation.

Employment Trends

Between 1960 and 1979 the employment rate at ages 16–19 rose from 40 percent to 49 percent and at ages 20–24 from 60 percent to 71 percent, despite a large increase in school enrollment rates and despite the huge surge in the number of persons in the 16–24 age group. All the talk about youth unemployment has tended to obscure the fact that throughout the 1960s and 1970s more and more young people were finding jobs.

When the data are disaggregated by sex and race, large differences in employment and school enrollment trends emerge. The proportion of nonwhite men in school increased by 13 percentage points between 1960 and 1979 and employment rates fell by a comparable amount. White male enrollment rates were virtually the same in 1979 as in 1960, and employment rates rose. Among women, both whites and nonwhites showed large increases in enrollment rates over the two decades, and employment rates of white women soared. Perhaps the most striking finding of the 1960–1979 comparison is that the group of greatest concern — those who are out of school *and* out of work — has not increased in relative importance (Table 4.1).

	Change in percent of population out of school and not at work, 1960 to 1979	
	Ages 16–19	*Ages 20–24*
White men	−2	−2
Nonwhite men	−3	1
White women	−8	−28
Nonwhite women	−6	−14

Although the proportion of young men who were out of school and out of work did not rise between 1960 and 1979, this proportion was very high among nonwhites in both years (about 20 percent at ages 20–24). The fact that this is an old problem rather than a new one does not make it any less serious. Indeed, the failure to reduce the race differential during two decades when public policies were nominally addressed to this problem should be a source of considerable concern. Not only has the employment rate of young nonwhites always been lower than that of whites, but their relative employment position worsened during the 1960s and 1970s, partly as a result of rising school enrollment by nonwhites, and partly because of a deterioration in their employment rates, holding enrollment status constant. In 1979 only 16 percent of nonwhite men ages 16–19 who were enrolled in school were also employed, whereas 42 percent of white men who were in school also had a job (Table 4.2). Employment rates of out-of-school nonwhite teenagers also deteriorated. At ages 20–24 the race differentials in employment are much smaller than at 16–19, but they were still substantial in 1979 and larger than they were in 1960.

The Race Differential

Why has the trend in employment rates of young nonwhites been worse than that of white youth? Racial discrimination has often been suggested as an answer, but this is almost surely wrong. Discrimination may help explain lower *levels* of nonwhite employment, but there is no evidence that discrimination *increased* between 1960 and 1979. Other reasons that have been suggested include minimum wage legislation, increasing size of cohorts, concentration of nonwhites in central cities, and increasing competition for jobs from adult women entering the work force. Attempts to measure the effects of these factors have not succeeded in proving that any one of them accounts for a major portion of the decline (Newman 1979; Bowers 1979; Iden 1980).

A highly original study by John Cogan of changes in teenage employment rates between 1950 and 1970 concluded that by far the most important explanation for the nonwhite decline is the mechanization of Southern agriculture (Cogan 1982). He also argued that extension of coverage of minimum wage laws in the 1960s contributed to the problem by limiting the opportunities of Southern black teenagers to find employment in retail trade, services, and construction. Using *Census of Population* data, Cogan showed that black teenage employment rates held steady outside the South despite a 215 percent increase in their population as a result of high fertility and interregional migration. He wrote: "The ability of northern urban labor markets to absorb such a massive influx of black teenagers without corresponding reductions in the employment ratio is both surprising and impressive. The widely held view that the root of the black teenage employment problem is the decline in employment conditions in northern central cities is strongly inconsistent with data for the period 1950 to 1970" (p. 624).

A more detailed examination of census data for 1960 and 1970 by school enrollment status as well as region supports the view that declining demand for labor in Southern agriculture is responsible for much of the decline in nonwhite youth employment. In both years the nonwhite employment rates by enrollment status were substantially below those of whites, indicating the disadvantaged position of nonwhite youth. The point that is most relevant for the present discussion, however, is that the ratio of nonwhite to white employment rates *fell* a great deal in the South during the 1960s while holding virtually *constant* outside the South (Table 4.3).

	Ratio of nonwhite to white employment rates, men ages 16–19	
	1960	*1970*
In school, non-South	.55	.56
In school, South	.75	.56
Out of school, non-South	.66	.61
Out of school, South	.95	.78

Cogan's argument (1981) that the minimum wage hurt employment prospects for nonwhite youth, especially in the South, seems reasonable for the following reasons. A minimum wage creates unemployment when it is higher than the equilibrium wage — that is, the wage at which employers find it profitable to hire all who are willing to work. The higher the minimum wage is above the equilibrium wage, the larger its adverse effect on employment. Thus, the minimum wage has a bigger effect on employment at ages 16–19 than at ages 20–24 because teenagers have less work experience than older workers, and a bigger effect in the South than in the non-South because wages have traditionally been lower in the South (Fuchs and Perlman 1960). The minimum wage also has a larger employment impact on nonwhite than white teenagers because many employers perceive the nonwhites as having, on average, lower skills and poorer preparation for work.

Trends in enrollment and employment are more complicated to analyze for women than for men because women's labor market choices are closely linked to decisions about marriage and childbearing. For instance, both white and nonwhite young women showed much bigger declines in the out-of-school, out-of-work category than did men because declining fertility affected women's employment and school enrollment much more than it did men's. At ages 16–19 white female employment rose rapidly but nonwhite did not; school enrollment rose for both races, but more rapidly for nonwhites than whites (Table 4.1). Further analysis of female employment requires a closer look at trends in marriage and fertility.

MARRIAGE AND FERTILITY

In order to understand changes in the labor market behavior of young American women, we must recognize that marriage and motherhood have traditionally been their principal careers. Throughout the twentieth century the majority of U.S. women have married in their teens or early twenties. Many are pregnant at the time of marriage and well over half of all women have a baby within twenty-four months of their first marriage. Since 1960, however, there has been a dramatic decrease in fertility at ages 15–19 and 20–24 (Table 4.4). There can be no doubt that a significant part of the increase in the employment rate of young women reflects a substitution away from marriage and childbearing toward work in the market. In addition, at ages 20–24 some of the increase reflects higher labor force participation by married women who have small children at home (see Chapters 3 and 5).

Although teenage fertility fell considerably over the past two decades, the rate of 52 per thousand is still double that of most countries of Western Europe, five times that of the Netherlands and Switzerland, and more than *fifteen times* as high as teenage fertility in Japan (Alan Guttmacher Institute 1981). The relatively high U.S. rate is mostly the result of the growing fertility of *unmarried* teenagers. The number of babies born to unmarried women ages 15 – 19 jumped from 87,000 in 1960 to 240,000 in 1978, while births to married teenagers fell from 507,000 to 316,000, thus tripling the illegitimacy ratio in less than two decades. Some of this increase in the ratio reflects changes in the propensity to marry, and some of it reflects changes in fertility patterns within each marital status. The proportion of 15 – 19-year-olds who were married fell from 16 percent to 9 percent between 1960 and 1978; married teenage fertility fell from 484 to 359 per thousand, while unmarried teenage fertility rose from 16 to 25 per thousand.

Why are there so many babies born to unmarried teenagers? The oft-heard answer that these births are the *unintended* consequences of increased sexual activity among teenagers is unsatisfactory. Sexual activity has undoubtedly increased, but there is good reason to believe that many, possibly more than half, of these babies are wanted by their mothers at the time of conception. They are not "accidents." This is true even though the large majority of *pregnancies* of unmarried women are unwanted, because most unwanted pregnancies are terminated by abortion. A hypothetical calculation illustrates this point. Suppose that a thousand young, unmarried women become pregnant, 80 percent of them unintentionally. At current rates, about 600 of the 800 unwanted pregnancies will be terminated by abortion. Thus, of the 400 babies born, only 200 are the result of unintended conception. Although this simple illustration ignores the effects of miscarriages and postconception marriages, and the actual proportions in each category may be slightly different from those in this example, the general point is indisputable.

A sharp decline in the willingness of unwed mothers to offer their babies for adoption provides additional evidence that these births are wanted (Zelnik and Kantner 1977). This is particularly true of whites, for whom the ratio of adoptions to births out of wedlock fell rapidly between 1960 and the mid-1970s. Potential parents who seek a white baby from adoption agencies face long delays and usually pay substantial premiums for babies obtained through private arrangements. Thus, the decline in the proportion of white babies given for adoption must reflect an increased demand for children by unmarried white mothers rather than lack of demand by potential adopters.

This demand for babies by unwed young women may seem like a new and strange phenomenon. In one sense it is new, but in another it is not a remarkable departure from the past and not so difficult to understand. Most of these births are to young women from low-income families who have little education and poor employment opportunities. For young women in such circumstances motherhood often appears to offer an opportunity to leave the parental home, to improve one's status, and to develop a more satisfying life. The only difference between the present and the past is that in the United States this formerly had to be accomplished within the bond of matrimony. Without the sanction of church or state there was great social stigma for mother and child, and no reasonable prospect of financial support. Recently, the social stigma has been greatly reduced, and government has come forward as a source of support. AFDC payments, food stamps, day care centers, Medicaid, and other subsidized programs make it possible for unwed mothers to establish a separate household and raise their children, albeit at a low level of living. Some are completely supported by transfer payments while others use government programs to supplement low earnings. A small proportion of the babies are born to young women with relatively good jobs who have opted for a life without a husband for themselves or a father for their children.

An analysis of teenage pregnancy by Rand researchers concluded that economic factors play a significant role in the choices made by unwed pregnant teenagers among marriage, abortion, or birth out of wedlock (Leibowitz, Eisen, and Chow 1980). They analyzed the behavior of 297 pregnant teenagers who visited health care providers in Ventura County, California, for either prenatal care or abortion during 1972–1974. In this sample, 15 percent married before delivery, 62 percent chose abortion, and 23 percent were unwed at delivery. Holding constant age, school enrollment status, grades, religion, and ethnicity, the women who were eligible for public aid were significantly more likely to deliver out of wedlock. The study also found that young women who were enrolled in school were significantly more likely to choose abortion, and, within the enrolled group, the higher the grade point average the greater was the likelihood of abortion. The authors believe that school enrollment and higher grades indicate a greater value of time, which increases the demand for abortion. Another significant finding is the reluctance of the Mexican-Americans in this sample to choose abortion. Other things equal, they were more likely to keep their babies whether or not they were married. Other than the Mexican-Americans, Catholics and non-Catholics did not differ in their choices, indicating that the Mexican cultural values do affect behavior, but not simply as a result of their Catholic religion.

Differences in marriage and fertility behavior between whites and nonwhites are substantial, but the basic trends for both groups have been similar in recent decades (Table 4.4). Both whites and nonwhites are currently less likely to marry or give birth in their teens than they were in 1960 or 1950. Instead, they stay in school longer and, when they do leave school, they join the labor force. In relative terms, young white women have reduced their fertility more than nonwhites, and their employment rates have grown relatively more rapidly.

When young women do give birth, a higher proportion do so out of wedlock. Despite improvements in contraception, more teenagers become pregnant now than in the past because of increased sexual activity. When unmarried white teenagers become pregnant a significant number marry; about 70 percent of those who don't marry have legal abortions (ignoring miscarriages). Nonwhite teenagers who become pregnant while single are less likely to marry, and fewer than half of them terminate their pregnancies with legal abortions.

These trends in marriage and fertility among young women have important implications for infants and children, and the trends in school enrollment and employment affect future earnings. All of the trends discussed in this chapter are relevant to the question of equality between men and women, a major subject of Chapter 5.

HEALTH

Although the vigor and vitality of most young people are the envy of their elders, a significant range of serious health problems are present at ages 15–24, including venereal disease, alcoholism, and drug abuse. Moreover, a large number of adolescents and youth are making themselves vulnerable to future health problems through cigarette smoking, poor diet, and inadequate exercise (Institute of Medicine 1978). One of the most disturbing trends is rising mortality among youth at a time when death rates at all other ages are declining rapidly. Male death rates at ages 15–19 and 20–24 were 12 percent *higher* in 1977 than in 1960, while mortality at other ages *declined* an average of 12 percent (Table 4.5). A large differential in mortality trends by age is also evident for women. The deaths of young people take a tremendous emotional toll and are also particularly costly because these men and women are at the threshold of productive lives during which they and society could realize a return on the investment that has been made in them.

The principal reason for the divergent trends in mortality by age is the increase in self-destructive behavior by young men and women (see the tabulation below). Among young men, suicide and motor vehicle accidents now account for half of all deaths, and among women for well over 40 percent. More youth die from suicide alone than from cancer, cardiovascular disease, diabetes, pneumonia, and influenza combined. The rising death rate from homicide also contributes to the rising death rate among the young. Homicide rates have approximately doubled at most ages, but because it is a relatively more important cause of death among the young, this doubling has had more of an impact on their overall rate. The high homicide rate among nonwhite men is particularly shocking, averaging about 50 per year per hundred thousand at ages 15 – 19 and over 100 per hundred thousand at ages 20 – 24. These rates imply that almost one out of every 100 black youths who turn 15 becomes a homicide victim before the age of 25! Apart from violent deaths, the trends in mortality of young men and women have been as favorable as at older ages.

	Percent change in age-sex-specific death rates, 1960 to 1977	
	Ages 15 – 24	*Ages 25 and over*
Suicide	145	6
Motor vehicle accidents	25	−15
Homicide	113	83
All other causes	−22	−21

Suicide

Why did suicide rates among young people increase so rapidly in the 1960s and 1970s? It is much easier to rule out answers to this question than to find ones that will withstand critical examination. For instance, it is highly unlikely that the trend is a result of differences in the reporting of suicides, although reporting practices do vary considerably over time and in different areas. Changes in reporting, however, would affect the suicide rate at all ages, and there was no comparable increase at other stages of life. The emotional trauma of the Vietnam War was felt more keenly by young people and this may have contributed to the increase in suicides, but there are two problems with this explanation. First, after the war ended the suicide rate among young people kept on rising, rather than falling back to prewar levels (see Figure 4.1). Second, suicide rates at ages 15 – 24 in Canada and Sweden have been rising as rapidly and are as high as in the United States. Neither country was much affected by the Vietnam War.

Suicides have been blamed on deteriorating economic conditions, but Figure 4.1 shows that the rate has been rising in good times as well as bad; the long-term trend is much stronger than

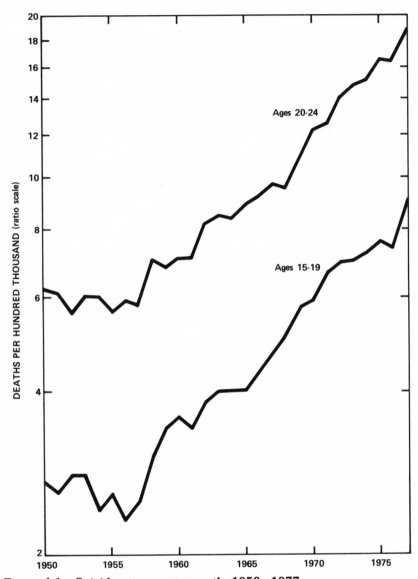

Figure 4.1. Suicide rates among youth, 1950–1977.
(*Sources:* U.S. Bureau of the Census, *Vital Statistics of the United States,* 1950–1977; idem, *Current Population Reports,* series P-25, nos. 310, 519, 721, and 870.)

any response to business cycle fluctuations. Furthermore, the suicide level is slightly higher among white than nonwhite youth and the rate of increase has been as rapid for whites as for nonwhites, despite the large race differentials in youth employment. One of the more mischievous arguments currently in vogue is that the problems of children and youth are the result of high unemployment and that their solution lies in better macroeconomic policies. Of course low unemployment is better than high, and price stability is preferable to inflation, but anyone who believes that the increases in suicides among youth, births to unwed mothers, juvenile crime, and one-parent homes are primarily the result of macroeconomic conditions is ignoring readily available evidence. All these problems were increasing particularly rapidly during the second half of the 1960s, when the unemployment rate averaged 3.8 percent and economic growth was extremely rapid.

Richard Easterlin attributed the rapid increase in suicides among youth to cohort size (1980, p. 104). I tested this hypothesis by examining separately the trends for age groups 15–19 and 20–24, but the data do not yield conclusive results. Cohort size probably plays some role, but it seems unlikely that it is the whole explanation for the suicide epidemic among the young.

Some mental health experts attribute the increase in suicides among the young to the rapid changes in the American family that are discussed in this book. A study at Bellevue Hospital in New York City of 102 teenagers who attempted suicide showed that only one-third of them lived with both parents (*Newsweek,* August 28, 1978, p. 74). Parents may be failing to provide enough structure and security for children either because they are not present or because they are preoccupied with their own lives and careers, or simply because they are too permissive. In a review of psychosocial literature on adolescence, Elder (1975) concludes: "Adolescents who fail to receive guidance, affection, and concern from parents — whether by parental inattention or absence — are likely to rely heavily on peers for emotional gratification, advice, and companionship, *to anticipate a relatively unrewarding future,* and to engage in antisocial activities" (italics added). On the other hand, some experts contend that too many demands and the setting of unrealistic standards by parents also predispose young people toward suicide.

Some evidence of a relation between family background and suicide appears in a long-term longitudinal study of fifty thousand male students of Harvard University and the University of Pennsylvania that compared the characteristics of 381 men who eventually committed suicide with a set of living control subjects randomly chosen from the same school and year as the suicides (Paffenbarger, King, and Wing 1969). One of the strongest results was a positive relation between suicide and loss of father. At the time of the original interview (average age 18) the future suicides were more likely than the controls to have a deceased father (12.4 percent versus 8.1 percent) or to have parents who had separated (12.6 percent versus 8.9 percent). The difference in paternal loss through death or separation was statistically significant at a high level of confidence. The future suicides also differed from the controls by having a larger percentage of fathers who were college-educated (69.1 percent versus 56.6 percent) and who were professionals (48.8 percent versus 38.4 percent). Loss of mother did not differ between the suicides and the controls.

It must be emphasized that the rapid increase in suicide rates among youth is unique to that age group—there is nothing comparable at other ages. By contrast, the doubling of death rates from homicide at young ages reflects a general increase in violent crime that has affected all age groups, although not in exactly equal degree. Suicide can be regarded as the extreme point on a continuum of self-destructive behavior that includes drug abuse, alcoholism, and cigarette smoking. The latter, though not as destructive in the short run, may be the most harmful health behavior among youth because smoking is a major cause of ill health and premature death in the United States.

Cigarette Smoking

Among men the difference in life expectancy at age 24 between nonsmokers and those who smoke a pack a day is over six years. Even within a relatively homogeneous, health conscious population such as regular participants in the Kaiser-Permanente Multiphasic health checkups, the age-sex-race-adjusted death rate for cigarette smokers is double that of nonsmokers. Cigarette smoking contributes to excess morbidity and mortality from coronary heart disease, lung cancer, chronic obstructive lung disease, and many other adult diseases. In addition, babies born to women who smoke during pregnancy are (holding other determinants constant) more likely to have retarded fetal development (see Chapter 2). This means that they are more likely to require expensive neonatal care, are more likely to die soon after birth, and, if they survive, may experience physical, mental, and emotional problems in childhood. The 1979 *Report of the Surgeon General: Smoking and Health* states flatly, "Overwhelming evidence indicates that maternal smoking during pregnancy affects fetal growth rate directly and that fetal growth rate is not due to characteristics of the smoker rather than to the smoking, nor is it mediated by reduced maternal appetite, eating, and weight gain" (p. 1-21). This is another striking example of parental choice affecting the well-being of the next generation.

The cigarette-smoking habit is usually acquired at an early age; approximately one-half of all smokers begin by age 17, and nine out of ten begin by age 24. Widespread discussion in the popular press about the harmful effects of cigarette smoking first appeared in 1953 and was reinforced by the first *Surgeon General's Report on Smoking and Health* in 1964. Since then there has been an appreciable decline in smoking by young men and a small decline by young women.

National surveys show a strong negative relation between education and smoking. In 1975, for instance, high school graduates (men and women) were 50 percent more likely than college graduates to be regular cigarette smokers. This was not always the case. A detailed analysis of the smoking histories of 1,200 white California men and women ages 24–75 (in 1979) who had 12–18 years of schooling revealed that the probability of smoking at ages 17 or 24 was only slightly related to education *before* the bad health effects of smoking became widely known (see Figure 4.2). After 1953, however, the probability of smoking by persons who had—or who were going to obtain—many years of schooling dropped sharply (Farrell and Fuchs 1981).

What explains the strong negative relationship between years of schooling and the probability of smoking among recent cohorts? One category of explanations asserts that schooling has a

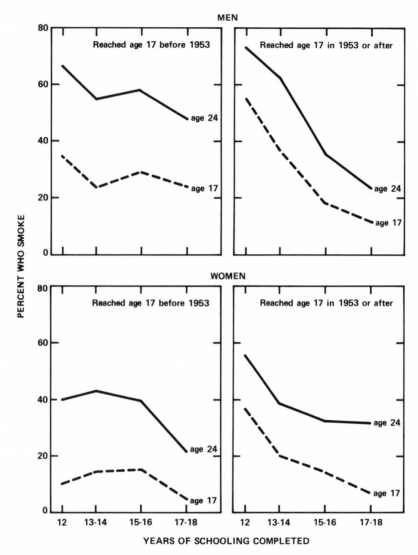

Figure 4.2. Cigarette smoking at ages 17 and 24, by years of schooling completed, sex, and cohort.
(*Source:* Farrell and Fuchs 1982.)

direct effect on smoking behavior. Additional schooling may increase knowledge about the harmful effects of smoking, it may change preferences, or it may increase the individual's ability to develop strategies of self control. A second category of explanations denies any causal role for years of schooling and asserts that the correlation is attributable to one or more "third variables" that affect both schooling and smoking behavior.

The results presented in Figure 4.2 strongly support the third-variable hypothesis. The negative relationship between schooling and smoking is *as strong at age 17 as at age 24.* At age 17, however, the individuals were all still approximately in the same grade. The difference in the probability of smoking that is observed at age 24 between persons with different years of schooling is already present at age 17, before the additional schooling is obtained. The additional schooling, therefore, cannot be the *cause* of the difference in smoking behavior. Differences in family background, type of school attended, or other factors probably account for both differences in schooling and in smoking behavior. One possible explanation is that both schooling and smoking behavior are related to individual differences in time discount — that is, the willingness and ability to incur current costs for future benefits (Fuchs 1982b). Schooling has long been recognized as a form of investment; decisions about cigarette smoking have a similar character because they involve a tradeoff between current pleasure and future ill health.

PUBLIC POLICY ISSUES

The preceding discussion has revealed numerous problems affecting adolescents and youth, problems ranging from rising mortality to teenage pregnancies to the decline of employment of nonwhite men. For some problems, such as the sharp increase in suicides, no simple or even moderately complex public policy solution is in the offing. Young people may be succumbing to what Abraham Maslow (1959) forecast as the ultimate disease of our time — "valuelessness." The rise in suicides and other self-destructive behavior such as motor vehicle accidents and drug abuse may be the result of weakening family structures and the absence of fathers, as suggested by the study of Harvard University and University of Pennsylvania students. We can't be sure of the cause, but if it's along the lines suggested above, the challenge to public policy is staggering.

Some problems of youth, especially those related to sex and alcohol, pose a different kind of problem — a failure to agree on what the goal of public policy should be. As an Institute of Medicine volume (1978) on adolescent behavior and health noted: "In a society as heterogeneous as ours, there are few standards of behavior which are universally embraced. For example, views vary widely on what constitutes acceptable sexual activity in adolescents; some advocate that adolescents consume no alcohol, while others speak of learning to drink responsibly, and so forth. In the absence of agreement on such issues, it is difficult to form a compelling national consensus on policies, programs and services for adolescents" (p. 6).

On two of the subjects we've discussed, there is wide agreement concerning problem definition, but not solution. These are the high rate of births to young unmarried women and the large percentage of nonwhite youth without employment. Almost everyone would welcome reductions in both areas, but there is great disagreement over causes and possible solutions.

Births to Young Unmarried Women

In New York and many other leading American cities, more than one out of every three births are to unwed mothers. Nationally, more than four hundred thousand babies are born each year to unmarried women under the age of 25; more than half of these births are to teenagers. As we have noted, these babies are frequently delivered at low weight, with all the potential risk implied by inadequate fetal development. Even if normal at birth, such babies will typically face many handicaps in life, including inadequate financial resources, the absence of a father, and a mother who is probably poorly prepared for the responsibilities of parenthood. Although most of the mothers eventually marry, most of their marriages end in divorce. Almost half of the children living with one parent are supported by AFDC payments, and many of the others depend upon food stamps, day care centers, Medicaid, and other subsidized programs. Definitive studies are not available, but there is some evidence suggesting that children from one-parent homes show lower achievement in school, present more discipline problems, and are more likely to be in poor health. Liberals and conservatives alike agree that a reduction in the number of births to unwed mothers would be desirable. There is strong disagreement, however, over why the illegitimacy ratio is so high and how it can be reduced.

As indicated previously, to make progress on this problem it is necessary to recognize that many — possibly most — of these babies are in some sense desired by their mothers, at least at the time of birth. Motherhood confers a positive change in status and creates entitlements to income and services. The baby is seen as someone to love and be loved by, and some young women attach importance to proving that they are fertile. The degree of desire for children varies, of course. At one extreme, some of the births are so strongly wanted that physicians report visits by unmarried teenagers seeking advice as to why they have not become pregnant. Some young women become pregnant because there are costs — monetary and psychic — to preventing pregnancy, and they carry to term because they prefer giving birth to having an abortion. Still other women do not want to give birth but do not contracept effectively and do not abort for a variety of reasons, including lack of information, inadequate financial resources, or moral objections.

What is to be done? If, as I have suggested, many of these babies are born as the result of conscious choices, policies aimed at reducing such births must either change underlying values or change the incentives and constraints that influence these choices. The economic perspective has little to offer concerning changes in values, but does contribute to our understanding of how public policy might affect the incentives and constraints that face young women.

One possible line of attack is to lower the costs of averting birth by making contraceptives and abortions cheaper and more readily available. More sex education in the schools has also been advocated as a method of reducing the number of teenage pregnancies. There is little doubt that a decrease in the price of averting births would result in some decrease in the number of births, but it would have no effect on those pregnancies that are desired. Even if an effective program of sex education and free contraceptives substantially reduced the number of unintended *pregnancies,* the most likely result would be a large reduction in *abortions* (a worthwhile objective), but only a small decrease in *births.* A program that increased the availability of abortions rather than contraceptives would also have limited potential because most unintended conceptions are already terminated by abortion. Further liberalization would not affect those infants who are carried to term because they are wanted by their mothers. This analysis makes it easier to understand why those states that are most liberal in providing sex education, family planning, and abortions do not have noticeably lower illegitimacy ratios.

In the early 1980s there is not much discussion of liberalizing abortion policies; a good deal of effort is being directed toward making abortions less readily available. If these efforts succeed, the problem may get worse. Making abortions more expensive and more difficult to obtain will probably result in a decrease in the number of unwanted pregnancies (the incentive to avoid pregnancy will have increased), but will also probably increase the total number of births to unwed mothers and increase the proportion of those births that are unwanted.

An alternative to lowering the cost of averting births is to decrease the attractiveness of having a baby by reducing AFDC payments, food stamp programs, and other government subsidies, and by establishing work requirements for unwed mothers. Such policy changes would probably result in some decrease in these births, but would mean increasing misery for those babies who would nevertheless be born. It is difficult to imagine administrative mechanisms that would take a hard line on the mothers (many of whom are still children themselves) without also punishing the babies, who surely bear no responsibility for their situation.

Occasionally it is suggested that society should make young men more responsible for the babies they father. It is undoubtedly true that in earlier generations the threat of a "shotgun" wedding prevented some pregnancies, and the fulfillment of that threat converted many premarital conceptions into births to married women. However, unless society is also prepared to make divorce more difficult and to enforce compulsory child support, this approach cannot have much impact.

Another strategy for reducing the number of births to unmarried women would be to *improve the alternatives* to early motherhood. It would not be easy to accomplish such an objective. However, an imaginative program that included schooling, counseling, work experience, and the opportunity to leave an unfavorable home situation might be effective. The current cost to society of maintaining an unwed mother and her children is very high and in many cases grows even higher when the children become adolescents. Thus, even a generously funded residential program that put young women on a different life course prior to pregnancy might have lower short-run direct costs and far greater long-run benefits for society, for the women, and for the children they would eventually bear.

Perhaps all three strategies should be pursued simultaneously: make it easier for women to avoid unwanted births; make it less attractive for young, poorly educated, unwed women to become mothers; and improve the alternatives available to them.

Employment Problems of Nonwhite Men

The large number of nonwhite youths who are neither in school nor at work is perceived as a major social problem by nearly all segments of society. Without some meaningful activity, many of these youths fall prey to drug abuse and alcoholism and some turn to criminal activity. Although it is widely believed that the problems of nonwhite men have become increasingly severe in recent decades, the data we have examined do not support that view. The percentage of the population out of school and out of work actually fell slightly between 1960 and 1979 at ages 16–19, and rose slightly at ages 20–24. The stability of the proportion, however, is at a much higher level than that of white men, and is the result of rising school enrollment rates for nonwhite men that offset major decreases in the percentage of out-of-school youth who are employed. These decreases occurred during a period when employment rates of white out-of-school youth were rising.

The papers by John Cogan that have been referred to and the data I have presented indicate that the *decline* in nonwhite employment rates, given enrollment status, has occurred primarily in the South. Thus, many of the discussions that have assumed that the decline was primarily a problem of the big cities of the North have been beside the point. The question of decline aside, the *level* of employment of young nonwhites is much below that of whites in all regions, especially for teenagers who are enrolled in school. Almost everyone agrees that this is a serious problem, but there is far less agreement regarding the reasons for it and possible solutions. Amid the large number of explanations that have been offered and remedial policies that have been proposed, several major themes can be identified.

Discrimination. Because there is a long history of prejudice against blacks (and other minorities) in this country, and because the gap between white and black youth employment rates is so large, many people understandably assume that this gap is attributable to discrimination by employers. Although such discrimination may be present in some cases, it is doubtful that employer prejudice alone accounts for the racial difference in employment levels or the changes that have occurred in recent decades. With respect to relative levels of employment, these were much *more favorable* to blacks in the *South* in 1960 than they were in the non-South, yet few would argue that there was less discrimination in the South at that time. With respect to the changes, every other indicator of segregation and discrimination in the political and social spheres shows improvement for blacks since 1960, not deterioration. This is especially true in the South, where the nonwhite employment declines have been heavily concentrated. The discrimination hypothesis is also rejected by the fact that the race differential in employment rates drops sharply as the men become older. If racial prejudice by employers were the major factor affecting black teenagers' employment prospects, why would employers be so much less prejudiced against them after they turned twenty?

For the discrimination argument to carry more weight, it must be expanded to include more than employer prejudice. For instance, discrimination in housing keeps some blacks from moving to areas where employment prospects for young people are better. It hardly pays to commute a long distance for part-time employment or even a low-wage, full-time job. Policies aimed at eliminating racial discrimination in housing are desirable in themselves and would probably also make a positive contribution to labor market problems. Young blacks entering the labor market are, in addition, handicapped by the less than equal opportunity they experienced as infants and children. To the extent that this inequality in opportunity is tied to discrimination, there is a double case for attempting to reduce it.

Macroeconomic conditions. Some critics like to pin the high unemployment rates of black teenagers on the failure of macroeconomic policies. The argument is as follows: if only aggregate demand were strong enough to keep the economy at full employment, the problem would, by definition, be solved. It is true that black teenage employment is particularly sensitive to changes in overall employment rates, and reasonably full employment is desirable in itself, but this explanation does not take us very far or provide any special insights for policy. For one thing, employment rates of black teenagers have been low, and the disparity between black and white rates has been great, even in prosperous years. More important, it is now widely recognized that when government attempts to constantly pump up the economy through easy money and deficit spending, the result is highly disruptive inflation. We need to be wary of so-called solutions that are only stop-gap measures. Trying to remedy unemployment through policies that produce inflation will probably make unemployment worse in the long run.

The statement "The economy should provide a job for everyone who wants to work" sounds innocuous until one asks, "What kind of job?" and "At what wage?" A more realistic approach would recognize that many young people have limited skills, no previous employment experience, and perhaps negative work habits. To increase their employment, their ability would have to be raised or they would have to be available at a wage commensurate with their contribution to production. Because work experience itself is an important way of increasing employability, the barriers to employment created by high minimum wages are particularly damaging. As economist Thomas Sowell (1981) has written, "Improving the lot of the poor means enabling them to move up the ladder, but they have to get on the ladder before they can move up. The minimum wage law prevents that."

Minimum wages. Some economists agree with Sowell that the minimum wage has a large negative effect on nonwhite youth employment; others believe there are no effects; and still others think that the effect is small. My own reading of the literature and related data leads me to conclude that the *long-run* effects are probably substantial. I emphasize long-run because I don't think that elimination of the minimum wage would immediately produce a big gain in teenage employment.

Considerable time would be required to see the effects of removing the minimum wage because business firms need time to adapt to a new wage structure.* At first, their capital equipment, their work flows, and their personnel policies would all be geared to the existing structure, based on a high minimum wage. If the minimum were permanently removed, existing firms would begin slowly but surely to adapt, and new firms (even new industries) would come into the labor market. Before minimum wages priced many retail clerks out of jobs, customers usually found ample sales help, even in the lowly five-and-ten-cent stores. Today sales help is scarce, not only in the equivalent of the five-and-tens but also in retail outlets that carry more expensive merchandise. Currently, the minimum wage is wiping out tens of thousands of jobs for teenagers in service stations that are converting to self-service. There are, in addition, many human-service organizations that could use more personnel — for example, nursing homes, day care centers, and after-school recreation programs.

One of the concepts plaguing discussions of youth employment is the "lump of labor" fallacy — the idea that there is only so much

---

* The public's response to higher oil prices provides a useful analogy. At first not much changed. But over time, modifications in automobiles, electric power plants, housing, transportation patterns, and other aspects of life had a substantial impact on trends in oil consumption.

work to go around and that any new employment of youth must mean displacement of some adult. In fact, there is virtually no limit to the work that needs to be done; the critical question is the cost. For instance, between 1965 and 1979 sixteen million additional women found paid employment. If there had been only a limited amount of work available, this huge increase would have been at the expense of male employment, but in fact ten million additional men found jobs during the same period. This was a bigger increase in the male work force than had occurred in the fourteen years preceding 1965. Furthermore, teenage employment grew by three million from 1965 to 1979, the largest increase ever recorded for a comparable span of time.

Another argument that is frequently made to defend the minimum wage, or to get it raised, is "How can you expect a family to live on X dollars per week?" This is an irrelevant argument when discussing teenagers. Indeed, it is irrelevant for the majority of people working at the minimum wage because they are usually not the sole or even main source of support for a family. There is an important distinction between minimum wages and minimum incomes, but minimum-wage proponents often argue as if putting a floor under wages is a big help to low-income families. It is not. In fact, high minimum wages and concomitant increases in wages of more skilled workers (to preserve skill differentials) contribute to inflation, thus reducing the real income of many of the nation's poorest households. The really poor lose more than they gain from wage inflation because they are usually too old, too sick, or too occupied with child care to be able to work. A policy of minimum incomes would be far more helpful to them than a policy of minimum wages.

Dead-end jobs? Even if elimination of the minimum wage did eventually create a large number of new employment opportunities for teenagers, many social critics would dismiss these jobs as "dead end." They are mistaken. *Jobs* are not dead end; the value of work experience depends on what an individual brings to a job and the effort he or she is prepared to make. Every job can be a stepping stone to a better job for someone, and every job can be a dead end if the individual does not have the motivation or capacity to benefit from and advance beyond it. The founder of the famous New York restaurant Sardi's started work as a dish-washer. Most service station owners began their careers by pumping gas, and millions of successful men and women once worked as stock clerks, office assistants, shipping clerks, messengers, and busboys. Among the tens of thousands of occupations listed by the U.S. Department of Labor in its dictionary, there is probably not a single one that doesn't provide an opportunity for someone to advance in the world of work.

A more careful analysis would reveal that the basic problem is the poor skills, work habits, and motivation that many teenagers bring to their initial jobs. To say this is not to pass judgment on these young people. Their circumstances of birth and their experiences as children may have ill prepared them for the world of work. But blaming it on the jobs, or the employers, or the economy does not help either. Many adolescents who function poorly in the world of work have the potential to improve their skills and attitudes, but special efforts are required for them to realize that potential. Employers will usually be unwilling to make such efforts unless they can hire these workers at low wages. The employer bears the costs of training, but the employee acquires general skills which can easily be transferred to another firm.

As a way of stimulating such employment and training, the government could supplement the low wages with stipends to the young people, conditional on their participation in approved jobs. Another approach is for the government to create training and work opportunities through a youth corps or similar program. Real jobs with private employers would probably be more effective if these could be properly arranged; unfortunately there is a big incentive for employers to hire those *least* in need of training. This problem occurred with great frequency in the programs established by the Comprehensive Employment Training Act (CETA). On the other hand, special programs not directly connected with actual jobs may result in poor articulation between what is being taught and the needs of the workplace.

One suggestion that has surfaced repeatedly in recent years is that a "National Youth Service Corps" be created to provide youth with a new environment, education, and opportunities for work and service to the community. Ideally, this corps would include young men and women from all sectors of society, not just the disadvantaged (Potomac Institute 1979). Participants would receive living expenses plus postservice benefits similar to those given veterans after World War II. There is ample work to be done by members of such a youth corps; but would the opportunity for service prove attractive to youth from all walks of life? If membership in the corps were drawn only or mainly from the most disadvantaged sectors of society, the same problems of low morale and local community hostility that plagued the Job Corps programs would probably arise again.

To summarize, there are two principal ways of addressing the problems of youth. One route emphasizes new government programs aimed at increasing their skills. Recent psychological research asserts that disadvantaged young men and women can be helped in this way (Hobbs and Robinson 1982). If cognitive skills can be increased at this stage of life, such programs could help reduce unwed motherhood and teenage unemployment. The other route emphasizes changing current policies, such as the minimum wage, that do more harm than good. We must recognize the extent to which even adolescents make the choices that seem best to them, given their incentives and constraints. If we want to change their behavior, one good way is to change those incentives and constraints.

5

A Time to Sow

Adults 25–44

For everything there is a season.
— *Ecclesiastes 3:1*

AFTER THE STORMY YEARS of adolescence and youth, the two decades from 25 to 44 often seem relatively calm and uneventful. For most men and women these are years of good health, work, marriage, and child-rearing. Although this is the "settling down" stage of life, it is far from static. During these years earnings grow much more rapidly than after 45, especially for well educated men. College-educated men earned 70 percent more at ages 40–44 (in 1979) than at 25–29; the differential is smaller for college-educated women and for men with less schooling. Among those women with only high school diplomas the increase in earnings with age is only 5 percent.

Workers change jobs more readily and migration across state lines is much more likely between ages 25 and 44 than at older ages. Most divorces take place at this stage of life, and remarriages are also frequent: currently about half of all weddings in the United States involve at least one person who has been married before. As the chapter's title suggests, this is the stage when men and women invest in careers and families with the hope that these investments will yield a good return later in life. The choices they make regarding work, migration, marriage, and fertility reflect in part their willingness and ability to incur current costs for future benefits — the wanting versus the waiting.

Conflicting demands of investment in career and family are felt particularly keenly by women because recent decades have witnessed major changes in gender-determined roles and relationships. As someone wryly observed, "More and more women are bringing home the bacon, but then they have to cook it too." In 1950 nine out of ten married women with children under 6 did not work for pay, but by 1980 almost half of this group were in paid employment. Moreover, the proportion of mothers of children under 18 who did not have a husband present rose by 10 percentage points between 1950 and 1980. Women in such circumstances have always had a high rate of labor force participation.

This chapter begins with an analysis of the growth of women in the work force and considers human capital investments that men and women make after leaving school. The second section looks at choices about family and describes many dramatic changes in marriage, fertility, divorce, and remarriage. We will use the economic perspective to explore the relationship between changes in the labor market and in the family, and seek to determine the causes and consequences of these changes. The chapter concludes with a discussion of public policy issues that are particularly relevant for relations between men and women at this stage of life and for their children.

Fifty years ago H. G. Wells predicted that "the family can remain only as a biological fact. Its economic and educational autonomy are inevitably doomed." Others contend that "the family is here to stay" (Bane 1976). Many recent trends seem to support the Wellesian view, but the demise of the conjugal family is not inevitable. This chapter shows that its future will depend primarily on the choices made by men and women ages 25–44, and on the public policies that influence those choices.

WORK

When a man explicitly vows to the Lord, the equivalent for a human being, the following scale shall apply: if it is a male from 20 to 60 years of age, the equivalent is 50 shekels of silver by the sanctuary weight; if it is a female, the equivalent is 30 shekels. —Leviticus 27:1-4

Women earn less than men, a lot less. They always have. This difference in earning power is partly a result and partly a cause of lower labor force participation by women. It is also related to gender differences in postschool investment in human capital and has a pervasive influence on marriage, divorce, and remarriage. This section on work concerns both men and women, but women receive most of the attention because their behavior is changing rapidly and their search for equality with men has significant economic and social consequences.

Female Labor Force Participation

In nearly all societies most adult women work most of the time. Women gather and prepare food, raise crops, tend animals, care for children, make clothing, and perform a variety of other types of work. The notion of "female labor force participation" takes on special significance only in a modern, urban society where there is a clear demarcation between work in the market and work at home. Female participation in market work has been rising in the United States for a long time, from 15 percent (at ages 25–44) in 1890 to 60 percent by 1980. The pace of increase was fairly constant (except for a temporary spurt during World War II) at about 3 percentage points per decade until 1950, but since then women's participation in market work has grown at the unprecedented rate of 9 percentage points per decade.

An understanding of the causes and consequences of this transformation is central to the explanation of many of the topics discussed in this book. Unwed motherhood, divorce, family size — even the expansion of nursery schools for children (Chapter 3) and the growth of nursing homes for the elderly (Chapter 7) are related to the rise in female labor force participation, although social scientists are not in full agreement regarding the direction and magnitude of the causal connections. Many economists have attempted to explain trends in female labor force participation as well as differences among individuals and groups at given points in time (Mincer 1962; Cain 1966; Bowen and Finegan 1969; Smith 1980). The following synthesis draws heavily on their work, but also incorporates my own judgments and speculations.

Before beginning systematic consideration of possible explanations, it is important to note that most of the increase in women working for pay has occurred among *married* women with husband and children present in the home. Among single women ages 25–44 four out of five work for pay, and this proportion has not changed since 1950. Divorced and separated women have also traditionally worked, and their participation rates (about 75 percent) have grown only slightly. The truly astonishing changes have taken place in the behavior of married women with children, as shown in Figure 5.1. This large increase in the propensity of married mothers of small children to work for pay is all the more remarkable because it coincided with a rapid decrease in the proportion of mothers who *are* married. Thus, the proportion of all mothers of small children (regardless of marital status) who are at work rose even more rapidly than the trends shown in Figure 5.1.

Why has the participation of married mothers grown so *rapidly* and so *steadily?* Popular discussions frequently attribute this growth to changes in attitudes that were stimulated by the feminist movement, but the time pattern portrayed in Figure 5.1 does not lend much support to this view. Betty Friedan's *The Feminine Mystique,* which is often credited with sparking the modern feminist movement, was published in 1963, long after the surge of married mothers into the labor force was under way. Moreover, there is no evidence of any sudden acceleration in response to this movement. Similarly, widespread public expressions of feminism *followed* rather than preceded the rise in the age of marriage and the fall in the birth rate. Divorce is the one variable whose change coincided with the burgeoning feminist movement, rising rapidly between 1965 and 1975. Thus, the feminist writings and discussion, valid as they may be in their own terms, will probably not be viewed by future historians as a basic cause of social change but primarily as a rationale and a rhetoric for changes that were already occurring for other reasons.

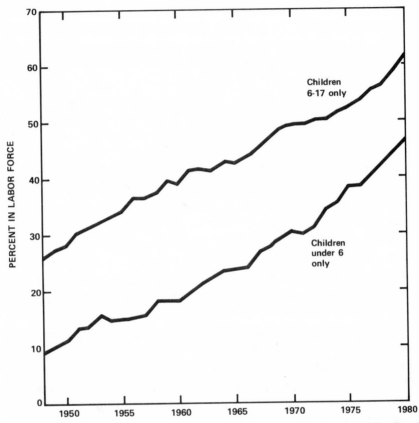

Figure 5.1.   Labor force participation rates of married women with husband present, by presence and age of own children, 1948 – 1980.
(*Sources:* Employment and Training Administration, *Employment and Training Report of the President, 1980,* table B-4; idem, *Employment and Training Report of the President, 1981,* table B-7.)

Government affirmative action programs are regarded by many as fostering female employment, but the timing again suggests that too much has been claimed for this explanation. These programs, which did not gain force until well into the 1960s, cannot explain the rapid rise in participation of married mothers in the 1950s — a rise that was even more rapid for older women with grown children. The timing of changes in the occupational distribution of employed married women is also contrary to what one would expect if the feminist movement or government affirmative action had a great deal of effect. The proportion who were in professional and technical occupations rose rapidly between 1948 and 1965, from 7.7 percent to 14.7 percent, but thereafter the rate of increase was more modest, only to 17.7 percent by 1979.

One of the most popular explanations for the two-earner family is that the wife's earnings are "needed to help make ends meet." This answer is the one most frequently given by women to survey researchers, and it receives some support from analytical studies that attempt to explain why, at any particular time, some wives work and some don't. There is a strong consensus among economists that, other things held constant, the higher the husband's income, the less likely it is that the wife will work for pay.

This explanation, however, does not contribute much to an understanding of changes over time. "Need," in an absolute sense, can hardly be the reason for the rapid rise in labor force participation of married mothers in the 1950s, when the real hourly earnings of their husbands were increasing at an unprecedented pace. Nathan Keyfitz (1980) observed that when women are asked why they work outside the home, they tend to reply that they need the money. "But," he writes, "the answer cannot be correct, since in earlier decades their husbands were earning less, presumably families needed money, and yet wives were content to stay home. Needing money is a universal, a constant, and a first rule of method is that one cannot explain a variable . . . with a constant."

One frequently mentioned but inadequately evaluated explanation for the surge of women into paid employment is the spread of time-saving household innovations such as clothes washers and dryers, frozen foods, and dishwashers. There is little doubt that it is easier to combine paid employment with home responsibilities now than it was fifty years ago, but it is not clear whether these time-saving innovations were the *cause* of the rise in female labor force participation or whether they were largely a *response* to meet a demand created by working women. Confusion about this point is most evident in comments that suggest that the rapid growth of supermarkets and fast-food outlets is a cause of women going to work. Similar time-saving organizations were tried at least sixty years ago, but with less success because the value of time was much lower then. The absence of supermarkets and fast-food eating places in low-income countries today also shows that their rapid growth in the United States is primarily a *result* of the rising value of time and the growth of women in the work force, not the reverse.

Within the economics profession the explanation that commands the widest consensus is that *higher wages* have attracted more married mothers into the labor force. This explanation is more firmly grounded in economic theory than many of the others and is reasonably consistent with observed behavior, both over time and among families at a given point in time. Ever since the pioneering work of Jacob Mincer (1962), numerous cross-section analyses — studies that examine differences among individual families or groups of families — uniformly report that the probability of a wife's working is *positively* related to her potential wage rate, holding constant spouse's education. This is the opposite of the previously noted *negative* effect of the husband's wage rate on the wife's labor force participation.

In explaining changes over time, economists argue that the growth of real wages increases the attractiveness of work outside the home because the value of the wife's time in the marketplace grows relative to the value of time at home. The time series data generally support this hypothesis, but there are some inconsistencies. For instance, real wages were also rising during the nineteenth and first half of the twentieth centuries, but the influx of married women into the labor market was much slower, and in some countries (such as France) it may actually have been in the reverse direction for part of the period. One possible reason why the effect was much stronger after 1950 is that wages must cross a certain threshold level before it pays for married women to enter the labor market (Becker 1981, p. 250). The fact that, on average, better-educated women joined the work force before those with less schooling supports the threshold hypothesis: the higher wages of the better educated meant that they reached the threshold sooner. In 1950 the participation rate was 40 percent higher for women with sixteen or more years of schooling than for women with twelve years, but by 1979 the difference was only about 10 percent. (This differential pattern of entry has *lowered* the average educational attainment of working women relative to working men over the last twenty years, despite the sharp increase in female college enrollment.)

The higher-wage hypothesis is also less than perfect in explaining why the rate of increase in participation of married mothers continued unabated during the 1970s — a decade marked by abnormally slow growth in real earnings. It may be that during this period the perceived-need explanation became more important — not because families were, in an absolute sense, worse off in 1980 than in 1970, but because the earnings of husbands failed to grow as rapidly as had been expected.

In addition to higher wages, the rapid expansion of jobs in the service sector has contributed to the rise in female labor force participation (Fuchs 1968). The service industries (retail trade, financial services, education, health, personal services, public administration) have traditionally offered much greater employment opportunities for women than have mining, manufacturing, construction, and other branches of the industrial sector. For instance, 73 percent of nonfarm female employment was in the service sector in 1960, whereas the comparable figure for males was only 44 percent.

There are many reasons for this large differential. First, most occupations in the service sector do not place a premium on physical strength. Second, hours of work are frequently more flexible in service industries and there are many more opportunities for part-time work. Other things held constant, mothers of small children are more likely to be working in those metropolitan areas where there is large variation in the weekly hours of men (King 1978). This variation is a good indicator of the existence of part-time employment opportunities, and, as will be shown in the next section, women are much more likely than men to seek part-time employment. Third, service sector jobs are more likely to be located in or near residential areas, thus making them more attractive to women who bear large responsibilities for child care and homemaking.

The propensity of women to seek service sector employment is particularly relevant because it is this sector that has provided nearly all of the additional job opportunities in the U.S. economy since the end of World War II. Between 1947 and 1980 U.S.

employment expanded by 39 million; the service sector provided 33 million of these additional jobs. To be sure, some of the growth of service employment is the *result* of the increase in female labor force participation rather than the cause (Fuchs 1981a). Families with working mothers are more likely to eat out, to send their children to nursery school, and to purchase a wide range of personal and professional services. This feedback effect, however, accounts for only a part of the growth of service employment. The major explanation is that rapid increases in output per worker in agriculture and industry cut the demand for labor in those sectors and shifted employment to services. A secondary reason is that consumer demand shifted slightly toward services in response to the growth of real income.

I conclude that the growth of real wages and the expansion of the service sector have been the most important reasons for the growth of female labor force participation. This participation, in turn, has had important effects on marriage, fertility, and divorce, but there is also some feedback from fertility and divorce to labor force participation. Better control of fertility makes a career in the labor market more promising to women, not only because of a reduction in the *number* of children but also because women now have better control over the *timing* of births. The increase in the *probability* of divorce contributes to the rise in female labor force participation because women recognize that complete commitment to home and husband can leave them in a perilous economic position if the marriage should dissolve. Alimony and child support payments are often inadequate, and are not paid at all in a large proportion of cases. An old song says that "diamonds are a girl's best friend," but today the ability to earn a good wage is likely to prove a more reliable asset. That ability is strongly influenced by the choices women make after they leave school.

Postschool Investment in Human Capital

In Chapter 4 we saw how education can be considered an investment in human capital and how the higher earnings associated with greater education can be viewed as a return on that investment. This type of activity does not end with the completion of formal schooling. In varying amounts, individuals continue to invest in human capital through formal on-the-job training, informal work experience, job search, migration, and other activities that involve a current cost in order to increase expected future earnings. Much of this postschool investment occurs between the ages of 25 and 44, because at older ages there are fewer years of working life left in which to realize a satisfactory return.

When men and women invest in formal schooling, their wage rate is zero (or negative, if one considers tuition). When workers undertake postschool investment, they usually receive a positive wage, but it is lower than the one that they could obtain if they were not also adding to their human capital. For instance, in order to acquire additional skills a physician may work for several years as a resident in a hospital for only one-half or one-third of what he or she could earn as a general practitioner. In the case of migration or job search, the worker will frequently incur current out-of-pocket expenses as well as time costs in order to enhance future opportunities.

The amount of postschool investment undertaken can rarely be measured directly; it is usually inferred from the way a worker's earnings change as he or she ages. Other things held constant, the greater the investment the faster earnings rise with age, because earnings are lower than normal during the period when the investment is taking place and higher when the return is being realized. Occupations such as law and medicine, which are characterized by large amounts of postschool investment, have particularly steep age-earnings profiles.

Sex differences in postschool investment are important in understanding the large male-female wage differentials. The average man earns 60 percent more per hour than the average woman and this gap has persisted for a very long time. Several possible explanations have been proposed. When most jobs required heavy labor, sex differences in size and strength were important, but given the present occupational structure of the U.S. economy, it is implausible to attribute such a large gap to inherent differences in physical ability. *Discrimination* by employers, other employees, and consumers plays a role, but most of the differential is attributable to gender-specific *role differentia-*

tion, which begins in early childhood and continues through adult life (Fuchs 1971 and 1974b). The different ways that little girls and boys are treated by parents, teachers, and other adults affect their choice of subjects in school, occupation, and location and hours of work. A major consequence of role differentiation is that women undertake less postschool investment, as evidenced directly by the more limited commitment to work of those women who are in the labor force and indirectly by the resultant slower growth of female earnings over the life cycle.

Consider the question of continuous commitment to work. Although female participation in the labor force has increased enormously, less than half of employed women work full time the year round.* At ages 25–44 the proportion is even smaller (Table 5.1). Among whites in 1979 only one out of three women worked full time the year round, whereas three out of four men did. The percentage of white women who worked part time (either less than a full work week or less than a full year, or both) was actually larger than either the percentage working full time or not working at all. Black women are more likely to work full time than are white women, probably because a higher proportion are unmarried or married to a husband with low earnings. The greater commitment of black women to full-time work helps explain why their wage rates virtually equal those of white women of comparable schooling, despite the handicaps faced by blacks.

Why do so many women work part time? When asked this question by the Bureau of the Census, most women said the main reason was "keeping house." Among men the main reason given was "could not find work"; less than 3 percent said "keeping house." The greater responsibilities that working women bear for home and child care cut into their earnings in several ways. First, if they work fewer hours, they earn less per *year* even if the wage per hour is the same as that paid to men. Second, wage *rates* are frequently lower for part-timers because there are fixed costs to the employer associated with each worker, regardless of the

---

* In 1979 24 percent were full time (at least 35 hours per week) but less than full year; 11 percent were full year but less than full time; and 21 percent were part time and part year.

number of hours worked. These costs may include interviewing and hiring, supervision, payroll and other administrative expenses, some fringe benefits such as health insurance, and the provision of space and equipment to the worker.

Family responsibilities also depress women's earnings through their effect on location of work. Many more women than men seek employment near their homes, but jobs located in residential areas pay less on average than do comparable jobs elsewhere because in such areas labor supply is usually large relative to demand. Finally, the more limited commitment to work, as evidenced by part-time participation and by the greater frequency with which working women periodically withdraw from the labor force, reduces the incentive of employers to provide on-the-job training and, more important, reduces the incentive of women to seek jobs requiring that type of investment.* Other things equal, lower investment in human capital results in lower earnings.

As a result of greater responsibilities at home, women's earnings do not grow as rapidly as men's over the life cycle. At every level of schooling the growth of annual earnings from ages 25–29 to 40–44 is appreciably higher for men than for women, suggesting that sex differences in work experience and postschool investment cut more deeply into the earning power of women as they get older (Table 5.2).

	Percent change in earnings from ages 25–29 to 40–44, 1979	
	Men	Women
Some high school	17	10
High school graduate	27	5
Some college	31	−2
College graduate	69	6
Beyond college	74	24

---

* Some women may work part time because of difficulty in finding full-time work, but there are probably as many or more women working full time who would prefer to cut back to part time if they could keep their current jobs.

This pattern is changing. Young women today seem to be more committed to continuous and full-time work, and are more likely to enter occupations that have large postschool investment opportunities and steep age-earnings profiles. The increased enrollment of women in schools of law, medicine, engineering, and business administration suggests that many traditionally male high-wage occupations are on their way to becoming less segregated. The employment data currently available do *not* show that this has happened yet to any large degree. Between 1960 and 1970 there was some slight reduction in sex segregation *within* the professional and technical occupations, but for the economy as a whole there was relatively little change. Women's share of most occupations tended to rise because of the large increase in female labor force participation, but the great majority of women were still heavily concentrated in "female" occupations such as clerical work, health services, and teaching.

Greater equality in occupational structure is probably the most important step toward greater equality in earnings between men and women. Equality of earnings already exists to a large extent *within* occupations, especially if the occupations are narrowly defined. It is important, therefore, to note Karen Mason's observation that "occupational segregation appears to be caused by the operation of *most* social institutions, not just the labor market itself. Such segregation is, in other words, just one reflection of a society-wide system of sex differentiation which promotes different roles, temperaments, opportunities and rewards for women and men" (1976, p. 81).

Mason goes on to suggest that probably the most serious barrier to occupational equality is "parenthood" (ibid., p. 82). I agree. So long as parents are responsible for children and this responsibility is borne disproportionately by mothers, inequality in the labor market will persist. The implications of this for public policy will be discussed in more detail in the last section of this chapter.

Migration

Migration is an important form of investment for young men and women after leaving school. For instance, in 1980 over 18 percent of 25-year-olds were living in a state different from the one they lived in five years earlier. Geographic mobility is greatest in the early and late twenties, but even among 35-year-olds 12 percent had migrated across state lines from 1975 to 1980. By contrast, less than 5 percent of persons age 55 had made a similar move (U.S. Bureau of the Census, *Current Population Reports* P-20, no. 368). The principal reason why young adults migrate is to improve their economic opportunities. This does not mean that they always move from low-wage to high-wage areas; other factors such as employment and unemployment rates, cost of living, amenities, and government subsidies also influence the direction of flow. Furthermore, many individual migration decisions are motivated by purely personal considerations — for example to live farther away from, or closer to, a particular person.

The tendency to migrate rises rapidly with years of schooling (Table 5.3). Human-capital theory predicts this relationship because the absolute costs of migration are usually similar regardless of schooling level, whereas the absolute benefits are usually greater the higher the level of schooling. For instance, suppose that wages in one state are 10 percent higher than in another at all levels of education. The absolute differential for college graduates who earn $25,000 per year will be $2,500, whereas it will only be $1,500 for high school graduates who earn, on average, $15,000. The costs of moving are not likely to vary proportionately with schooling; therefore, the return from moving will be greater for the college graduate.

Women tend to migrate as much as men do, but decisions about when and where to relocate have typically been dominated by the husband's employment and earnings prospects, not the wife's. This is understandable if the couple are trying to maximize their joint income and if the wife's potential earnings are substantially lower than the husband's. In most families the wife does earn considerably less than the husband because of a lower wage rate, shorter hours, and less continuous labor force attachment. Thus, a 20 percent increase in his annual wage will usually add a lot more to the family income than will a 20 percent increase in her wage. The consequence of a male-dominated location strategy, however, is to further worsen women's earnings prospects because families often relocate to an area where demand is strong for the husband's occupation but weak for the wife's. Also, the timing of the move is often inopportune for the wife. As the earnings of wives come closer to those of their husbands, the economic perspective suggests that their employment prospects will be given more weight in couples' migration decisions.

Americans have always been highly mobile. Not only are we a "nation of immigrants," but a comparatively large number of people have always been willing and able to pull up stakes and move to a different part of the country in an effort to improve their chances or those of their children. The British economist Alfred Marshall believed that this internal migration was a key factor in the continued growth and vitality of the American economy. Early in the twentieth century Marshall wrote: "The people of the United States differ from other European colonists of the New World in that their nervous energies have been stimulated not only by one great migration across the ocean, but by an exceptional persistence to migration within their own large country" (1920).

Up to the mid-1960s the principal net flow of internal migration was from the Northeast, North Central, and South to the West; but blacks had a different pattern, with large outmigration from the South to the Northeast and the North Central regions (Table 5.4). Blacks left the South partly because of generally weaker economic conditions there and partly because race differentials in wages and educational opportunity were much larger in the South than in the North. As economic conditions in the South improved, an inflow of whites began in the late 1960s. By the late 1970s blacks also showed *net* migration from the North to the South, as the North-South difference in race differentials in education disappeared and the gap in earnings was also reduced.

The timing of migration into and out of the large cities has also differed by race. Since 1950 these cities have been losing their share of the white population, but blacks continued to head for the big cities, with the result that by 1970 one in four residents of large cities in the Northeast was nonwhite and in the North Central region the proportion was one in three. Between 1975 and 1980, however, there was an appreciable net migration of blacks out of central cities into suburbs. Whites also continued to leave the central cities for the suburbs, but the rate of flow was slower than between 1970 and 1975. With race differentials in education and family size sharply reduced for recent cohorts, future location patterns are likely to become more similar for blacks and whites, especially if racial discrimination in housing is reduced. A recent study of migration concluded, "Blacks are increasingly affected by social forces that determine population redistribution for the nonblack population, suggesting that blacks are being integrated into the mainstream of American society" (Heaton, Lichter, and Fuguitt 1982, p. 19). The same authors note, however, that racial differences in geographic distribution are likely to persist for a long time unless migration rates accelerate markedly.

FAMILY

A man leaves his father and mother and clings to his wife, so that they become one flesh. —Genesis 2:24

Dramatic changes in rates of marriage, fertility, and divorce have led some observers to predict the end of the family as we have traditionally known it. Others point to very high rates of remarriage as evidence that the family is not disappearing, simply changing. The future of the conjugal family is uncertain, but the economic perspective helps us understand recent changes and provides some clues regarding what is likely in the decades ahead. It also offers guidance regarding public policies that could influence the structure and viability of American families.

Marriage

Marriage is one of the oldest, most universal, and most distinctive of human institutions. There is no record of any society, however ancient or however simple its economic and political system, that does not have marriage as one of the key elements of its social structure. Examples from other primates that are biologically close to humans, such as chimpanzees and orangutans, show that a long-term commitment between a male and a female is not essential for the perpetuation of a species. Human societies, however, usually treat marriage as a matter of great importance with well-defined and often elaborate rules and rituals for arranging, sanctifying, and preserving the union of man and woman.

Most people marry. In the United States there has not been any cohort in this century in which more than 10 percent have never married by the age of 45. The tendency to postpone marriage in recent years has caused a good deal of comment and concern, but the current propensity to marry is low only in relation to the unusually high marriage rates of the 1950s and early 1960s. If one takes a longer time perspective — say, back to 1920 — we find that the percentage of women married at various ages is about the same now as then, and the percentage never married is substantially lower than it was in 1920 (Table 5.5).

During the last quarter-century there has been a gradual rise in the median age of women at first marriage, from a low of 20.1 in 1956 to 22.1 in 1980. The median age for men rose from 22.5 to 24.6. It was the 1950s, however, and not the current period, that was unusual. Current marriage ages are not that different from those at the turn of the century, when the median was 22 for women and 26 for men. In a similar vein, the jump in the proportion of women single (never married) at ages 25–29 from 10 percent in 1960 to 21 percent in 1980 seems less extraordinary when we realize that this percentage was always above 20 from 1900 until World War II.

Although the proportion of persons 25–34 who were single in 1976 was similar to what it was in 1950, their propensity to *live alone* was very different. In the earlier year only 4 percent of single men and 6 percent of single women headed their own households. The others were living with their parents or other relatives or sharing living quarters with roommates and friends. By 1980, 29 percent of single men and the same proportion of single women in this age group were living in one-person households. Analysis of interstate and interpersonal variations in the propensity of young men and women to live alone in 1970 reveals that *higher income* is the principal reason for this enormous change (Michael, Fuchs, and Scott 1980). Autonomy and privacy are apparently highly valued by many young Americans, and, when their income permits, those who are not married often choose to live alone. Not only does income explain cross-sectional differences in living alone, but the relationship estimated from the cross-sectional data can explain most of the changes that have occurred over time.

In addition to the growth of one-person households, the number of unmarried couples living together almost tripled between 1970 and 1980. The most frequent ages for this type of living arrangement are 25–34. Most unmarried couples are childless, but about one-fourth of these households include children who were either born out of wedlock or are the offspring of previous marriages.

What about the future of marriage? Does the increase in living alone, unmarried cohabitation, and divorce signal the demise of this ancient institution? Probably not, but the character and the basis of marriage are changing, and not for the first time. In most preindustrial societies the marital union was part of a more elaborate and more extended network of family and clan relationships. These relationships served to enhance production, to distribute risk, and in general to contribute to the economic and social welfare of the larger group. The interests and preferences of the individual bride and groom were usually subordinated to those larger concerns. Decisions about the timing of marriage, choice of mate, living arrangements for the married couple, and the like were typically not left to them, but were the responsibility and prerogative of their elders. These decisions were frequently made only after consultation with others who would be affected by the union.

With the coming of the Industrial Revolution, the growth of markets, an increase in formal education, greater mobility, and increases in private and public insurance programs, marriages became less the concern of the extended family and more that of the individual man and woman. The basis for marriage shifted primarily to that of a partnership entered into for affection, intimacy, children, and the benefits of the division of labor. Women typically specialized in home production, including child care, cooking, and cleaning, while men specialized in work in the market.

In this partnership the husband usually contributed more goods and services than the wife, except when there were small children at home, in which case the longer hours worked by the mother tended to offset the differential in explicit or implicit wage per hour. The earnings potential of men was higher than that of women for two principal reasons. First, the fact that women usually bore several children and were at risk of additional pregnancies sharply reduced their opportunity to successfully pursue a remunerative career. Second, physical strength was an asset in most jobs prior to the development of modern production techniques and the growth of the service industries. Although the economic power of the husband was usually greater than that of the wife, their consumption of goods and services was usually equal. Such marriages, therefore, were typically hierarchical rather than egalitarian in social and power relationships. The inequality in economic power resulted in deference of the wife toward the husband, a double standard with respect to sexual behavior, and other gender inequalities. Most women accepted these hierarchical marriages because the alternative seemed worse. As Jessie Bernard has written, women "remained even in brutalizing relationships because there were, in effect, no genuine alternatives . . . They had to settle for what they could get" (Levinger and Moles 1979).

Perpetuation of such inequality is morally indefensible. Fortunately, another transition in the nature of marriage is under way. The economic opportunities available to women in postindustrial society are far better than they were previously, and women have much better control over their fertility. These economic and demographic changes will reduce economic inequality, there will be less specialization, and male dominance is likely to diminish. Even Lady Diana Spencer, the bride of the future king of England, did not promise to "obey" when they were married in 1981.

There is, however, one large obstacle remaining in the path of economic equality for women: their demand for and concern about children. If, as current behavior suggests, this demand and concern are not as great among men as among women, two outcomes are possible. On the one hand, concern for children may prevent some women from committing themselves as whole-heartedly as men to paid careers, and an earnings gap will remain.

On the other hand, full commitment to careers by women may result in further decline in fertility and less parental attention to children. Solution of this dilemma will require imaginative and courageous action in both the private and public sectors.

Fertility

The extraordinary swings in American fertility since World War II, which were discussed in Chapter 2, are shown in greater detail in Figure 5.2. Three features of the changes are particularly relevant for this chapter. First, the peak in fertility was reached in 1957, one year after the average age of marriage reached its lowest point, and long before the feminist movement attracted public notice. Second, all age groups show more or less the same cyclical pattern, implying that the determinants of fertility were changing in a way that affected different cohorts simultaneously.

The third major implication of the data in Figure 5.2 is rejection of the view that the fertility decline is only a postponement of child-bearing — that is, a change in the age at which women become mothers. In relative terms, fertility actually declined more rapidly at ages 30 – 34 than at 25 – 29, and even more rapidly at ages 35 – 39. This finding is contrary to the popular impression that there was a large upsurge of births to women over 30 in the late 1970s and early 1980s, but there is a good explanation for the apparent paradox.

The number of *first* births to women ages 30 – 34 and 35 – 39 did increase rapidly between 1970 and 1979, for two reasons. First, there was a large increase in the number of women at these ages. Second, a much higher percentage of these women had no previous children. Thus, despite a huge absolute increase in the number of first births, the proportion of childless women in their thirties who gave birth was no higher in 1979 than in 1970. Furthermore, the rate of second- or higher-order births per thousand women declined appreciably over the nine years and the rate for all births declined by 16 percent at ages 30 – 34 and by 39 percent at ages 35 – 39 (Table 5.6).

Why did fertility rise and then fall as dramatically as shown in Figure 5.2? The most likely explanation is the pattern of change

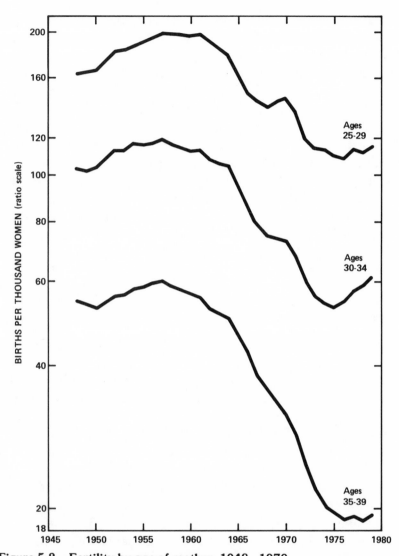

Figure 5.2. Fertility by age of mother, 1948 – 1979.
(*Sources:* U.S. Bureau of the Census, *Historical Statistics of the United States, Colonial Times to 1970,* series B11 – B19; idem, *Statistical Abstract of the United States, 1981,* table 85, and Statistical Abstracts for 1975 and 1980.)

in average hourly earnings. From 1947 to 1957 earnings (adjusted for inflation) were growing at the unusually rapid rate of 2.7 percent per annum. With real living standards booming, it is hardly surprising that most couples felt they could afford to have several children. From 1957 to 1967 the comparable growth rate was only 1.8 percent per annum, and between 1967 and 1977 it dropped still further to 0.7 percent per annum. Therein lies the changed perceptions about the ability to "afford" children.

In addition to the slow growth of earnings, the increase in employment opportunities for women, improvements in contraception, and legalization of abortion have also contributed to the fall in fertility. More problematic is the role of divorce. Divorce, and expectations about divorce, can lead to lower fertility, but in this recent period of rapid change the decline in fertility preceded the upturn in divorce by several years. Moreover, both phenomena are probably the result of the major economic changes of recent decades, particularly the rapid increase in women working for pay and, in the 1970s, the abnormally slow growth of real earnings of men.

Divorce

Among the many aspects of American society considered in this book, none has changed more suddenly since 1965 than the divorce rate. As shown in Figure 5.3, the number of divorces per thousand married women has tended to rise very slowly over the long term. A sharp increase in the rate during and immediately after World War II was quickly followed by a return to a more normal level by 1948. From 1950 to 1965 the rate was remarkably stable. The slight decline evident in Figure 5.3 was largely the result of a shift in the age distribution of married women (the divorce rate is lower for older women) rather than a decline in age-specific divorce rates. Between 1965 and 1975, however, the annual rate doubled, jumping from 10 to 20 per thousand married couples. Since 1975 the increase has been at a slightly slower pace.

Some insights concerning the unusual pattern of change can be obtained from cross-sectional studies that attempt to discover differences among couples that are good predictors of the probability of divorce (Ross and Sawhill 1975; Becker, Landes, and Michael 1977). These studies generally agree that, other things held constant, the probability of divorce is higher if the marriage occurs at a very young age, if the husband and wife do not know

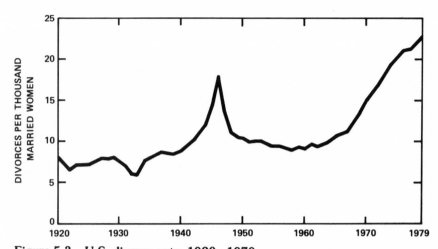

Figure 5.3. U.S. divorce rate, 1920–1979.
(*Sources:* U.S. Bureau of the Census, *Historical Statistics of the United States, Colonial Times to 1970,* series B217; idem, *Statistical Abstract of the United States, 1981,* table 124, and Statistical Abstracts for 1974 and 1980.)

each other well before marriage, and if they come from different backgrounds (often proxied by race or religion or large differences in education). Also, a strong negative relationship is found between duration of marriage and the probability of divorce. Most divorces occur early (over half by the seventh year of marriage), for at least two reasons. First, the longer the couple have been together, the more likely it is that they have many mutual investments in children, home, friends, and the like, and the more costly (in psychic terms) the divorce will be. Second, there is undoubtedly a selection process at work whereby those husbands and wives who are most incompatible split early, leaving the more compatible ones in the pool of married couples.

Another important finding of cross-sectional studies is that *unexpected* changes tend to be maritally destabilizing, regardless of whether the changes are in a positive or negative direction. Consider, for instance, the effect of changes in income. In cross-sectional studies, higher income is usually positively related to marriage and negatively related to divorce. If a husband or wife, however, experiences a large, *unexpected* increase in income, the probability of divorce goes up. The probability also rises if there is a large, unexpected decrease in income. Unexpected changes in health and fecundity have a similar effect (Becker, Landes, and Michael 1977). The economist's conclusion that unexpected change is maritally destabilizing is echoed by a marriage expert, Helen Singer Kaplan. In response to the question of whether a marriage would be adversely affected if the wife had more income than the husband, she wrote, "Not necessarily . . . If, however, there is a change in the relationship, if she used to earn less and now she starts to earn more, it usually does create a crisis in a marriage . . . If a man marries into a very wealthy family . . . he marries knowing this, and they can have a compensating contract" (1981, p. 82).

The number and ages of children are systematically related to divorce, although the interpretation of the relationship is not entirely clear-cut. As might be expected, the more young children present, the less likely the marriage is to dissolve. One obvious reason is that when a couple have several small children, divorce is likely to be quite costly to both the father and the mother in psychic and material terms, and they are also likely to consider possible adverse effects on the children. The relationship can, however, also be explained in part by a causal connection running in the opposite direction. A husband and wife who believe there is a high probability that their marriage will end in divorce (they know much more about themselves and their relationship than the researcher can possibly include in the analysis) are likely to have fewer children.

These results of studies based on behavior at a given point in time contribute to our understanding of the changes in divorce that have occurred over time. The sharp rise in divorce associated with war, for instance, is related to the haste with which many marriages are entered into at that time, and the young age of many of the brides and grooms. Some divorces also result from the separations and unexpected changes that the war produces. The stability in the 1950s and early 1960s is probably the result of the huge increase in fertility of that period, which tended to offset the early age of marriage that might have led to a rise in divorce.

Many factors probably contributed to the very steep increase that occurred after 1965. The United States was at war in Vietnam, although the scale of involvement was considerably less than in World War II. Fertility was down sharply, and this decline preceded the increase in divorce by several years. Robert Michael, a leading investigator of the economics of divorce, believes that improvements in contraception — specifically birth control pills and intrauterine devices — were important factors for three reasons: (1) they made it easier to reduce the average number of children per couple; (2) they reduced *uncertainty* about subsequent fertility, thus encouraging women to be more career-oriented and to increase their economic independence; and (3) they decreased inhibitions concerning extramarital sex because of the reduced risk of pregnancy (Michael 1982).

The large increase in the size of AFDC payments (see the discussion of the illegitimacy ratio in Chapter 2), the relaxation in eligibility requirements, and the growth of other economic subsidies probably also increased the chances that a mother of small children, finding herself in what she regarded as an unsatisfactory marriage, would choose the option of divorce.

The effect on divorce of women working for pay is one of the most difficult to understand. Becker's economic theory of marriage (1981) focuses on the gains from division of labor and suggests that these gains will be smaller if both spouses work in paid employment and also work at home. The available data provide some support for this theory, but are open to several different interpretations. Most studies that look at a sample of families at a given point in time find that the probability of divorce is higher when the wife has paid employment, holding constant other influences on divorce such as number of children, duration of marriage, and income. The total explanatory power of these models of divorce is small, however, and there may be other variables not included that affect both wife's working and subsequent divorce. For instance, if a husband and wife are not getting along with each other, the wife may go to work because she wants more economic independence, or because she anticipates that the marriage has a high probability of ending in divorce.

One bit of evidence in favor of the hypothesis that the causality runs from wife's work to divorce is that the rise in labor force participation by married women with small children at home preceded the rise in the divorce rate by several years. It would be very difficult to support the proposition that an increase in divorce, or even anticipation of an increase, was causing mothers to enter the labor force in the 1950s. In recent years, however, the labor force participation of mothers has continued to rise rapidly, but the divorce rate is not rising as rapidly as before. If wives' labor force participation is truly causal, the divorce rate should have continued to climb rapidly. One way to reconcile the disparate implications of the time series data is to recall the destabilizing effect of *unexpected* changes. The entry of wives into the labor market in the 1950s and 1960s may have contributed to the rise in divorce because in many cases this entry was unexpected. The high and rising labor force participation of young mothers in the 1970s may not be as destabilizing to marriage because most recent marriages have been entered into with this expectation. Indeed, withdrawal from the labor market by the wife might actually contribute to divorce if such withdrawal was contrary to the expectations at the time of marriage.

Heather Ross and Isabel Sawhill, in their study of the increase in divorce and of births to unmarried mothers, hypothesize that "the changing economic and social status of women is a major source of the behavioral evolution leading to female-headed families" (1975, p. 5). They write that the rise in divorce in particular may be attributable in part to the rapid shift in the economic role of women. They say that this shift may have occurred more rapidly than changes in beliefs about traditional sex roles, thus setting up "increased ideological dissonance" (p. 49). They go on to suggest that "if and when attitudes change in accord with the facts, more marriages will be stable," although they foresee somewhat less stability than in the traditional relationships of the past.

In summary, the years from 1965 to 1975 were marked by several unusual changes which contributed to the rapid rise in divorce. There were the technological changes in contraception, economic changes such as the slowing down in the growth of real earnings and the increase in government entitlement programs, and social and cultural changes, including a resurgence of feminist ideology and widespread criticism of traditional institutions and norms. Unless new transformations of comparable magnitude emerge, it seems highly unlikely that the divorce rate will continue its rapid rise. Whether it will stay at its current level or fall to a lower one is more difficult to predict.

Remarriage

Remarriage occurs frequently in American society. Approximately one out of every three persons marrying has been married at least once before, and almost half of all weddings involve at least one person who has been previously married. Those writers who like to emphasize the persistence of marriage as an institution cite the high rates of remarriage as evidence in their favor. For young widows and divorcees the statistics are rather astounding. Those under 25 have an *annual* remarriage rate (the number marrying, divided by the number who are eligible to marry) of 30 percent. This is double the marriage rate of *never-married* women under 25. Remarriage prospects fall with age, especially for women. At ages 25–44 the annual rate is approximately 13 percent.

Although remarriage rates are high, they have been falling. In 1978 the annual rate for widowed and divorced women ages 25–44 was 12.5 percent, down from 15 percent in the late 1960s. Moreover, during this period there was a shift in the composition of the group toward more younger divorcees and fewer older widows, a shift that should have raised the remarriage rate because remarriage prospects are better for younger women and a desire to remarry is frequently the cause of divorce. Adjustment for changes in age and marital status lowers the 1978 rate to 8.5 percent. The sharp decline in the remarriage rate since the late 1960s may be attributable in part to the huge increase in the number of divorced women and the fact that some time must elapse between divorce and remarriage; but even if remarriage does occur eventually, there is a clear trend toward divorced women remaining divorced for a longer period of time. This may be the result of improved employment opportunities for women or the growth of government transfer programs such as AFDC. A carefully controlled study of families in twenty states found that remarriage rates were lower, the higher the level of AFDC payments (Hutchens 1979).

Gender differentials are quite large in the remarriage "market." At ages 25–44 remarriage rates are almost twice as high for men as for women, and there tends to be a larger difference in age between groom and bride in remarriages than in first marriages. When the marriage is a first one for both bride and groom, the grooms are, on average, two years older than their brides. When the groom is remarrying but the bride is not, the average differential is about seven years, and when both bride and groom are remarrying the average differential is three to four years. If the bride is remarrying and the groom is not, the bride will be older than the groom about 40 percent of the time, the same age in 10 percent of the cases, and younger in only half the marriages (National Center for Health Statistics 1973b).

The gender differential in probability and age of remarriage lends support for the view that many marriages are still something other than symmetrical partnerships. The stereotype of the older, richer, divorced man marrying a younger woman receives enough support in the data to suggest that his higher income is being exchanged for her youth and attractiveness. As some women acquire higher earning power in the professions and business it will not be surprising to see them marrying younger men, either on first marriage or, more likely, on remarriage. In such cases the roles of buyer and seller will have been reversed.

PUBLIC POLICY ISSUES

By far the most important public policy issues at ages 25–44 are those that bear on the roles of men and women, the relations between them, and the consequences of these roles and relations for children. To be sure, role differentiation begins to develop long before 25 and there are important implications of gender after 45, but this chapter's discussions of work and family indicate that issues of gender become critical between those ages. It is during the years when men and women are engaged in building *careers* and *families* that biological and cultural differences between the sexes have their greatest impact.

Men and women have traditionally had different (and some would say unequal) roles in society, primarily because of women's involvement in child-bearing and men's greater size and strength. When fertility was high and life expectancy short, child-bearing occupied a significant fraction of a woman's life, precluding equality with men in the labor market, except in unusual cases. In addition to differences due to child-bearing, the average man had an advantage in most jobs because of his physique. Men were also more likely than women to receive college and postgraduate educations, but this differential was more a *result* of the basic factors discussed above rather than an independent cause of their labor market advantage.

Economic growth and technological change have sharply reduced these sources of role differentiation and gender inequality. In particular, better control over fertility and longer life expectancy imply that women can consider spending many more years in the labor market. The rise of a service economy implies that differences in size and strength no longer confer an advantage to men in most occupations. The hospital, the classroom, and the shopping center have replaced the coal mine, the steel mill, and the assembly line as the major work sites of modern society. "Industrial man" has been succeeded by "postindustrial person."

These changes have heightened the expectation and desire of many women (and some men) for complete gender equality at *work* and at *home*. To date, these expectations and desires have not for the most part been realized. Many observers believe that the only way women can attain greater autonomy and greater social and political power is by raising their earning power in the marketplace. In order to do this, they would have to be as committed to work, as continuously attached to the labor force, and as varied in their occupational choice as men. If they do take this route, what will happen to marriages, homes, and families? One possibility is that men will assume equal responsibility in the home, but this has not yet happened to any large extent.

Many women believe that they are at an economic disadvantage relative to men, and the large sex differential in earnings certainly supports this view. Some of this disadvantage stems from the social and cultural legacies of an earlier era, when child-bearing and job requirements presented major obstacles to women. As these obstacles have diminished in importance, the

major remaining source of disadvantage is the conflicting demands of family and work — a conflict that is usually greater for
women than for men. Women appear to have a greater demand for
children — both in terms of wanting to be a parent and of caring
about the children after they are born — and this difference
between the sexes is exacerbated by the fact that the child-bearing
years are more restricted for women. The differential pressure
from this source on women in their middle and late thirties is
obvious.

The relevance of differential demand can be seen by imagining
the opposite case. Suppose that men wanted to have children and
cared about their welfare more than women did. In order to induce
women to bear their children and help raise them, men would have
to make major concessions with respect to allocation of time,
economic decision making, and the like. In other words, women
could call the shots. It is obvious that this is not the case today.

The stronger concern for children by women may be rooted in
biology, or it may be culturally determined, or both. Whatever the
cause, most women are much more sensitive to the conflicting
demands of family and career than are most men. Betty Friedan,
one of the earliest and most perceptive leaders of the "women's
movement," said that young women in 1981 were asking the
following questions:

"How can I have the career I want and the kind of marriage I
want and be a good mother?"

"How can I get my husband to share more responsibility at
home?"

"How can I have it all? Do I *really* have to choose?"

Friedan's answers to the dilemmas facing young women re-
volve primarily around day care for children and changes in the
labor market. In an article entitled "The Myth of the Super
Mom," she recommends " 'quality' day care," "tax incentives for
day care," "better company benefits," "part-time work," and "a
new concept of work." Similar recommendations have been made
by many other writers; let's consider each one in turn.

Day care. One of the complaints most frequently voiced by
women who are trying to juggle career and family is the absence of
high-quality day care. The problem is often stated as if there were

a failure of *supply,* but a closer look indicates that the real problem is one of weakness in effective *demand.* There are virtually no barriers (except those that governments impose in the form of unrealistically high standards) that inhibit the supply of day care if there is a willingness and ability to pay for it.

Day care does not depend on a limited supply of exhaustible raw materials. It does not require a unique location, a huge capital investment, or extremely scarce skills. The production of day care, unlike automobile manufacturing or even hospital care, can be carried out efficiently in a small organization. The chief input into quality day care is warm, loving, intelligent service by men and women who expect to be fairly compensated for their efforts. There is no evidence that, given appropriate compensation, the supply of such services would not be forthcoming, especially where there is not excessive government regulation.

The harsh reality is that the quantity and quality of day care available are limited primarily by what men and women are willing to pay for. If we want more and better care, we must be prepared to say how we will meet its cost. The problem is not solved by simply saying that "business firms" or "the government" should pay for day care either through direct provision of services, subsidies, or "tax incentives." Surely we have learned by now that there is no magic wand that can divert resources to day care without taking them away from something else. If business firms provide day care (and it may be good business for them to do so), the cost of that care must come primarily out of the wages or other fringe benefits of employees, or be added to the price of the goods and services they produce. If government bears the cost (and there may be good reasons why it should), this must result in higher taxes or in lower expenditures for other services.

Regardless of the funding mechanism, the average family will have to pay the average cost of care, and this has led some economists to conclude that subsidies for child care will not help the wife at the expense of the husband in such families. They argue that as long as the husband is making financial transfers to the wife, he can fully offset the effect of the public policy by cutting back on these transfers (Becker 1981). I disagree. The husband is probably receiving services or deference from the wife in return for those transfers, and he cannot arbitrarily reduce them without experiencing some change in her behavior. At the limit, if he cuts these transfers too much, the wife may decide she is just as well off without the husband. I conclude, therefore, that a subsidy for child care, even if fully offset by a tax on the family, will benefit the wife if the wife cares more about the children than does the husband, as explained in Chapter 3.

Better company benefits. One of the proposals made by Friedan and others is that companies should offer individual employees a *choice* of benefits among vacations, retirement, medical insurance, maternity/paternity leave, and so on, rather than having a standard package for all workers. This seems like a reasonable proposal in principle, but there are several possible objections. Many fringe benefits such as a retirement plan or health insurance are made compulsory in order to avoid the problems created by allowing some workers not to participate and then having them become a burden to others in time of need. (This is the so-called free-rider problem.) Also, if workers are free to choose and change benefits as their circumstances change, the problem of adverse risk selection would be severe. For instance, one can imagine a worker opting for the parental leave package when young and for the retirement benefit when old. At the extreme, consider the implications of allowing a worker to choose health insurance only after illness strikes. Such benefit hopping and shopping would raise the cost to all and would destroy the concept of mutual insurance which underlies most of these programs. Assuming these objections can be met, however, there is a case for allowing flexibility in the way a worker's total compensation is divided between wages and fringe benefits and among those benefits.

Part-time work. Earlier in this chapter we noted that more than half of all working women work part time or part year. In what sense, then, can part-time work be regarded as a new solution? Probably the main argument is that *all* workers, men and women, should be free to convert *any* job into part time and that the hourly wage and benefits should not be adversely affected by the exercise of such an option. As in the case of day care, there needs to be some discussion of the costs of such a policy. If there are no costs — that is, if part-time workers are just as valuable in every respect as full-time workers — there is no need for a special public policy to deal with the problem. Employers would be just as happy to hire part-timers, and if there are many workers who prefer part-time jobs, they will be hired.

Part-timers, however, are often not as valuable as full-timers (several reasons were given earlier in the chapter); therefore, a policy that forced equal pay would have some undesirable effects. It would *decrease* rather than increase part-time employment opportunities because many employers would be reluctant to offer part-time work, and those who did might have difficulty making a profit and staying in business. If *all* firms were *forced* to hire part-timers, the extra costs would come out of the wages and benefits paid to full-time workers or would be passed on to consumers in the form of higher prices. Although full-time workers and consumers would suffer from such a policy, women would probably be better off because they comprise the bulk of the part-time work force. However, women who work full time would bear the costs along with men.

A new concept of work. The "new concept of work" advocated by Friedan and others calls for recognition of housework, child care, care of the elderly, and similar work at home as the equivalent to wage work. They say it should be rewarded by the government through tax breaks, Social Security benefits, and the like. As with the previous recommendations, it is necessary to raise the question of costs. The tax system is *already* biased in favor of work at home compared to work in the market, because the former is not taxed whereas market earnings are subject to both income and Social Security taxes. Subsidies for work at home could not benefit the average family (their additional taxes would be at least as great as the subsidies they receive), but they could benefit women for the reasons already given.

Public policy could be used to improve the position of women in our society; the fact that such policies may impose costs does not mean that they are not desirable. It does mean, however, that we should carefully consider the prospective benefits and costs and the distributional implications of such policies. Also, the experience of other countries should be used to gain insight regarding the feasibility and consequences of proposed changes.

The limited ability of government to eliminate all differences between men and women is apparent in Sweden, a country that has gone further than most in attempting to remove or compensate for the handicaps that women face because of their gender. An article on equality in Sweden, "Some Are (Still) More Equal Than Others," states that "a complete overhaul of marital and social legislation, which has wiped out the illegitimacy of children and removed all handicaps for the unmarried woman and mother, has resulted in a complete freedom of life style for women, with no fears of financial hardships on any score . . . But problems continue to abound." These problems arise primarily from the failure of men to take their share of responsibility for work at home and care of children. The author states: "Tension over the sharing of daily tasks — an unbearable physical load for one person without assistance — has become a major factor for the breakup of homes. There is a divorce for every other marriage and a reluctance to marry at all in the circumstances" (Chabra 1980, p. 22).

It appears that children are central to the question of sex role differentiation and inequality in the labor market. If the demand for children is stronger among women than men, and if women feel more responsible for children after birth, they will be economically disadvantaged relative to men. On the other hand, to the extent that women become less interested in bearing children or less concerned about their welfare after birth, the future of the family and of society looks bleak because there is little evidence that men are prepared to take up the slack. The bottom line for public policy must be to assure a socially desirable level of investment in children, both with respect to numbers and quality of care.

6

A Time to Reap

Adults 45–64

*Whatsoever a man soweth, that shall
he also reap.*
—*Galatians 6:7*

BETWEEN THE AGES of 25 and 44 men and women invest in the
future by raising families and building careers; the following two
decades, from 45 to 64, are a time to reap returns on these earlier
investments. Children grow up and begin to form families of their
own. Life continues to improve for some older adults, others are in
a holding pattern, while still others begin to feel that their best
years are behind them. At this stage of life major differences in
work, income, and health emerge, partly as a result of differences
in previous investments in human capital. The earnings of some
men peak at age 45 or even earlier, while others continue to
experience increased earnings right up to 65. Income inequality
among men is present at all ages, but is much greater at 60 than at
40 because of widening differences in wage rates and differential

withdrawal from work. At ages 55 – 64 over 80 percent of men with a college degree are still in the work force, compared with only 60 percent of men with an elementary school education.

The educational level of older men has been rising in recent decades, but paradoxically they have been leaving the labor market at an unprecedentedly high rate. In 1980 fully 28 percent of men ages 55 – 64 were not in the labor force; as recently as 1970 that proportion was only 17 percent, and in 1960 it was 13 percent. Even at ages 45 – 54 the proportion of men neither employed nor seeking work rose from 6 to 9 percent during the 1970s. Never before in U.S. economic history has there been such a massive withdrawal from work by men who are below the conventional retirement age of 65. This withdrawal places an increasing burden on those still at work to pay the disability, retirement, health care, and other benefits of those who have stopped.

Withdrawal from work is related in considerable degree to health problems. Poor health increases the probability of early retirement and is the basis for the collection of disability payments prior to retirement age. Although there is no reason to believe that there was any deterioration in the average level of health in the 1970s, government expenditures for disability and early retirement grew enormously during that decade. Poor health may determine *who* stops working, but the changes in the 1970s are the result of other factors such as the increased attractiveness of Social Security retirement and disability payments relative to what the recipients could earn by continuing to work.

After age 45 health worsens, on average, and individual differences in health become much larger. Some differences are genetic in origin, but many are the result of behavioral choices concerning life style that were made as adolescents or young adults. Differences in death rates between men and women also increase after age 45, and the excess mortality of men, combined with the propensity of older widowed and divorced men to marry younger women, results in a significant sex difference in marital status. At earlier ages the proportion married is about the same for men and women, but by 65 one out of every three women has no spouse while only one man in seven is unmarried. Although women at this stage of life face less conflict between work and family than do younger women, the sex gap in earnings is greater because of the commitment that women made to their families earlier in life when men were building their careers.

Thus, health, work, income, and marital status are closely interrelated at this stage of life, and are discussed in this chapter in the first four sections. Because inequality among individuals is greater at this age than at any other, the chapter concludes with an examination of public policies that bear on inequality.

HEALTH

A healthy body is the guest-chamber of the soul. —*Francis Bacon*

Until someone discovers Ponce de Leon's fountain of youth, health will decline with advancing age. Particularly after age 45 mortality rates rise, self-assessed health status worsens, and the utilization of medical and hospital care increases. Not only does the average level of health decrease between 45 and 64, but differences in health among individuals increase, the relationship between health and income becomes more pronounced, and health differences between men and women get larger. These changes, through their effects on work, income, and marital status, are a major determinant of how men and women live at this stage of life.

The average 45-year-old American man's chances of dying within one year are 5 per thousand; the probability for a woman of that age is about 3 per thousand. By age 65, however, the annual probability of death is 30 per thousand for men and 15 per thousand for women. Declining health leads to much greater use of health services after age 45. In 1978 each thousand men ages 45–64 received 1,619 days of care in nonfederal short-term hospitals, compared with only 614 days for men ages 15–44. The comparable figures for women (excluding childbirth) are, respectively, 1,656 and 772 days per thousand. Visits to physicians and use of prescription drugs also rise substantially as adults move through middle age. Per capita utilization of medical care is even higher after age 65 than before, but because there are currently so many more people at ages 45–64 than at 65 and above, aggregate health care expenditures in the United States are at a maximum at the former stage of life.

The deterioration in health implied by the foregoing statistics is the result of an accumulation of chronic health problems, not a higher incidence of acute conditions. In fact, the rate of acute conditions (such as upper respiratory infections) and the number of days of restricted activity and bed disability attributable to these conditions are *lower* at ages 45–64 than at 17–44. Chronic conditions such as low back pain, however, result in almost four times as many days in bed per thousand people at ages 45–64 than at 17–44.

It is well known that the *average level* of health declines after age 45; it is not as widely recognized that the *variability* in health among individuals increases. At earlier ages most men and women are usually in good health, despite occasional spells of acute illness. Some people continue to enjoy excellent health up to 65 and beyond, but many others begin to experience substantial disabilities and deficiencies, including impaired sight and hearing, high blood pressure, diabetes, diseases of the heart, and pulmonary disorders. One indication of an increase in variability can be found in measures of blood pressure, which not only rise with age but also show an increase in relative variation among individuals. This variation reaches a maximum among people 55–64 (National Center for Health Statistics 1981, p. 42).

Health deteriorates after age 45 partly as the result of biological factors that are beyond the individual's control, and partly as the result of choices made earlier in life regarding smoking, diet, and other aspects of personal behavior. Worsening vision provides a good example of the former; emphysema resulting from cigarette smoking illustrates the latter. The percentage of people with corrected vision 20/20 or better is virtually constant — about 85 percent — from ages 18 to 44, but drops sharply to 56 percent at ages 55–64, largely because of physiological changes. Cigarette smokers have a higher probability of dying than do nonsmokers at every stage of life, but if we compare the future mortality of a thousand male smokers age 35 with the mortality of a thousand nonsmokers, we see that the absolute difference between these groups will be greatest at ages 50–65. The differential in mortality is not large before age 50 because it takes a long time for lung cancer to develop and for the harmful effects of cigarette smoke on the heart to reach a critical level. After age 65 the differential in mortality between smokers and nonsmokers declines because both groups become increasingly vulnerable to a large number of diseases (Harris 1981).

	Number of deaths per thousand men age 35		
	35–50	*50–65*	*65–80*
Smokers	55	223	421
Nonsmokers	18	94	315
Excess deaths of smokers	37	129	106

The disastrous effects of cigarettes on health and the tendency for better-educated persons to smoke less is one reason why there is a strong relation between schooling and health. This relationship holds regardless of whether health is measured by mortality, morbidity, disability, or self-evaluation, and is readily apparent in comparisons of individuals or group averages. At one time it was thought that the better educated were in good health because of their higher income (Antonovsky 1967), but several econometric studies during the past decade have shown that the relationship between schooling and health holds even after controlling for differences in income (Auster, Leveson, and Sarachek 1972; Grossman 1972; Taubman and Rosen 1982).

Although there is no doubt that schooling and health are related, the *way* in which schooling affects health is less clear. Michael Grossman believes that additional years of schooling help individuals to achieve better health, both for themselves and their families, by enabling them to make wiser use of medical care and more informed choices about cigarette smoking, diet, and other elements of life style. One of his interesting results is that the health of middle-aged men is better the higher the level of their *wives'* schooling, even after controlling for their education and income (Grossman 1976).

Schooling probably does affect health by increasing efficiency, as described above, but this explains only part of the relationship. As shown in Figure 4.2 and the accompanying discussion of smoking, another likely explanation is that both greater schooling and better health are the result of some third variable such as individual differences in willingness or ability to invest in human capital. Both schooling and health-related activities (for example, preventive visits to physicians) involve incurring current costs for the sake of future benefits. Individuals differ in the rate of return that will induce them (or their parents) to undertake such investments, partly because of differences in access to financial resources. Even when access to capital is the same, investments in human capital may vary because individuals differ in their skills of self-control or in their ability to visualize the future.

Given the strong relation between education and income, it is not surprising to find that income is also related to health. The reasons for this relationship, however, have changed. In very poor countries the causality runs primarily from income to health because income means command over food, shelter, and other basic necessities of life. In the United States and other developed countries, however, income is not a major determinant of health because basic necessities are available to people at almost all levels of income. Indeed, higher income can actually result in poorer health if it leads to the consumption of fatty foods, less exercise, and other unhealthy behaviors.

In postindustrial societies the causality runs primarily from poor health to lower income, especially at ages 45–64. The difference between being in excellent or poor health is most strongly related to income at this stage of life because health problems become severe and significantly impair the ability to work. Below 45 or above 65 the relation is weaker because at young ages the health problems are usually not as serious, and at old ages few people are working regardless of health (Table 6.1).

WORK

Between the ages of 25 and 54 more than nine out of every ten men participate regularly in the labor force, but the rate falls sharply to

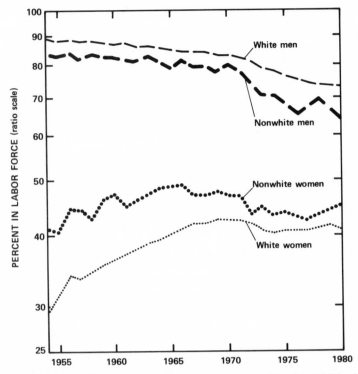

Figure 6.1.   Labor force participation rates at ages 55 – 64, 1954 – 1980.
(*Source:* Employment and Training Administration, *Employment and Training Report of the President, 1981,* table A-5.)

less than three out of four at ages 55 – 64. This low participation is a relatively new phenomenon in the United States; as recently as 1965 fully 83 percent of men ages 55 – 64 were in the labor force and most of the decline occurred after 1970 (see Figure 6.1). Poor health is often given as the reason for retirement prior to age 65, but there is no evidence that the health of older men has been deteriorating in recent decades. Thus, the sharp decline in their labor force participation must be the result of other forces. Changes in Social Security retirement and disability benefits are probably the main explanations.

In 1961 men gained the option to collect benefits at age 62 (women have been able to since 1956) and benefit levels at all ages were raised faster than the cost of living, especially in the late 1960s and early 1970s. As a result, early retirement became common and the labor force participation rate of 62-year-old white urban men fell twelve percentage points, from 78 percent to 66 percent, between 1969 and 1973 (Hurd and Boskin 1981). Disability benefits under Social Security were increased and eligibility requirements eased, resulting in an *eight-fold* increase in aggregate payments between 1965 and 1978. Injuries and illness did not increase and neither were jobs becoming more physically demanding, but many low-wage workers found these government-financed alternatives to work increasingly attractive. One study of men ages 45–54 concluded that "the increase in SSD [Social Security disability] benefits relative to earnings can explain roughly half of the decrease in labor force participation" (Leonard 1979, p. 25).

The participation rate of women ages 55–64 increased sharply in the 1950s and 1960s, but then leveled off at a rate substantially below that of men. Most women are married to men several years older than themselves. When the husband retires, the wife is likely to do so as well in order to keep him company, travel with him, or move to a retirement location. Other women at this age are widows and the income they receive from Social Security, private pensions, and life insurance benefits enable many of them to live without paid employment. The high rates of labor force participation now being recorded by young women suggest that the rates at ages 55–64 may swing up again when these younger cohorts reach this stage of life. The gender difference in labor force participation at older ages in not likely to disappear, however, as long as wives are younger than their husbands (and follow them into retirement), and as long as many women are widows with substantial nonwage income.

One of the most striking aspects of labor force participation at ages 55–64 is the extent to which it varies with level of education (see Figure 6.2). Men who have not attended high school have participation rates of only about 60 percent, compared to over 80 percent for those who have a college degree or more. The differential for women is even more striking. Differences in health explain part of this relationship, for two reasons. First, we know that men and women with less schooling have, on average, poorer health. Second, even when the same health problem afflicts both the well

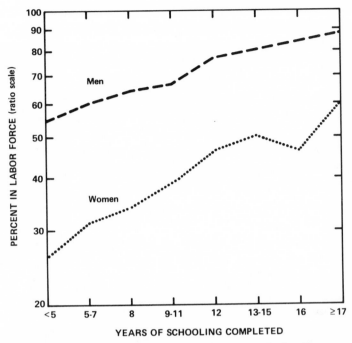

Figure 6.2.   Labor force participation rates by years of schooling completed, at ages 55 – 64, 1979.
(*Source:* National Clearinghouse on Aging, *The Older Worker,* Statistical Report on Older Americans, no. 6.)

educated and the poorly educated, its effect on labor force participation is greater for the poorly educated because they are more likely to be in physically demanding occupations.

In addition to enjoying better health, better-educated workers typically earn higher wages and frequently derive more satisfaction from their jobs. Thus, men with less education are more likely to find disability payments or early retirement benefits an attractive alternative to work. Donald Parsons used the National Longitudinal Surveys of 45 – 59-year-olds to investigate the decline in male labor force participation, with special emphasis on the sharp fall in the rate for nonwhites. He concluded that "the decline in labor force participation, particularly among blacks, is the result of increasingly attractive alternatives to work. The differentially large decline among blacks is due simply to their relatively poor market alternatives and the increasingly progressive structure of Social Security benefits" (Parsons 1980, p. 919). For women, the relevant comparison is often between working in the market and working at home; the lower the wage, the more attractive the alternative of home production.

One anomaly in the schooling–labor force participation relation shown in Figure 6.2 is the dip in the rate for women with sixteen years of schooling (college diploma). The explanation seems to be that married women with college degrees have husbands who earn considerably more money than do the husbands of women with thirteen to fifteen years of schooling, but who earn only slightly less than the husbands of women with postgraduate education (seventeen or more years of schooling). Furthermore, women with sixteen years of schooling are more likely to be married than are women with more than sixteen years (67 percent versus 51 percent, respectively, among white women ages 55–64 in 1970).

Regardless of education, women are more likely to work part time or part year than are men, but the gender difference is much smaller at this stage of life than between 25 and 44 because the competing responsibility of child care eases after the age of 45. The impact of family responsibilities on the work careers of women was demonstrated by David Salkever in an unusual study that compared the labor market behavior of mothers of *disabled* children with that of mothers similar in all respects except that their children are without disabilities (Salkever 1982). He found that, on average, the mothers of disabled children work significantly fewer hours per week and have significantly lower earnings per hour than do other mothers. By contrast, there is no decrease in work or earnings among the *fathers* of disabled children. The negative effect on the mother's wages is greater the older the disabled child (as the human-capital model predicts) because of the cumulative effect of forgone experience on earnings. If the child's disability involves limitations in school attendance or schoolwork, the mother's hours and earnings are further decreased.

Although many studies show that women's wages and their labor force participation rise and fall together, it is often difficult to establish the direction of causality. Women who can earn high wages have more incentive to work (other things the same), but women who build up more labor market experience are likely to earn higher wages. In the Salkever study it seems unambiguous that the causality runs from the disabled child to less work experience to lower wages, rather than the reverse.

The greater commitment of women to family at the expense of career results in large sex differences in job tenure. At most ages men have worked at least 50 percent more years with their current employer than have women. The differential is greatest at ages 45–54, when the median tenure for women is only 5.9 years compared with 11.5 years for men. This difference is the result of the work and family specialization that has characterized most marriages in the past; it does not represent greater turnover by women who are fully committed to a lifetime of market work. Women who have never married have as much experience on the current job as do men of comparable age (U.S. Bureau of Labor Statistics 1975).

Women's commitment to the labor market is increasing, but the full effects will not be evident until the female labor force participation rate levels off. At present, many working women are planning a more continuous attachment to the labor market, and the time they will spend on the same job will lengthen. In recent decades, however, the female labor force has been augmented by relatively new entrants at all ages. These women obviously have only limited experience on their current jobs.

This influx of new entrants needs to be considered in analyzing the gap between male and female earnings. Many observers have been surprised and alarmed that the gap has shown little tendency to narrow despite the Equal Pay Act of 1963, numerous affirmative action programs, and other efforts to reduce gender inequality. The relative stability of the earnings differential, however, must be appraised in the light of the divergent trends in labor force participation. Female participation has been rising rapidly, especially among those with less schooling, at the same time that less-educated males have been leaving the work force. The new female entrants pull down the average earnings of women because they have less schooling and less experience than those already at work, and even at equal levels of schooling the soaring supply of women workers slows down improvement in their relative wages. In a study of changes in the female/male wage ratio between 1959 and 1969, I found that for workers with twelve or fewer years of schooling the ratio only changed from .61 to .62, but for workers with more than twelve years it rose from .59 to .66 (Fuchs 1974b). The real test of equality in earnings will come when the rapid increase in female labor force participation abates. There is good reason to think that at that point the male-female earnings gap will begin to narrow substantially, but it is unlikely to disappear so long as women are hindered in their careers by disproportionate responsibility for children.

INCOME

The income of most men and women varies considerably over the life cycle, usually rising at first, reaching a peak between the ages of 45 and 54, and then declining. This pattern primarily reflects the opposing influences of postschool investment in human capital and age-related deterioration in health. When a worker first leaves school, he or she does not necessarily take the job that offers the highest immediate wage. Instead, the worker may seek a job that offers opportunities to learn and to acquire valuable experience, and that has the potential of higher earnings in the future. This postschool investment tends to depress observed earnings in the early years of work, and the return on that investment raises earnings at older ages. Jacob Mincer has shown that the "cross-over point" — that is, the point at which the return on previous investment is equal to the earnings forgone by current investment — occurs on average about seven years after leaving school (Mincer 1974). Earnings of most workers continue to rise for many years after the cross-over, but eventually the adverse effects of aging on health causes actual or potential earnings to fall.

The amount of postschool investment, the steepness of the age-earnings profile, and the age of maximum earnings vary considerably, as evidenced by the ratio of earnings at ages 55–64 to earnings at 25–34 for men in a variety of occupations (U.S.

Bureau of the Census 1973e, table 1). These ratios are based on earnings of different workers in the same year and may differ slightly from the experience of a given cohort as it moves through the life cycle; the differential effects of age on earnings over time has been fairly stable, however, so the general picture can be accepted without major qualification. We see that earnings increase greatly with age in occupations (such as medicine and law) that involve a great deal of postschool investment; but there is no increase, and there may even be a decrease, in some other occupations.

Earnings at 55–64 relative to 25–34 in 1969

Physicians	2.45	Clerical	1.11
Lawyers and judges	1.95	Retail clerks	0.98
Engineers	1.26	Truck drivers	0.95

Failure to take account of interpersonal differences in the life cycle pattern of earnings leads to an exaggerated view of the extent of income inequality in our society. Imagine a young man or woman at age 18 considering two different careers with very different age-earnings profiles, as shown in Figure 6.3. Career A provides a steady wage of $15,000 per year from age 18 through age 65, for a total of $720,000. (All figures are in dollars of constant purchasing power.) Career B requires additional schooling until age 25 (with zero earnings), after which earnings rise rapidly to a peak of $40,000 per year at age 50 and stay at that level until age 65. Lifetime earnings in career B will total $1,147,300 — 59 percent more than in career A. Superficially, there appears to be considerable inequality.

The crucial point, however, is that in this example *there is no real inequality* in lifetime wealth. At age 18, when the choice must be made, the discounted value of the two earnings streams is approximately equal (at 4 percent per annum).* That is, the extra

---

* If money can be invested to yield a real rate of return of 4 percent per annum, one dollar that will be earned a year from now has a present value of 96 cents. A dollar earned 18 years from now has a present value of 50 cents at 4 percent interest continuously compounded. Nominal interest rates are frequently much higher than 4 percent because of inflation, but a *real* rate of 4 percent is in accord with long-term experience.

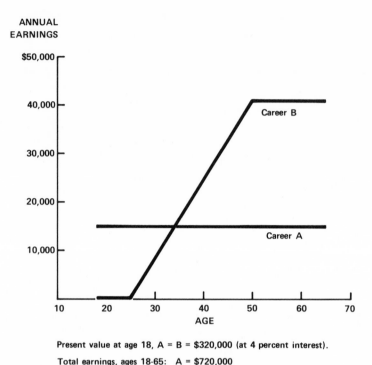

Figure 6.3. **Hypothetical example of two life cycle earnings streams, with equal present value at age 18.**

earnings under career B are equal to a real rate of return of 4 percent per year on the higher earnings that career A provides during the early years of the working life. Any 18-year-old who places a higher value on receiving immediate income (who has, in other words, a rate of time discount greater than 4 percent) will, other things equal, choose career A; those with a time discount rate lower than 4 percent will choose career B. Men and women do differ in their rates of time discount — their willingness and ability to wait. Unless they can easily borrow all the money they want to, these differences will affect choices about schooling and occupations and are likely to have an impact on life style and health.

The life cycle earnings pattern has special relevance for the economic position of women at ages 45–64. If a woman has not worked previously and then finds herself widowed or divorced at age 55, her income is likely to fall considerably unless offset by life insurance or alimony. Even if she has worked intermittently (as many women did in the past), she is unlikely to have experienced the same increase in earnings as men. Indeed, periodic withdrawal from the labor force not only eliminates normal life cycle earnings growth, but often results in women returning to work at wages lower than those they were receiving when they stopped (Mincer and Ofek 1980).

Solomon Polachek has shown that the negative impact of withdrawal from the labor force on wages varies among occupations. In some occupations, such as semiskilled work in manufacturing and domestic service, there is very little effect. Women in these occupations who stop work can return at wage rates similar to those they would have had if they had not dropped out of the labor force, because these occupations do not involve much postschool investment. By contrast, women in professional, managerial, and craft occupations experience a large wage loss from temporary withdrawal because of failure to maintain and improve their knowledge and skill.

Polachek based his conclusions on multiyear observations of a panel of white women who were between the ages of 30 and 44 at the beginning of the study. He showed that the more time a woman spends out of the labor force, the more likely she is to be in an occupation in which intermittent participation has only a small effect on wages. This is true holding constant education, age, and marital status. He recognized that being in an occupation with low cost of intermittent participation may encourage such behavior, but he demonstrated that at least some of the causality runs from labor force attachment to choice of occupation (Polachek 1981). One obvious conclusion from this analysis is that women who plan to spend all or nearly all of their adult lives in the work force are more likely to seek careers in professional and managerial occupations. Rising female enrollments at professional schools in the 1970s indicate that this is already occurring.

The major consequence of variations in health, work, and postschool investment is that income inequality across individuals and families increases over the life cycle. One good measure of inequality is the *interquartile ratio,* which is calculated by ranking all income recipients in order from the highest to the lowest, taking the difference between the incomes at the first quartile and the third quartile, and dividing that difference by the income at the median. The ratios for men at different ages in different years show that relative variability is consistently highest at ages 55–64. An alternative measure of relative inequality, the variance of the logarithm of income, shows an even greater peak at ages 55–64.

	Relative inequality in income of men		
	1960	*1970*	*1979*
Ages 35–44	.71	.77	.75
Ages 45–54	.79	.83	.84
Ages 55–64	.99	.98	1.03

The increased labor force participation of wives has caused some observers to fear that the growth of the two-earner family will result in greater disparities in family income, but two papers have concluded that this fear is unwarranted (Danziger 1980; Bergmann et al. 1980). Both studies reported that the relation between earnings of husbands and wage rates of their working wives is low.

Also, Bergmann and her colleagues showed theoretically what happens to inequality as the labor force participation of wives rises from zero to 100 percent, depending upon whether it is the wives from the high-income or the low-income families that enter first. If women married to high-income men enter the labor force first, increasing participation by wives would initially increase inequality, and then decrease it. If women married to low-income husbands enter first, inequality in family income would reach a minimum when about 60 percent of wives are participating and would tend to rise thereafter. In fact, actual participation rates of women follow neither of the extreme paths but are somewhere in between. On the one hand, high income of husbands acts as a deterrent to participation by the wife; on the other hand, high-income men tend to be married to better-educated women, whose higher potential wage attracts them into the labor force. The actual path, therefore, is between the two extremes, with the result that family inequality is not much affected by changes in the percentage of wives who are working.

MARITAL STATUS

A rapid change in the marital status of women (but not of men) between 45 and 65 both reflects and affects how we live. At age 45 the percentage not married is similar for both sexes — approximately 15 percent — but by age 65 more than 33 percent of women are without a spouse, while the proportion of men not married is unchanged. The most important reason for this shift is differential mortality. Men are more likely than women to die at all ages, but the difference becomes particularly large toward the end of this stage of life. At ages 40–45, for instance, the male death rate is 75 percent above the female rate; ten years later it is 88 percent higher; and at 60–65 the differential peaks at 104 percent. After age 65 the gender difference decreases to 71 percent at ages 70–75, and to 30 percent at ages 80–85.

If both spouses are 45, the odds are two to one that the husband will die before his wife if one of them dies before 65. In most marriages, however, the husband is older, and this is a second reason for the high proportion of women aged 65 who are without a spouse. If the husband is five years older, the probability of his dying first rises to three to one. So strong is the force of differential mortality that a wife would have to be eight years older than her husband in order for there to be an equal probability that she would die first during the years from 45 to 65.

A third reason for the rise in the proportion of women without a spouse, while men show no change, is that divorced men have higher remarriage rates because many of them marry women from younger cohorts. In the late 1970s the probability of remarriage by divorced men was more than double that of divorced women at ages 45–64. The probability of a widower remarrying is almost six times that of a widow at this age.

A fourth reason for the large number of unmarried women is the high death rate of unmarried men — almost three times that of unmarried women. There are two explanations for the strong relation between marital status and mortality among men. The first assumes that the causality runs from marital status to mortality. Men, it is argued, are more dependent on women to fulfill a nurturing role and to keep them healthy, while unmarried women are more capable of taking care of themselves. The second explanation assumes that the causality runs from health status to marital status and asserts that those few men who are not married at ages 45–64 are likely to be unmarried because they are in poor health, while the more numerous unmarried women are likely to be in that status for a wide variety of reasons.

The rapid increase in the number of widows at this stage of life leads to a big increase in the proportion of women who live alone. At ages 45–54 the proportion is the same for both sexes — about 7 percent — but when they are ten years older the situation changes substantially. At 55–64 fully 18 percent of women are living alone, compared with 8 percent of the men of that age. In addition to the rise in the number of widows, an excess of divorced women over divorced men also plays a small role. Within any marital status, there is no difference between men and women in the propensity to live alone.

Changes in marital status not only affect living arrangements and life expectancy, but also have significant implications for income. Moreover, these effects are different for women than for men. In households headed by a married couple (with no children under 18 years of age) average income per person (from all sources) was $9,998 in 1979 — a higher figure than in households headed by divorced women, or widows, or never-married women. Those women who have never married come closest to having the same per capita income as the women in married households — $9,568 (Table 6.2). Unlike divorced, separated, and widowed women, the never-married woman has probably been more continuously attached to the labor force and has maintained or even enhanced her earning power. For men the reverse situation holds. Per capita income is higher in households headed by divorced, separated, or never-married men than it is in married households because there are fewer persons to share their earnings.

The relation of these numbers to the themes about family and work is fairly obvious. Measured purely in income terms, most women are best off when they are married and share in the higher earnings of their husbands. This disparity in economic prospects helps explain why so many marriages were not and are not egalitarian in other respects. The men seem to be financially better off if they are not married, but this is deceptive even in narrow economic terms because it does not take into account the value of the goods and services produced by wives at home. If men are expected to share equally in the work at home, however, the household income statistics suggest that the economic advantages of marriage would be considerably reduced for many men.

PUBLIC POLICY ISSUES

The pervasiveness of inequality among individuals at ages 45–64, and especially at ages 55–64, is striking. Although inequality is present at all stages of life, its *consequences* are most evident in late middle age when interpersonal differences in health, work, and income are at a maximum. Many of the most controversial questions of public policy concern attempts to deal with these inequalities. As a society we are constantly deciding how much redistribution to undertake, and how to accomplish it. The answers that we give to such questions depend upon basic values and personal visions of what constitutes a "good" society. They should also be based on an understanding of the nature and causes of inequality and of the consequences of attempts to reduce it.

Consider first the question of income distribution. Detailed statistics on family and individual income confirm an easily observable fact: some Americans live extremely affluent lives while others are desperately poor. If all families in the country are arranged in order of income from the highest to the lowest, the family at the first quartile of the distribution has 2.7 times the before-tax income of the one at the third quartile. Before discussing what public policy can or should do about such inequality, we should consider some facts concerning U.S. income distribution.

First, it is clear that inequality in *earnings,* not income from capital, is the primary source of inequality in total income. A few

Americans receive large amounts of dividends and interest, but complete elimination of such income would have little effect on inequality. In 1979 the average income of families in the top half of the income distribution was 3.00 times the average of those in the bottom half. If all income from dividends, interest, rent, estates, trusts, and royalties were eliminated, the ratio would be virtually unchanged at 2.97 (U.S. Bureau of the Census, Statistical Abstract 1981, p. 443). The slogan "Tax excess profits" makes fine rhetoric for some, but is largely irrelevant to the question of redistributing income.

Second, some of the variation in earnings is not inequality in any meaningful sense, because it reflects the rise and fall of earnings over the life cycle. As we have seen, earnings tend to vary with age. Thus, even if every person had exactly the same age-earnings profile (if there were complete equality among individuals over the full life cycle), we would still observe considerable inequality at all times because different individuals would be at different stages of life. Younger and older men would earn less than those in their forties and fifties.

If everyone of the same age earned the same amount, but earnings varied with age, should public policy try to reduce this variation? It is difficult to see why it should, except for one possible reason. Suppose one feature of this completely egalitarian (over the full life cycle) distribution was very low or zero earnings during the last ten or fifteen years of life. Would society be willing to trust each individual to save enough during the years of high earnings to provide an adequate income during the years when earnings are low? And if an individual did *not* make such provision, would society let that person starve? Our present system of compulsory Social Security is designed, in part, to eliminate such a possibility.

Actual earnings not only vary with age, but at each age there is considerable inequality in earnings. Men and women with more education tend to earn more, and the effect of schooling grows larger at older ages when workers reap most of the return on their investment in schooling and postschool training. One attempt to adjust earnings for this return concluded that inequality in *lifetime wealth* (that is, lifetime earnings discounted back to age 18) is almost 30 percent less than the average inequality within narrow age groups (Lillard 1977). Discounting earnings back to age 18 adjusts for the fact that some workers realize more of their earnings early in life, whereas others must wait until older ages.

Even after adjusting for schooling, age, and all other measurable characteristics, however, earnings still vary greatly among individuals for several reasons. First, there may be differences in innate or acquired ability that are recognized by employers, although not known to those seeking to explain the earnings distribution. Second, even workers of equal ability and motivation may earn different wages (plus fringe benefits) for many reasons, including discrimination, union influence, or sheer chance.

The choice of policy to deal with inequality should depend at least in part on the reasons for the inequality. If blacks earn less than whites because employers discriminate against them, rigorous enforcement of antidiscrimination laws would eventually eliminate that inequality. If, however, much of the black-white difference in earnings is attributable to differences in quality and quantity of schooling, family living arrangements, and other aspects of investment in children, other policies need to be considered. There is considerable evidence that employer discrimination is not the whole story. Thomas Sowell (1981) noted that black immigrants from the West Indies and their children have achieved much higher earnings than blacks born in the United States, and that Americans of Chinese and Japanese ancestry have fared extremely well in United States labor markets despite longstanding prejudice against them.

Some observers see unions as a source of inequality, but the overall effect of unions is small. On the one hand, strong unions can secure above-normal wages for their workers relative to others, and it is rarely the poorly educated, low-skilled workers that are unionized. On the other hand, unions tend to reduce wage differentials among organized workers. Several studies put the union-nonunion wage differential in the range of 10–15 percent; but even in the case of strong unions, excesses tend to be self-correcting, as evidenced by the willingness of unionized workers to forgo pay hikes when faced with loss of jobs to foreign competition.

According to standard economic theory, competition in labor

markets results in wages that equal the worker's marginal contribution to production (at least on average over a substantial period of time). If wages are below that level, employers can improve their profits by hiring more workers, and in trying to do so they bid up wages. If wages are above that level, employers will want to lay workers off and the resulting unemployment will depress wages. This theory cannot be completely true because of discrimination, unions, exploitation by employers, and other market imperfections, but it provides a better explanation of why wages vary than does any other.

One reason for accepting this theory is that the earnings of millions of workers are *directly tied to their production.* Examples include self-employed workers, piece-rate workers, executives and professionals in personally owned corporations, commission sales personnel (in securities, real estate, insurance), and those who depend heavily on tips (waiters and waitresses, hairdressers, taxi drivers). It is significant that the inequalities in the earnings of such workers, who are essentially paid by performance, are similar in character and degree to those in the labor market as a whole.

A second reason for believing that there is some validity to the theory is that competition between firms in most industries would tend to eliminate large wage differentials that are unrelated to differential contributions to production and revenue. Labor costs are a substantial fraction of the total costs of most firms and are usually several times as great as profits. If large groups of workers were grossly and systematically underpaid while others were overpaid, those firms who by luck or design employed mostly the former would make huge profits, while firms that employed the latter would be forced out of business. Thus, competition among firms drives the system toward equality between wages and marginal contribution, regardless of what individual employers or workers would like to see happen.

Although I believe that the income distribution largely reflects differences in the contribution that workers make to output as valued by the consumer, it does not follow that this distribution is fair or even efficient in a broad social sense. The differences may be the result of great inequalities of opportunity that go back to birth or even the prenatal period. In Chapters 2, 3, and 4 we saw that there is great variation in the circumstances of birth, childhood, and adolescence. William Blake was surely right when he wrote, "Some to misery are born." Although most Americans subscribe to "equality of opportunity," we are still far from that goal. Public policy can be used to move us closer, but it is a mistake to think that all that is needed is good will on the part of the more fortunate or that there are only benefits and no costs associated with redistributive policies.

Some inequalities arise from circumstances beyond an individual's control; some are the result of choices individuals make as they move through life. Extreme egalitarians do not want to make this distinction, but most Americans feel more comfortable with policies that focus on inequality that is beyond individual control. Attempts to reduce inequality that stems from individual behavior create adverse incentives regarding that behavior.

The controversy over national health insurance provides a useful context for examining this issue. On the one hand there are those who believe that everyone should have unlimited free access to tax-supported medical care. They regard ill health, and the consumption of medical care, as beyond the control of the individual citizen. Direct payment by a sick person for care is viewed as analogous to an unjust tax; the purpose of national health insurance is to prevent medical bills from unjustly reducing an individual's welfare.*

Other participants in the health policy debate question this line of reasoning. They point out that individuals *can* affect their need for medical care by choices about cigarette smoking, drinking, diet, exercise, and other behaviors. In addition, they note that the amount of medical care consumed is not simply a function of health status. The more insurance a patient has, the more medical care he or she is likely to use. A large-scale health insurance experiment conducted by the Rand Corporation found that families receiving free care used significantly more than did similar families who had to pay 25 percent of the cost (Newhouse et al.

---

* There are, of course, other arguments made for national health insurance that involve externalities, adverse selection problems, and paternalism (Fuchs 1976).

1981). Other studies show that the incentives facing physicians also affect utilization. Families use less care (holding health constant) in systems such as prepaid group practice where physicians are compensated by an annual fee rather than on a fee-for-service basis (Luft 1981).

Some utilization of medical care is at the discretion of the individual but some is not; sometimes life itself depends upon expensive medical care that even affluent persons could not afford out of current income. The remedy for such risks is well known — insurance. But what if an individual refuses or neglects to buy such insurance? Will society deny that individual needed medical care? If not, society will probably make insurance compulsory, thus creating incentives for overuse of care.

Many economists want to deal with the problem of overuse by making the patient more cost-conscious. This can be done through the use of deductibles and coinsurance. I do not favor this approach. Patients often lack the information necessary to make good judgments about the benefits and costs of care, and, when they or their loved ones are ill, they are often too emotionally involved to make rational choices. The best way to achieve efficient use of health care resources is to give physicians a stake in holding down costs. Because of their training, physicians are usually in a better position than patients to judge which care is most useful and which is of small value. If physicians and hospitals were organized in competing groups and were paid a fixed amount per person enrolled in their plan, and if everyone had a choice of several plans (with government subsidies paying the premiums of the poor), we would probably achieve as good a combination of justice and efficiency as is possible in this complex area (Enthoven 1980).

With respect to income inequality, we have seen that the large individual differences at this stage of life are primarily the result of inequality in earnings. This inequality is related to differences in individuals' ability to contribute to national output. Differences in ability result from variation in inherited aptitudes, environmental influences early in life, and choices made by individuals in adolescence and young adulthood.

Many people would prefer less inequality in our society, but as we have seen from examples in this and earlier chapters, egalitarian policies can have perverse incentive effects on behavior. The challenge is to find methods of redistribution that have the least adverse effects and the most social return. Greater equality of investment in human capital at young ages appears to be a promising route. Redistribution policies aimed at improving opportunities for the disadvantaged *early in life* could yield a favorable return to the economy as well as contribute to a more just society. If there were more equality of opportunity in childhood, we would probably see less inequality later in life.

7

For Which the First
Was Made

Old Age

Grow old along with me!
The best is yet to be,
The last of life for which the first was made.
— *Robert Browning*

BROWNING'S nineteenth-century vision of old age as a time of peace and beauty stands in stark contrast to the dismal prophecies epitomized in the title of a book by Robert Butler, former director of the National Institute of Aging: *Why Survive? Being Old in America* (1975). According to objective measures, the current cohort of seniors enjoy the best physical health and the highest real income of any group of elderly in our nation's history. Why, then, do so many popular discussions emphasize misery and despair?

Historically, one of the strongest of all human aspirations has been to live to a ripe old age — to reach the Biblical "three score and ten." Before the modern era, however, only a small fraction of the population achieved that goal. It wasn't until 1900 that as many as three out of ten Americans survived until age 70. Now life expectancy has risen much higher: at current age-specific death rates, seven out of ten will reach 70, and four out of ten will celebrate their eightieth birthday. A falling birth rate and rising life expectancy have resulted in a large increase in the relative number of persons over 65. This increase, from less than 7 percent of the population in 1940 to over 11 percent in 1980, is one of the most important trends affecting the position of the elderly as a group and the relation of this group to the rest of society.

The rise in life expectancy has been much greater for women than for men. This differential, combined with the tendency for older men to marry younger women, results in huge sex differences in marital status and living arrangements among persons 65 and over. In 1980 there were more than five widows for every widower, and two-thirds of these widows lived alone. Another major change is the decrease in the labor force participation of men 65 and over, from 46 percent in 1950 to 20 percent in 1980. Most of the elderly population now rely almost completely on Social Security benefits for their living expenses.

We will look at the causes and consequences of these trends and show their relation to two of our themes: the fading family, and demography and destiny. Health will also receive major attention because of its direct importance to the elderly and its indirect importance to all age groups through its effects on medical care costs. The extremely high utilization of medical care by the elderly, especially in the last year of life, presents a severe problem for them and for society. The concluding section identifies major weaknesses in the Social Security system and discusses proposals for substantial reform.

NUMBERS AND WORK

How Many Elderly?

Almost every article and book about the elderly begins by noting that their relative numbers have grown appreciably over time. Why is there so much interest in the percentage of the population that is over 65? First, it is generally assumed that most of the elderly are not at work; therefore part of the working generation's output must be transferred to the elderly through Social Security payments or other means. The higher the percentage of elderly, the greater the amount that must be transferred. Second, consumption and saving patterns of people who are near the end of the life cycle differ from those of other adults, with important implications for health care, housing, financial markets, and other sectors of the economy. Last, the rise in the number of elderly increases their political power. This increase, coming at a time when economic issues are often resolved through the ballot box rather than the marketplace, and when family ties are weakening, raises the possibility of bitter conflict between the elderly and other groups in society. The elderly have many needs, but the resources used to satisfy these needs could be used to alleviate problems of children, teenagers, and women.

The upward trend in the relative numbers of elderly, from 4.6 percent of the population in 1920 to 11.3 percent in 1980, has resulted primarily from changes in fertility and only secondarily from the lengthening of life expectancy. To see why the birth rate is so important, imagine a world in which everyone lived until age 80 and then died. If the population were growing at 2 percent per annum (through an excess of births over deaths), one person in eight would be over 60 years of age.* If, however, the population were stationary (zero population growth), one person in *four* would be over 60 years of age, assuming everyone still lived until age 80. Thus, a change from 2 percent per annum growth to zero population growth, given the same life expectancy, would double the proportion of the population over age 60.

By contrast, the huge change in life expectancy of white men, from 48 years in 1900 to 70 years in 1976, when applied to a stationary population raises the fraction over 60 from 14 percent to only 19 percent. For most of this century, changes in life expectancy did not have much effect on the percentage of the population over age 60 because most of the decrease in mortality

---

* By assumption, each annual cohort is 2 percent larger than the one that preceded it. Thus, for every hundred people age 80, there would be 149 people age 60, 223 people age 40, 332 people age 20, and 495 people just being born.

occurred at *young* ages, primarily increasing the size of the population *under* 60. What was true of the past, however, will not be true in the future. Because death rates at young ages are now so low, future declines in mortality will mostly increase the number of elderly.

Now that one out of every six adults is over 65, there is also increasing interest in distinguishing the "young old" (persons between 65 and 75) from those who are 75 or more. The latter are more likely to be in poor health, less likely to be in the labor force, and much more likely to be institutionalized. Between 1900 and 1940 there was virtually no change in the *proportion* of elderly who were 75 or older (about 30 percent), but by 1980 it was 39 percent, and it is expected to be 45 percent by the year 2000 (Table 7.1). The decline in adult *female* mortality explains most of this increase, and also explains the large changes in marital status and living arrangements that will be discussed later in this chapter. In the early decades of the twentieth century there were approximately equal numbers of elderly women and men because the sex differential in mortality was small and men outnumbered women among immigrants. By 1980, however, there were three women for every two men at this stage of life. The fact that an increasingly large proportion of adults are over 65 has important consequences for the labor market, retirement costs, health care, and living arrangements.

How Many Elderly Are at Work?

The proportion of men 65 and over who are at work has decreased steadily in the United States, as can be seen in Figure 7.1. No completely satisfactory explanation of this long-term downward trend is available, but the growth of real wages and the increase in the relative number of elderly are the most likely candidates. The Social Security retirement system probably contributed to the acceleration of the trend in recent decades. Mandatory retirement rules, age discrimination, poor health, and several other factors that affect older workers also need to be considered.

Wages. Long-term growth of productivity has resulted in higher real wages and income, as evidenced by a four-fold increase

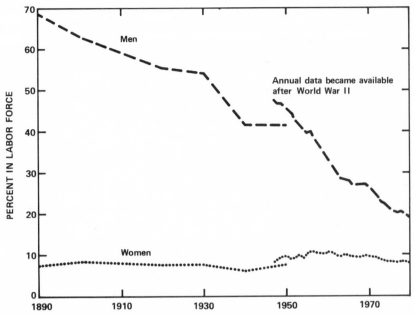

Figure 7.1. **Labor force participation rates at ages 65 and over, 1890–1980.**

(*Sources:* Decennial census data, 1890–1950, from U.S. Bureau of the Census, *Historical Statistics of the United States, Colonial Times to 1970,* series D29–D41; annual data, 1947–1980, from Employment and Training Administration, *Employment and Training Report of the President, 1981,* table A-5, and 1980 edition, table A-2.)

in GNP per capita between 1900 and 1980, after adjustment for inflation. Economic theory tells us that higher real wages have two opposing effects on labor force participation — a price effect and an income effect. These effects can most easily be understood by thinking of the alternative to work as leisure, and by thinking of leisure as a commodity, like coffee or steak. The wage a worker can earn (adjusted for taxes, fringe benefits, and the utility or disutility of work) represents the "price" of leisure. An increase in real wages, other things remaining constant, means an increase in the price of leisure, and this should decrease the quantity of leisure demanded (that is, the quantity of work should increase). On the other hand, an increase in real wages implies an increase in real income, and the quantity of leisure demanded should rise (and the quantity of work decrease) for that reason, just as the demand for any normal commodity rises when income increases.

Whether the price effect or the income effect will dominate behavior cannot be determined on theoretical grounds. It is an empirical question, and the answer varies depending on circumstances. For women of prime working age, for instance, the price effect dominates the income effect in both cross-section differences and the long-term trend. Higher real wages result in more labor force participation by women, not less, possibly because in most families total income still depends primarily on the husband's earnings. In the case of older men, it appears that the income effect dominates the price effect. This may be the result of age-related declines in health; when health is failing, there is a greater tendency to use higher income to buy more leisure.

One test of whether the growth of real income explains the long-term trend is to examine its effect on the labor force participation of older men in countries with different levels of real income. I find that this relationship is much weaker among the twenty-four countries of the Organization for Economic Cooperation and Development in 1970 than it was in the United States between 1890 and 1979. In the latter case, the rise in per capita income almost perfectly tracks the decreased participation by older men; but for the twenty-four OECD countries, income differences explain only half of the variation in participation rates.* In addition, average participation in these countries in 1970 was much lower than in the United States at a comparable level of real income. Many of them had rates of about 20 percent in 1970, with gross domestic product (GDP) per capita in the range of $3,000 to $4,000. When the United States was at that income level (about 1955), the participation rate of men 65 and over was about 40 percent (Table 7.2).

To be sure, the OECD countries typically had more generous public pension plans in 1970 than the United States had in 1955, and these plans induced men to retire. But why did these countries adopt generous public pension plans? The increasing num-

---

* I fitted curves of the form $L = e^{\alpha(G)^\beta}$ to the United States time series and the OECD cross-section. For the former, the coefficient of determination (R^2) between the actual and the predicted values is .96; for the latter it is only .48. (L = labor force participation rate of men 65 and over; G = gross domestic product per capita.)

ber of elderly may be the answer, partly because of the political power that numerical strength confers, and partly because younger workers wanted the older ones to leave the labor market.

Number of elderly. Although per capita income in most OECD countries is substantially below that of the United States, elderly people make up as large a proportion of their population because fertility and mortality rates are similar to those in the contemporary United States. The high proportion of elderly probably contributes to the low participation rate. When there are relatively few people over age 65, the population has a pyramidlike age structure similar to the hierarchical structure of most organizations, and the relatively few older workers can more easily progress up the organizational ladder. Currently in the United States and in the OECD countries the age distribution is more rectangular in shape, but organizations still have a pyramidlike hierarchy, with fewer and fewer openings the higher up one goes. Thus, if most older workers stayed in the labor force they would find it impossible to move up within their organizations. This may be one reason why they do not stay. An extreme example of this process can be found in the U.S. Armed Forces, where the age of retirement is related to rank. Those who rise in rank can retire later; those who do not advance must retire at an earlier age.

Social Security. One way that society encourages older workers to stop working is through public pensions which, in the United States, usually take the form of Social Security retirement benefits. The value of these benefits has been rising faster than wages; the difference in rate of change was particularly great between 1970 and 1980. Real benefits per retiree grew by more than three percent per year, while real earnings per worker did not grow at all (Table 7.3). It is most unlikely that retirement benefits can continue to grow more rapidly than wages over the long run. Indeed, the prospective increase in the number of elderly relative to the number of workers suggests that it will even be difficult to keep benefits growing at the same rate as wages.

There can be no doubt that public policy has made it increasingly attractive for older people to stop work—by offering an early retirement option at 62, by increasing retirement benefits relative to wages, and by withholding benefits from eligible retirees at the rate of 50 cents per dollar of earnings on any earnings above $5,500 per year (Burkhauser and Turner 1980). What public policy has done, however, it can undo, provided enough citizens of all ages understand why the trends of recent decades need to be reversed.

Decline of self-employment. Another factor that probably contributes to the downward trend in participation by older men is the declining importance of self-employment. A study based on the Retirement History Survey data for the 1970s showed that self-employed men are more likely to continue working after 65 than are wage-and-salary workers, holding constant education, age, health, wages, and other relevant variables (Fuchs, 1982a). One reason why the elderly self-employed keep working is that they find it easier to reduce their hours of work without changing their occupation or job. Wage-and-salary workers face more rigidity in hours and wages. The proportion of workers who are self-employed has declined drastically throughout the twentieth century because of the shift of employment from agriculture to industry and service. Even within each sector, self-employment has declined in relative importance as small farms and small businesses find it increasingly difficult to compete with larger enterprises.

Mandatory retirement and age discrimination. This discussion of the factors affecting labor force participation has, in the spirit of this book, focused on the choices workers make in response to changes in income and relative prices. The wide attention given to mandatory retirement and age discrimination in the popular press may led some readers to believe that the emphasis on choice is misplaced. According to some writers, most men stop working because they are forced to, or because they are the victims of discrimination. These explanations, however, find little support either in theory or empirical analysis.

James Schulz (1976), a specialist in the economics of aging and retirement, noted that about half of all currently retired men were never subject to mandatory retirement rules. Furthermore, he pointed out that many workers retire before the mandatory age, many retire willingly at the mandatory age, and some are not working for other reasons such as ill health. He concluded that only a small fraction of workers are truly affected by mandatory retirement. Dorothy Kittner confirmed this conclusion (1977), stating that only ten million workers — approximately 14 percent — in the private sector of the economy were subject to mandatory retirement in 1974. Moreover, some of those affected will retire before the mandatory age and others will go on to new jobs after their initial retirement.

Mandatory retirement rules rarely exist in a vacuum; they are usually part of a total labor contract, either explicit or implicit, that provides workers with stable or even rising wages until retirement, even though their productivity may decline during their last years of employment. Edward Lazear (1979) has hypothesized that some firms and workers choose such contracts — with wages below productivity at young ages and above it at older ages — as a way of ensuring that workers do not shirk or otherwise behave in a manner that would justify dismissal prior to the agreed-upon retirement date. Contracts of this type need to have mandatory retirement; otherwise rising wages and falling productivity would eventually bankrupt the firm. If older workers are being paid more than they are currently worth, when they lose their jobs through mandatory retirement they have difficulty obtaining a new job at their old wage rate. By contrast, when workers are paid directly according to performance, as in piece-rate work or commissioned sales, mandatory retirement is less common, and a new job is more easily obtained.

The gap that develops between the wages of older workers and their productivity is one of the principal reasons why we frequently hear complaints about "age discrimination." It is obvious that many employers prefer younger to older workers, but whether this constitutes "discrimination" in an economic sense is less clear. An employer can be said to be guilty of age discrimination if age influences hiring or other decisions independently of the relation between age and a full productivity/cost calculation. If age does affect productivity or labor costs, an employer who takes these effects into account can hardly be said to be discriminating on the basis of age.

From a productivity/cost point of view, there are several reasons why younger workers might be preferred. For instance, the older worker may expect a higher wage even though his productivity does not justify the wage differential. Even at equal wages and equal productivity the fringe benefits of older workers are often higher, especially for health insurance, life insurance, and pension benefits. Age differences in willingness to accept an employer's request to change location or occupation may affect the productivity/cost calculation. Also, the shorter prospective length of employment of newly hired older workers lowers the return to employer-provided investment in on-the-job training.

It is doubtful that there is widespread age discrimination by employers in an economic sense, but *individual* elderly workers may be the victims of what has been called "statistical discrimination." Employers frequently find it difficult to ascertain all aspects of an individual worker's productivity and costs prior to hiring. The employer may, therefore, ascribe to a worker the average expected values for workers with the same readily identifiable characteristics. Thus, when a 65-year-old man applies for a job, in the absence of other information the employer may assume that this man has the productivity, flexibility, health, and other traits of the average 65-year-old. If this particular worker actually has traits more favorable than the average, he will be discriminated against. Similarly, workers with traits less desirable than average will benefit from statistical discrimination.

Health. When older men are surveyed about their labor force status, those not participating frequently cite ill health as the reason. These replies have been viewed with some skepticism because ill health may be offered as a socially acceptable reason for not working when the true explanation lies elsewhere. Analysis of a large national sample of older men (the Retirement History Survey), however, has convinced me that ill health plays an important role in their labor force decisions (Fuchs 1982a). This study focused on white urban men ages 61–63, all of whom were at work in 1969 and were resurveyed in 1973. Those who reported a health limitation in 1969 were more likely to have stopped working by 1973 than were those men who had not reported a health-related work limitation in 1969 (other things held constant). Since all the men were working at the time they reported their health status, there is little reason to suspect any bias in their responses.

Health is a good predictor of which men stop working and which don't at any point in time, but it does not explain why participation by older men is so much lower now than it was thirty years ago. On average, the health of the elderly has certainly not deteriorated, and changes in the occupational structure — away from blue-collar jobs requiring heavy physical exertion — suggest that constancy in health status would have resulted in fewer men leaving the labor force for health reasons.

I conclude that poor health, mandatory retirement, and age discrimination may affect the employment status of individual older workers, but they do not explain why four out of five older men were not at work in 1980. The major reasons are the growth of real income, the relative increase in the number of elderly, the retirement incentives built into the Social Security and tax systems, and institutional changes such as the decline of self-employment.

HEALTH, MARITAL STATUS, AND LIVING ARRANGEMENTS

Though much is taken, much abides. — Alfred Lord Tennyson

At the aggregate level changes in health do not explain the trend in labor force participation, but at the individual level health is probably the most important factor affecting the lives of older people. Failing health causes withdrawal from work, increases utilization of medical care, heightens dependency on others, and eventually creates widows or widowers. In recent years the health of the elderly has improved considerably; but on average, health still deteriorates with age and the costs of medical care for the elderly have escalated greatly. Dramatic changes in the marital status and living arrangements of the elderly have also occurred, partly as a result of changes in health.

Improving Health

The most objective measure of health, age-specific mortality, has shown substantial improvement since 1965 for all age groups except adolescents and youth, and has been particularly striking for people over 65. Mortality declined for all race-sex groups, but women improved more than men, as was also true between 1950 and 1965 when the overall rate of change was much lower (Table 7.4). As a result, life expectancy at age 65 jumped almost three-and-a-half years for women between 1950 and 1978 (to 18.4 years), while increasing only a little over one year for men (to 14.0 years).

Why are older people, especially women, living longer after age 65? A dramatic decrease in age-specific death rates from heart disease explains most of the increase in life expectancy, but it has been extremely difficult to identify precisely the factors responsible for this decrease. Analysts who are technologically inclined attribute most of the reduction to better control of hypertension, special coronary care units in hospitals, open heart surgery, and similar medical innovations. Other observers credit changes in diet, smoking, exercise, and other aspects of personal behavior. We do not know the true explanation; there is probably some validity to both points of view.

The other major killer in old age, malignant neoplasms (cancer), has unfortunately not shown the same downward trend as heart disease. In fact, its age-adjusted rate *rose* between 1965 and 1977, and the rate of increase was more rapid than between 1950 and 1965. The absence of improvement in mortality from cancer is a puzzle, inasmuch as researchers and practitioners in that field have pointed with pride to breakthroughs in chemotherapy and radiotherapy and have heralded advances in early detection. The proportion of patients who survive at least five years has increased for most types of cancers. Unless this increase is only the result of earlier detection, the failure of age-specific death rates to improve suggests a rise in the incidence of the disease. The incidence of cancer may have risen as a result of increases several decades ago in cigarette smoking and environmental hazards. Although *deaths* from heart disease still outnumbered those from cancer by two to one in 1975, one study claims that the incidence of *new cases* in that year was about equal for the two diseases (Hartunian, Smart, and Thompson 1980).

Rising life expectancy for the elderly during a period of earlier and more widespread retirement certainly throws doubt on the popular notion that retirement is bad for health. Studies of this question using data on individual retirees have encountered severe methodological problems and yielded ambiguous results (Minkler 1981), but aggregate data lead me to conclude that the popular notion is wrong. If retirement from work adversely affected health, we would see a significant change in the male-female mortality ratio around retirement age because most men leave the labor force within a short span of years around age 65, whereas very few women are at work past the age of 60. The male-female mortality ratio, however, is approximately the same at age 70 as at age 60. Moreover, the introduction in 1961 of an early Social Security retirement option for men at age 62 produced no adverse change in the mortality of men ages 62–65 in subsequent years, even though retirement rates at those ages rose substantially. Indeed, death rates at ages 62–65 show a small decline from 1960 to 1970, while mortality at ages 55–60 and 65–70 actually rose slightly.

Health Care Costs

Although the health of the elderly has improved in recent years, it is still true that, on average, health worsens and health care costs increase with age. The male death rate at age 74 of six per hundred is approximately four times the rate at age 57; the female death rate is appreciably lower but also increases approximately fourfold between those ages. The notion that beyond some critical age there is a period of reduced probability of death is false. People over 65 are much more likely than younger people to have chronic conditions that limit their activities, are more likely to go to the hospital, and stay longer once they are admitted. Overall, the elderly consume about three times as much medical care per capita as do people under 65.

Scholars debate the role of medical care in the fall of death rates of those over 65, but there is no doubt about the huge increase in resources that society devotes to care for the elderly. Most of the increase dates from 1965. In that year personal health care expenditures for people 65 and over accounted for 1.3 percent of the gross national product, but by 1978 the proportion had grown to 2.3 percent. Much of the increase is the result of

Medicare (and to a more limited extent to Medicaid, which supplements Medicare for the poor elderly). To date, Medicare and Medicaid have represented a huge financial subsidy for the current cohort of elderly, supplementing retirement benefits which alone have been far in excess of the Social Security taxes this cohort paid while at work. In 1978 the average retired person received an additional 50 cents' worth of health care benefits for every dollar of Social Security retirement payments (Hurd and Shoven 1982).

Medicare and Medicaid were introduced in 1965 primarily to make access to medical care more equal for people at different levels of income, and it certainly has had this effect. The tabulation shows pre- and post-Medicare rates of surgery among the elderly by income class (adjusted for changes in inflation). The two lower-income groups showed large increases in surgery, while the highest-income group actually showed a decrease (Bombardier et al. 1977). Whether this differential change in access to care has narrowed socioeconomic differentials in mortality is not yet known. It seems unlikely, since life expectancy depends more on personal behavior and environment than on quantity and quality of medical care (Fuchs 1974a).

	Operations per thousand urban whites, 65 and over	
	1963	*1970*
Low income	67	86
Lower-middle income	65	84
Upper-middle income	96	98
High income	77	62

Although Medicare and other government health programs were designed to relieve the elderly of the financial burden of medical care, their *private* expenditures for personal health services have risen rapidly since 1970, following a decline in the first few post-Medicare years. In fact, after adjusting for inflation, the average person over 65 was spending more in 1978 than in 1965 (when there was no Medicare), even though the government was covering 63 percent of the individual's health care costs in 1978. The high cost of health care, which absorbs almost 10 percent of the nation's total resources, is emerging as a major problem for public policy.

A substantial fraction of the health care spending for the elderly occurs in the last year of life. Approximately 31 percent of Medicare expenditures in 1976 were accounted for by the 6.4 percent of beneficiaries who died in that year (Lubitz, Gornick, and Prihoda 1981). At one West Coast teaching hospital in 1980 the average cost per case for patients 65 and over who died in the hospital was $14,000. This reflects only the hospital costs during the patient's last admission; the addition of inpatient and outpatient physician charges and costs of previous admissions during the same year could bring the figure to $30,000 per patient. As technological improvements increase the possibility of keeping people alive, albeit frequently with sharply curtailed mental and physical capacities, society will have to face difficult questions concerning the allocation of resources to such purposes. The development of home care and hospice programs may provide more humane and less costly alternatives for the terminally ill.

Economic growth, medical advances, and social changes have raised the age of death and altered its site and circumstances away from home and family to institutions. In 1980 almost half of all U.S. deaths occurred after age 75, compared with less than one-fourth in 1940. More than half of the deaths over age 65 occur in hospitals, and an additional one-fifth in nursing homes. As is true of so many of the changes discussed in this book, this shift partly reflects the diminished role of the family. It also illustrates the way choices are biased by public insurance and private insurance coverage. In most instances families have an incentive to choose institutional care, which is usually reimbursed, rather than home care, which is not. Thus, public policy influences how we die as well as how we live.

Marital Status and Living Arrangements

The earlier mortality of men and the tendency of older widowed and divorced men to choose younger wives when they remarry create a large surplus of unmarried women above the age of 65, a surplus that has grown in recent years because female mortality has improved more rapidly than male mortality. The excess of male deaths may result partly from biological factors, but differences in lifestyle are also important. As gender differences in smoking, working, and other behaviors diminish, the differential in mortality will probably become smaller.

In 1980 there were almost four unmarried women 65 and over for every unmarried man of that age, a steep increase from a ratio of less than two to one in 1940. The ratio of women to men rose in every marital status, with the greatest change occurring among the widowed. In 1940 there were approximately two elderly widows for every widower, but by 1980 there were more than five. Without regard to marital status, there were 143 women for every hundred men 65 and over in 1980, up from 105 per hundred in 1940 (Table 7.5).

The huge rise in the number of elderly widows has been accompanied by a dramatic change in their living arrangements. In 1950 one in four was living alone; the other three were living with children, other relatives, or friends. By 1980 two out of three widows 65 and over were living alone, and only one in three was sharing living quarters with someone else. Most elderly men are married; even at ages 75 and above, two out of three are living with their wives. By contrast, only one woman out of five has a husband at that age (Table 7.6).

There has been a great deal of hand-wringing about the decline of three-generation households, but historians have hastened to point out that in Western Europe and the United States the three-generation household has always been the exception, not the rule. We can accept their conclusion that most households did not contain an aged mother or father, but it does not follow that only a small fraction of aged men and women lived with their children. When mortality is high and the population is growing rapidly, it is possible for *most* of the elderly to live with their children even though only a *minority* of children have elderly parents living with them. For example, if each woman has two daughters, and if half of the women survive into old age, only one daughter in four would have her mother living with her, even if every one of the survivors were living with a daughter.* As an indication of how longer life expectancy and falling birth rates have raised the mother/daughter ratio, the number of women 65 and over relative to those 35–44 *doubled* between 1950 and 1980.

In addition to demographic changes, rising real income contributes to the decrease in the number of mothers who double up with their children (Michael, Fuchs, and Scott 1980). Americans of all ages have always put a high value on autonomy; therefore, the rising income of recent decades and the particularly rapid rise in the income of the elderly have made it possible for an ever higher percentage of them to maintain their own households, health permitting.

Health is an important factor in living arrangements just as it is in the decision about retirement. In earlier times, poor health was often the reason why older men and women moved in with their children. At present, poor health often results in a move to a nursing home. The number of elderly in nursing homes increased at an astonishing 7 percent per annum between 1963 and 1977, to a total of over 1.1 million. On any given day 5 percent of all elderly live in nursing homes, but a much larger proportion enter a nursing home at some point in their lives. Of those who do enter, only one in four returns to a private or semiprivate residence. Half are transferred to another health facility (usually a short-term general hospital), and one-fourth die in the nursing home.

Why have nursing homes become so important? The answers have already been revealed in earlier discussions of rising income, increased propensity to live alone, higher mother/daughter ratios, and higher labor force participation rates by young and middle-aged women. There are many more elderly people who need care and attention, and relatively fewer children who are providing it within the home. Government policy also influences the decision because frequently the cost of nursing home care is paid by government (57 percent of the total in 1981) but the cost of home care is borne by the family.

---

* Let D = daughters with mother living with them ÷ all daughters; let M = mothers living with daughters ÷ all mothers; and let R = all mothers ÷ all daughters. Then $D = MR$.

INCOME AND WEALTH

A cynic once observed that "rich or poor, it's good to have money." From that perspective, today's older Americans are much better off than their predecessors. They have more income and more wealth (adjusted for inflation) than any previous generation of elderly.

Income

The real income of the elderly has risen not only in absolute terms but also relative to the income of the working population, primarily because of the rapid growth of Social Security retirement benefits. Although income per capita after age 65 is about 30 percent lower than at ages 55–64, the elderly enjoy many financial benefits including special tax concessions (for example, Social Security benefits are tax free), price discounts, and nonmonetary transfers (especially medical care). Moreover, low labor force participation frees time for home production (gardening, cooking, repair, and maintenance), reduces living expenses, and facilitates migration to a less costly area of the country. Interstate migration declines with age until about 60, but then rises to a new peak at about 65. Even among the elderly, the propensity to migrate increases substantially the higher the level of schooling, providing another example of the greater willingness or ability of the better educated to invest in the future.

Most of the financial problems of the elderly today are related to poor health. Not only do the ill face huge medical bills, but deterioration in health raises living costs by creating a need for special diets, special transportation, and personal services. When illness results in death, the surviving spouse frequently suffers a cut in income and, even if income *per capita* rises, it is often more difficult for the survivor to make ends meet because small households are not as efficient as larger ones in the use of space, equipment, food, heat, and light. Among households headed by someone 65 or over, 44 percent have only one person in them, and another 46 percent have only two persons. It could be argued that the elderly are free to double up or triple up in order to pool incomes and gain the economies of a larger household, but the difficulties and disadvantages of such pooling are apparently considerable. At present, fewer than 2 percent of elderly households include members who are unrelated, despite efforts by social agencies to encourage shared housing.

Although most of the elderly receive an after-tax income that compares favorably with what they earned while at work, there is a dramatic change in the *source* of income after age 65. From ages 25 to 54, labor income accounts for more than 90 percent of the total, and between 55 and 64 earnings still account for 78 percent of income. For people over 65, however, earnings provide only 20 percent; the balance is accounted for by other sources. Social Security retirement benefits are most important, with capital income such as interest and dividends next in importance, followed by government employee pensions, private pensions, and public assistance.

Does the source of income matter? I think it does, both for the individual older person and for society as a whole. It matters to the individual because Social Security retirement income does not flow from *assets* which the older person can pass on to children or consume at a pace that he or she determines. In an earlier era the aged had less total income relative to younger people than they do today, but more of it came from farms or small businesses or bits of real estate that they *owned.* Ownership usually contributes to a sense of power and control. If seniors today are "doing better and feeling worse," it may in part be because of this loss of control over their economic status.

Society is also affected by the fact that the elderly get most of their income from Social Security retirement benefits, because these transfer payments must be financed by the working population. A major problem looms in the coming decades, when the number of workers will decline relative to the number of retired people. At present the ratio is more than three to one, but it will fall to two to one in the next century if present trends continue. This fall must result in a large increase in taxes or reduction in benefits. The only alternative is to reverse the trend toward earlier retirement.

The relationship among taxes, benefits, and the worker/retiree ratio can easily be understood by considering a simple example of an economy with only active workers and retired people. Suppose part of what the workers produce is taxed and transferred to the retirees, as in our Social Security system. The size of the tax, as a fraction of production, depends upon the ratio of workers to retired people and on the ratio of benefits per retiree to after-tax income per worker. The smaller the first ratio and the larger the second, the larger must be the tax.* For instance, if there are three workers for each retired person and if the average income of retirees is to be 60 percent of workers' income, a tax of 17 percent on production will be sufficient. On the other hand, if the ratio falls to two workers to every retired person, the tax would have to rise to 23 percent in order to maintain relative income at 60 percent. To keep the tax rate at 17 percent, the relative income of the elderly would have to be slashed to 41 percent. Notice that in an economy with zero population growth there *will* be only two workers for each retiree if every man and woman works for forty years and is retired for twenty years.

The drastic decline in the labor force participation of older men during the last thirty years would already have had a large effect on the ratio of workers to retirees if not for two offsetting trends discussed in earlier chapters: the rapid growth in female labor force participation, and the large influx of young workers into the labor force in the 1970s as a result of the baby boom of the 1950s. These trends will *not* continue. The labor force participation rate of women is likely to remain high and will probably even increase, but there is no possibility of its continuing to increase at as fast a rate during the next thirty years as it did in the past thirty. Furthermore, the number of young people entering the labor force will surely decline because of the fall in the birth rate in the 1960s and 1970s. Thus, unless retirement patterns change, the ratio of workers to retirees will decrease substantially, and further improvement in life expectancy will intensify the decrease.

---

* Let P = production = income; let T = tax on workers = income of retirees; let $P - T = S$ = income of workers; let W = number of workers; and let R = number of retirees. Then the tax rate = $T/P = (T/R + S/W) \div [W/R + (T/R + S/W)]$.

Another important effect of the growth of Social Security retirement benefits is a change in the distribution of income among the elderly. Because these benefits are higher (relative to previous earnings) for those who had low earnings during their working lifetime, there is much greater *equality* of income after age 65 than at earlier ages. Men 65 and over with sixteen years of schooling have a mean total income only 55 percent above that of men with twelve years of schooling, whereas at ages 55–64 the differential is 80 percent. Income differences between men and women also narrow after age 65. For instance, among the elderly, widows receive 76 percent of the income of widowers, divorced women receive 82 percent of the income of divorced men, and the income of single women actually exceeds that of single men. At ages 45–64 the sex differential in income is greater within each marital status.

Wealth

Relative to other stages of life the income of the elderly is more equally distributed, but the opposite is true for the ownership of controllable, transferable *wealth* in the form of real estate, securities, bank accounts, and the like. Using 1972 Internal Revenue Service data, I estimated that the top 1 percent of wealth holders 65 and over own 28 percent of the elderly's total wealth, and the top 10 percent own 63 percent of the total; this is greater concentration than exists at ages 50–64. The per capita holdings of the wealthiest 10 percent of elderly were $241,000 in 1972, while the remaining 90 percent owned only $16,000 per capita. The existence of the Social Security system probably fosters inequality in the ownership of transferable wealth because many people rely on Social Security to provide their retirement income, and they thus reduce or eliminate private saving during their working years.

Why do people accumulate wealth? According to some economists, the primary purpose is to maintain consumption spending after labor income falls or disappears (Modigliani 1966). This is known as the "life cycle" hypothesis. The central idea is that people want to smooth their consumption over their life cycle rather than allow their spending to fluctuate with earnings.

Opposed to this is the "intergenerational transfer" hypothesis. Economists who hold this view argue that the primary motivation for the accumulation of wealth is to build an estate for the next generation (Kotlikoff and Summers 1981). They claim that if the only purpose of saving were to smooth life cycle consumption, a much smaller amount of personal wealth would be accumulated.

There seems to be merit in both arguments. For most *people* the life cycle motivation may be the more important one. Considering the large inequality in wealth, however, most of the *assets* may have been accumulated in order to leave an estate for the next generation. Furthermore, many people accumulate wealth with neither goal firmly in mind. Their behavior, especially once they leave the labor force, is heavily influenced by *uncertainty*. For instance, people don't know how long they are going to live. Thus, some cling to and even add to their wealth in old age rather than consume it because they are worried about outliving their money and becoming financially dependent on others. The average 65-year-old man has a 60 percent chance of dying before 75 (at current age-specific death rates), but he also has a 20 percent chance of living past 85. Furthermore, his 60-year-old wife has much better than a 50 percent chance of living for at least twenty years and almost a 40 percent chance of living for at least twenty-five years.

Uncertainty about length of life would not be a problem if good annuities existed. In that case the retired person could use his or her wealth to purchase an annuity that would provide income until death. Available annuities, however, do not offer attractive payout rates, partly because the insurance companies and other institutions that sell annuities must protect themselves against *adverse selection*—that is, the likelihood that only people with above-average life expectancy will purchase the annuities. The problem is exacerbated by uncertainty about inflation because annuities typically do not provide protection against decline in the value of the dollar. A third uncertainty is about health and the possibility of large expenditures for medical care, nursing home, special nursing, and other services. As a result of these uncertainties, many older people try to conserve their wealth rather than consume it, and thus leave larger estates (more intergenerational transfer) than they would in a world of perfect certainty.

Another problem arises because a substantial portion of the average older person's wealth is in real estate — specifically in the house in which he or she lives. About two-thirds of the personal wealth of the elderly is held in the form of physical assets such as real estate, about one-sixth is in stocks, and one-sixth in bank accounts, bonds, and similar assets that are fixed in nominal value. Among the rich elderly — the top 10 percent — about 60 percent of wealth is in physical assets and 25 percent in stocks.

Although many older people own their homes free and clear of any mortgage, it is difficult to convert this wealth into current income without moving out — a step that they are reluctant to take. Short of selling and moving, the older homeowner could raise cash by taking out a conventional mortgage, or by entering into a less conventional financial arrangement such as sale or philanthropic donation with the right to live in the house until death. There seem to be many psychological barriers to such action, however, including confusion over the nature of novel financial arrangements. Some elderly say that they do not want to sell their house or risk losing it because they wish to leave it to their children, thus supporting the intergenerational transfer hypothesis.

Whether intended or not, a substantial portion of the wealth held by the elderly is transferred to the next generation. What is known about the distribution of such transfers? Are sons favored over daughters? First-borns over their siblings? Are there systematic patterns of preference in favor of, or away from, children based on their financial position? A few economists have begun to look at these questions, with conflicting results. A study of estates probated in Connecticut in various years from 1931 to 1944 found a strong tendency toward *equal division* among children regardless of sex, birth order, or other characteristics (Menchik 1980). In this sample of 379 estates where there were two or more children, the share going to sons was roughly equal to the proportion of sons among the children, and first-borns received the same as their siblings. The author concluded that "in most cases the children received equal, or within one percentage point of equal, shares." On the other hand, a study based on interviews with heirs in the Cleveland area in 1964–65 found substantial inequality in the distribution of inheritances among siblings, concluding that "children with low incomes received greater bequests of material wealth than their better-endowed contemporaries" (Tomes 1981).

The problems parents face in allocating gifts and bequests to their children parallel those faced by society in redistributing income, and an analysis of the family's dilemma provides insights concerning national issues. The parents want to be fair, they want to be efficient, and they want to foster the cohesiveness of the family. It would be most efficient to invest more (for example, provide more schooling) in children who will benefit most from the additional investment, but justice will require that they transfer more in other ways to children who receive less investment. The conflicting goals of equality of opportunity and equality of outcome are present within a single family no less than in the total society. What should parents do if one child has a much higher income than his or her siblings? Compensate the latter with larger bequests? Should the parents' policy vary depending upon whether the income differential results from the high-income child's possessing more natural ability, working harder, investing more wisely, or benefiting from sheer chance? And should income be the only criterion for making compensatory allocations? What if the child with less income has a happier marriage? More capacity to enjoy art and music? Better health?

Incentives need to be considered as well. If the parents' policy is known, will the behavior of the children be affected in undesirable ways? For instance, a policy of compensating for income differentials might lead some children to work less, or to save less. Finally, for a family as for a society, it is important that the policy be *perceived* as fair by those most directly affected. A policy devised by a committee of ethicists and economists might be a disaster for a family if it led to disputes among the children and recriminations toward the parents.

PUBLIC POLICY ISSUES

The increasing health problems experienced by men and women as they age create many issues for public policy. Poor health leads to lower earnings or complete withdrawal from work toward the end of the life cycle and establishes a need for retirement income. Illness and impairment also raise the demand for medical care and for supplementary services for the frail and the disabled. Finally, death creates widows and widowers who must learn to cope with loneliness, and often to manage on a smaller income. Although the root cause is biological, the immediate problems of the aged often appear to be economic, and the proposed solutions almost always involve spending more money.

Probably the most important public policy issues concerning the elderly are those that are related to the Social Security retirement system. Controversial aspects of this system include its pay-as-you-go compulsory character, its less than universal coverage, its mixing of income redistribution and benefits that are contribution-related, the implicit tax on benefits if a worker does not retire at 65, the rate of growth of benefits, and the age of eligibility.

Pay-As-You-Go versus Saving-Investment

A central feature of the United States Social Security retirement system is that it taxes *today's* worker to support *today's* retirees. It is a transfer system as opposed to a saving-investment system: in the latter, individuals save and invest during their working lives and then consume the income from the investment and the investment itself during old age. At its inception in the 1930s, the system was designed to accumulate a large reserve fund, but after several years there was a gradual conversion to pay-as-you-go. The fact that the size of the retirement benefit is partially related to previous earnings leads some people to think that the system is based on saving and investment, but it differs from such a plan in two important respects. First, the taxes previously paid by current retirees were *not* invested in income-producing assets; they were used to pay benefits to other retirees in the past. Second, there is no contractual obligation to pay any stated amount of benefits to retirees; the size of and eligibility for benefits are determined by federal legislation and can be changed at any time.

One reason frequently given against basing Social Security on a saving-investment approach is that "people can't *afford* to provide for their old age." This is a weak argument. In a country with a stationary population and constant output, any generation of individuals can afford to provide for their own old age with exactly the same ease or difficulty as they can afford to provide for the previous generation's. A growing population and growing output may make the burden slightly easier under a transfer system, but declining population and output make the burden worse. The "can't afford" argument sounds plausible for people with low earnings in the sense that they experience more difficulty in saving; but unless there is *redistribution,* such people are at a disadvantage regardless of the financing method, and with redistribution they could afford to save.

According to some economists, the fact that Social Security is pay-as-you-go has sharply reduced the total amount of capital investment in the economy (Feldstein 1974, 1982). They argue that the average person thinks of his or her prospective Social Security retirement benefit as a substitute for income on *real* investments he or she might have made, even though there is no investment corresponding to the benefit. Thus, total national investment is reduced. Other economists question whether Social Security has this effect. They claim that the transfers made in the form of retirement benefits merely replace other transfers that the working population would make to the elderly if there were no Social Security (Barro 1978). Still others take the position that the negative effect on investment has been small thus far, but may get larger in the future (Munnell 1974).

Whatever the merits of saving-investment in principle, it would be exceedingly difficult for the United States to change to such an approach now because the present generation of workers would have to provide for their own old age while simultaneously meeting the income needs of those who are already retired. For better or for worse, we are probably locked into our existing pay-as-you-go system; the feasible policy options include some strong medicine but not radical surgery. A saving-investment component could be gradually phased into the Social Security system over the next several decades. Alternatively, the growth of

Social Security benefits could be kept below the rate of growth of real wages, allowing more scope for private saving and investment.

Compulsion versus Voluntarism

The present Social Security system is compulsory for most workers. Setting aside questions of redistribution, is there any reason why the government should have a compulsory system for providing retirement income? In a free society why shouldn't provision for retirement be left to individual choice, much as decisions about occupation, marriage, fertility, and other important aspects of life are left to the individual? The two principal answers given to this question are that compulsion is needed to eliminate free riders, and as a precommitment strategy to deal with problems of self-control. In the first instance, individuals favor compulsion because they are concerned about the behavior of *others* — people who don't provide for old age and thus become a public burden. In the second instance, individuals favor compulsion because they are worried about their *own* behavior. They know that they should provide for their old age and they want to, but they think that they lack the self-control to do so on a purely voluntary basis. A third reason for favoring compulsion arises from the difficulty in obtaining satisfactory annuities through private markets because of adverse selection and uncertainty about inflation. These problems become more manageable if everyone must participate in the government program.

It seems to me that a completely voluntary system is not a feasible option. The relative importance of the compulsory component could be changed, however; more voluntarism could be introduced over time by slowing the rate of growth of benefits financed from the compulsory system.

Universal Coverage?

When the Social Security system was first introduced in 1935 a substantial fraction of the labor force was not covered, but in the

1950s and 1960s most of the exempt workers were brought into the system. One large group of workers — federal government employees — are still not covered. State and local governments and nonprofit organizations can choose to be excluded from Social Security. Many have taken this option and many others are considering doing so. The failure of Congress to bring all workers into the Social Security system is unfair to those workers who *are* covered for two reasons. First, the system has a substantial redistributive component because workers with low earnings obtain benefits that are high relative to the taxes that they pay; the difference is financed by taxes on the workers with higher earnings. Most government employees enjoy average or above average earnings, but they are exempt from Social Security taxes and thus escape their share of the redistributive burden. Second, many government workers obtain enough covered employment (either on a part-time basis of full-time after retiring from the government) to qualify for Social Security benefits. These benefits are typically large relative to the amount the government worker has paid in Social Security taxes. In the interest of justice, government workers should be brought into the system as promptly as possible. The exemption of its own employees from a government-enacted compulsory program that is allegedly universal is the least defensible aspect of the system.

Redistribution versus Contribution-Related Benefits

One of the central features of the present Social Security system is that it combines income redistribution with benefits that are related to previous earnings. It has a progressive benefits structure that pays out proportionately more to those who earned less when they were employed. As a result, income inequality falls after age 65.

Many experts have recommended separating the two aspects of the program. The government could, for instance, enact legislation guaranteeing a minimum income to every elderly person regardless of his or her previous employment, and fund this program through general revenue. With minimum income guaranteed, the retirement benefit financed from Social Security taxes could be strictly proportional to the taxes that the individual paid over his or her lifetime.

Imagine a system that covered *everyone* who worked. Each individual would build up a retirement income credit based on Social Security taxes paid, plus a rate of return set by Congress based on the growth of the economy. At a specified age each individual would begin to receive an annual price-indexed annuity based on his or her accumulated credits, with no penalty if the beneficiary continued to work. Annual annuities that did not reach the established minimum level would automatically be raised to that level (without a means test) with funds from general revenue. Thus, social adequacy would be assured and the redistributive portion of the system would be financed from the more progressive general tax structure. Retirement income above the minimum would be strictly proportional to the taxes previously paid.

Political acceptance of such a two-tiered system would probably be enhanced by making the minimum benefit a matter of "right." This would help the elderly to maintain their pride and sense of dignity and would also reduce the incentive for individuals to misrepresent or manipulate their financial position in order to qualify for the benefit. If this two-tiered approach resulted in the government's paying out too much, or was not sufficiently redistributive, an offset could be introduced by including a portion of Social Security benefits in the individual's taxable income.

A system based on individual credits with a guaranteed minimum should also help reduce or eliminate some of the inequities of the present system in its treatment of wives and divorced women. The first tier — the universal minimum — would ensure a basic level of subsistence for all individuals, regardless of whether they had worked in covered employment or had worked at home as housewife or mother. The second tier — benefits directly proportional to the taxes paid by the individual — would ensure that women who worked in covered employment received full credit for that work regardless of marital status or size of spouse's benefit. At present, many women do not receive benefits based on their former employment because they collect a spouse's benefit.

In the event of divorce the credits accrued by both spouses could be split equally or divided in some other way consistent with the overall divorce settlement or premarital agreement.

Conditional or Unconditional Benefit

The present system makes benefits conditional on the older person's retiring from work. It does this by reducing benefits by 50 cents for every dollar of earnings above $5,500 per year (from retirement until age 72). Many critics find this "tax" inequitable and inefficient. It is inequitable because the older person who wants to keep on working has paid taxes along with his (or her) peers. In the spirit of the system, he should be entitled to the benefit that was "earned" regardless of whether or not he retires. It is inefficient because it biases the choice in favor of leisure and against labor, thus reducing national production and the total real welfare of society.

The two arguments usually advanced in favor of this earnings "tax" are that its removal would increase the total amount of benefits paid and that it would result in more older people staying in the labor force, thus limiting employment opportunities for younger workers. The first argument ignores the fact that by staying in the labor force the older person is contributing to the total output of the nation and is paying taxes, thus making the total transfer burden less than it would otherwise be. The second argument is partially true and partially false. It is true that if all older workers kept positions of leadership in every organization, they would impede a desirable flow of younger men and women into those positions. It is false, however, to assume that by simply staying in the labor force, older workers necessarily deny employment opportunities to others. This is the "lump of labor" fallacy previously discussed. The history of this nation rejects the view that there is only a fixed amount of work to be done. Imagine what the economy would look like if this position had been taken in recent decades with respect to women (as it once was). We see how erroneous and how harmful it would have been to argue that every time a woman obtains a job a man must lose his. As previously noted, an additional 24 million women joined the work force between 1950 and 1980, but male employment increased by 14 million during the same period.

Another disadvantage of the earnings tax is that it biases investment away from human capital and toward financial investment: a worker who retires and enjoys a large income from stocks and bonds does not experience any reduction in benefits, but one who acquires human capital through schooling or post-school investment and wants to realize a return on that investment in his later years loses part of that return through a reduction in retirement benefits.

Age of Eligibility

The preceding discussion has indicated that there are a large number of policy issues concerning the Social Security system — issues of fairness in its treatment of different individuals, and issues of efficiency such as the effect of the system on capital formation and labor force participation. Although these issues are important, probably the most important one for most people is the financial integrity of the system itself. As we have seen in this chapter, longer life expectancy, declining birth rates, earlier retirement, and rising benefits are undermining its financial foundations. During the 1990s, for instance, 7 million fewer young people will reach working age than did in the 1970s. The prospective shrinkage in the worker/retiree ratio will necessitate a large increase in taxes or reduction in benefits. Either option is likely to set generation against generation and prove extremely disruptive to our society.

Many analysts believe that the most reasonable way out of this dilemma is to gradually and steadily raise the age at which workers become eligible for retirement benefits. For instance, by raising the eligibility age two months per year for 18 years the early retirement option would change to age 65 and eligibility for regular retirement would be at age 68. This simple change would ultimately provide a large financial boost to the Social Security system by increasing the worker/retiree ratio. Because it would take place gradually, there would be minimal disruption to workers, families, and firms. Workers who are already close to retirement would not be much affected by the small changes, whereas those who are still many years away from retirement would have ample opportunity to make the necessary adjustments in their plans. Most private pension plans would probably adapt to the changes in Social Security, and mandatory retirement has already been raised by Congress from 65 to 70.

The retirement age of 65 was chosen at a time when people started work at an early age and most died before ever reaching 65. Currently, men and women begin full-time work at a later age and, given present trends in life expectancy, people who retire at age 68 in the year 2000 can expect to enjoy as many years in retirement as did the worker who retired at 65 in 1960.

Probably the principal objection to raising the age of eligibility is that there are some workers who find it difficult to continue to work late in life because of ill health. The Social Security system already provides disability insurance, and presumably there would be some increase in the use of this option. Another possible objection is that if large numbers of older workers continue in their jobs, it would be more difficult for younger workers to move up within organizational hierarchies. The way to meet this objection is through greater flexibility in job assignments of older workers and in their wages and hours of work. It would be easier to accommodate older workers in the labor force if they could cut back on their responsibilities, if their wages were free to fall along with declining productivity, and if they could choose shorter and more flexible hours. The *self-employed* elderly are more able to make such adjustments, which helps explain why more of them continue working after age 65.

A Final Note

Reform of the Social Security system should be very high on the agenda of every policy maker interested in the long-run welfare of our society. It is one of the clearest examples of a situation where a severe problem can be anticipated in sufficient time to take the necessary actions.

Even successful reform of Social Security, however, will not solve all the problems of old age. Despite their improved economic position, the present generation of elderly must contend with circumstances very different from those of earlier generations. Perhaps most significantly, the elderly are no longer a rarity. When only a small proportion of each cohort survived beyond the age of 65, there was more reason for the rest of the population to look upon them with awe and reverence. When the elderly are more numerous, they are not so regarded. Also, because there are so many more elderly now relative to the younger generation, it is more difficult to provide the needed physical and emotional support. The problem is exacerbated by the mobility of our population and by the sharp rise in female labor force participation. In the past a great deal of care for the elderly was provided by their middle-aged daughters and daughters-in-law.

Many elderly feel a loss of control because they pass on much of their wealth to the next generation early in life by paying for college educations and in other forms of investment in human capital. In the past, wealth was often held in the form of land or ownership of a small business, and typically was not transferred to the next generation until death. Also, new elements of uncertainty for the elderly have been introduced in the form of rising health care costs and general inflation. Even some of the relatively affluent among the elderly have seen the real value of their wealth sharply reduced by rising prices, and almost all aged people realize that extraordinarily high medical and nursing expenses can quickly exhaust a lifetime's savings.

The bottom line, however, is probably not so much a question of money as of relationships, and these are the most difficult issues for public policy to address. The fragmentation of families hits particularly hard at the old because even when they are in reasonably good shape physically and financially, the quality of their lives depends a great deal on family ties. This became very evident to me on a trip through Western Europe when I visited many attractive, well equipped communities for the aged. The administrators of these residential centers invariably echoed the director of an especially fine one in Copenhagen who, when asked what was the biggest problem, replied, "The children never come to visit."

8

The Policy
Perspective

*The interests of society are
the great rails on which
humanity moves, but the
ideas throw the switches.*
— *Max Weber*

THE ECONOMIC APPROACH to understanding human behavior
emphasizes the inescapability of choices and provides a set of
concepts useful for analyzing those choices. These concepts —
price, quantity, demand, supply, equilibrium, elasticity, the
margin — have usually been applied to behavior in markets for
commodities, labor, and capital, but we have seen in this book that
they can also be used to analyze such diverse phenomena as
marriage, divorce, fertility, education, and health. The virtues of
the economic approach are its simplicity and its generality. It is
simple because it emphasizes only a limited number of variables,
primarily income and prices. It suggests that many changes in
behavior over time (or differences between groups at the same
time) can be explained at least in part by variation in these
external constraints and incentives. It is general because phe-

nomena as different as unwed motherhood, school enrollment, labor force participation, and the utilization of nursing homes can all be treated within the same framework, and the interrelations among these diverse phenomena can be more fully understood.

My primary focus has been on U.S. experience since the end of World War II, but the analysis has relevance for other developed countries and for the future as well as the more distant past. When I began work on this book I was impressed with the apparent novelty of the social changes that have occurred in the United States in recent decades, but I now believe that these changes are best viewed as a continuation of trends evident in the first half of the century, and even foreshadowed before then. What is unusual about recent decades is the *pace* of change, particularly with respect to fertility, divorce, household living arrangements, and the labor force participation of married women with small children.

In approaching these phenomena, I have tried to use the economic perspective as a flexible mold that would help give shape to huge masses of data rather than as a procrustean bed to which all data must be made to conform. Even this flexibility, however, does not do full justice to the complexity of the problems discussed. The economic perspective is *necessary* for formulating good private and public policy, but it is not *sufficient*. Most of the phenomena under study have dimensions that can be understood only with contributions from other disciplines. Moreover, policy depends on *values,* as well as on analytical understanding. This chapter, therefore, not only draws on the insights that flow from economic analysis but reflects my own judgments and values concerning the kind of society that I hope my children and grandchildren will inherit.

MAJOR THEMES

The Fading Family

One of the most persistent themes that emerges from the data presented in this book is the fading role of the conjugal family as the major institution in U.S. society. At every stage of life, one sees evidence of this change: the growing proportion of unwed mothers, the proliferation of one-person households, the increasing importance of nursery schools and nursing homes. Shrinkage in the economic, social, and cultural roles of the family is not a new phenomenon, nor is it entirely unexpected. More than a century ago radical writers such as Friedrich Engels were predicting that the industrialization and urbanization that capitalism had unleashed would undermine the family, and, from their point of view, the sooner the better. They viewed the family as a barrier to the creation of a centrally controlled communist society.

By the end of the nineteenth century there was already considerable speculation and discussion about the rising divorce rate, the falling birth rate among the better educated, the changing position of women, and the so-called revolution in morals (Lasch 1977, p. 8). Half a century ago a book entitled *Recent Social Trends in The United States* (President's Research Committee on Social Trends 1933) called attention to the decline of the institutional functions of the family, and in 1935 sociologists Carle Zimmerman and Merle Frampton contrasted the "limited" family of their day with that of an earlier American period: "The family with its home was a domestic institution, a factory, and a well-integrated social institution . . . As an educational institution, it instilled the religious beliefs necessary for facing the world. As a social institution, it was a gathering place for play and recreation . . . Many of the activities connected with consumption, such as the refining of food and the making of furniture and clothing, have left the home. In a similar way the functions of protection, education, religious instruction, and recreation have developed in extrafamily circles to a much greater extent than within the home" (p. 8).

Joseph Schumpeter, a conservative economist, predicted that socialism would replace capitalism in large part because of the "disintegration of the bourgeois family" (1942, p. 157). According to Schumpeter, "the capitalist process, by virtue of the psychic attitudes it creates, progressively dims the values of family life and removes the conscientious inhibitions that an old moral tradition would have put in the way toward a different scheme of life" (p. 158).

Reactions to the fading of the family differ enormously. There are those who welcome the trend, those who deplore it, and those who deny that it is happening. The denial takes two different forms. Some writers define the term "family" to describe a mother and child without a father, a man and woman who live together for a short period of time, two persons of the same sex who live together, an elderly person living alone — in short, whatever suits the purpose at hand. This looseness of terminology obscures the real issue. Definitions are admittedly arbitrary and can be changed. A free society should allow alternative life styles so long as they do not impose large costs on others. The real point, however, is that different living arrangements have different consequences for individuals and for society. Throughout history one of the great strengths of most *human* families has been the presence of an identifiable father with a long-term commitment to his children and their mother. Currently, one out of every four American children does not live in that kind of family, and it is estimated that 40 percent of the children born since 1975 will live with only one parent at some stage of their lives prior to age 18 (Hofferth 1982).

The other form of denial has come from scholars who claim that reduction of the family's functions actually strengthens it. "The advocates of the 'new family,'" wrote Zimmerman and Frampton, "believe that personality reaches its greatest development when the family concentrates its entire strength on 'affection,' leaving education to the schools, religious teaching to the church, protection to the state, and support to industry or the state" (1935, p. 9). Subsequent developments have not confirmed these optimistic expectations. As Mary Ann Glendon, an authority on family law, has written: "In our own time the trend toward attenuation of family ties has gathered force, reaching into the core of the nuclear family, simultaneously loosening its legal bonding and emphasizing the autonomy and independence of its individual members — husband and wife, parent and child" (1981, p. 11).

The family has faded relative to the market and the government for several reasons. First, economic growth has increased the advantage of both large-scale and specialized production units. As Adam Smith so acutely noted more than two hundred years ago, productivity rises with division of labor, and division of labor is limited by the size of the market. As markets have expanded, the processing of food, the making of clothing, the education of children, and the production of many other goods and services have moved from the home to specialized institutions. Technological change involving economies of scale frequently contributes to this shift; some elements of modern hospital care, for instance, could not possibly be delivered within the home.*

The declining importance of home production of most goods and services, far from strengthening the family, seems to be leading to further reductions in its most intimate, most central functions. It is not at all unusual today for men and women to purchase child care services from institutions or other individuals, seek advice about education, health, and careers from professionals, depend on the workplace for emotional support and assistance with smoking and drinking problems, and delegate care of dying relatives to hospital and nursing home personnel.

Not only has the market taken over many activities formerly carried out in the family, but government has also been assuming many family functions such as providing social insurance for widows and orphans, the sick, and the elderly. Occasionally, universal government insurance is more efficient than private insurance because it overcomes the problem of adverse selection. The main reason for the proliferation of government programs, however, is the pressure for income *redistribution*. Almost all government "insurance" programs, from Aid to Families with Dependent Children to Social Security retirement benefits, contain significant elements of redistribution. When the family was the dominant social and economic institution in society, it redistributed resources among its own members, but there was great inequality among families.

---

* Technological change need not always favor market over home production. At least two activities — men's shaving and the laundering of clothes — moved from the market to the home as a result of new technologies, namely the safety razor and automatic washers and dryers. Prospective changes in computers and television may also work in the same direction.

The driving force behind most social legislation in the United States and other developed countries is the pressure for a more egalitarian society; the conditions of modern life compel a more equal sharing of material goods and political power. In *Equality and Efficiency: The Big Tradeoff,* Arthur Okun (1975) assumes that this sharing occurs because people prefer more equality to less and that as a society's income rises it can more readily afford to satisfy this preference. Although this may be true for some people, it is also likely that many who have power and goods prefer not to share them, but find it more difficult to perpetuate inequality as average income rises.

The more affluent and complex a society becomes, the more it depends on the willing, cooperative, conscientious efforts of the people who work in that society and the more difficult it is to obtain satisfactory effort through the use of force. When the main task of society consisted of hauling large blocks of stone from a quarry to a pyramid, it was a relatively simple matter to rope hundreds of slaves together and use a whip and the threat of starvation to secure compliance. In feudal societies the predominantly agricultural workers were kept in line by force, by taking advantage of their limited mobility and their need for protection, and by preaching to them the promise of Heaven and the threat of Hell. But when a nation's workers are airplane mechanics, teachers, and operating-room nurses, for example, such techniques will not succeed. The complexity and interdependence of a modern economy make it highly vulnerable to disruption by disaffected workers. Furthermore, a regime based on force and terror is incompatible with the widespread education, free flow of information, and geographic and social mobility necessary for a highly productive economy.

In advanced industrialized societies the problem of getting everyone to "go along" is compounded by the waning power of religion, nationalism, and other traditional control structures. Calls to serve God and country do not meet with as enthusiastic a response as they once did, whether that service is military or some onerous and not particularly rewarding civilian task. Modern governments use egalitarian social welfare legislation to induce mass participation and cooperation in the tasks of society. Paradoxically, this same legislation also can create negative incentives for work and investment. For example, subsidization of food and medical care is in part an attempt to placate the poor and bring them into the mainstream of society. These attempts succeed, at least to some extent. But subsidies that are available only to individuals and families with income below specified levels tend to discourage work and saving because greater income would result in a loss of benefits.

The expansion of government at the expense of the family is exacerbated when, as is often the case, public assistance is provided only if individuals use *nonfamily* sources for the subsidized services. Nursery schools, hospital care, and nursing homes provide examples of the way in which government policy biases choices in the direction of obtaining services outside the home, even though some of them could be provided within the family. Government agencies undoubtedly find it more difficult to monitor the use of financial aid in a family than in an institution, but some of the biases embedded in present programs of subsidized care could be eliminated. For instance, subsidies for home care of chronically ill elderly could result in reduced expenditures for hospitals and nursing homes.

The same pressures for equality that result in redistributive social welfare legislation also lead to weaker hierarchical relations within the family — as well as in the church, the workplace, the school, and other institutions. We have only to contrast present with past relations between priests and parishoners, employers and employees, or teachers and pupils to realize that the weakening of parental authority over children or of husbands' authority over wives is part of a larger phenomenon. As historian Carl Degler has stated, "The great values for which the family stands are at odds not only with those of the women's movement, but also with those of today's world. Democracy, individualism, and meritocracy, the values most closely identified with the last two centuries of Western history, are conspicuous by their absence from the family" (1980, p. 471).

How can the family be saved? Romantics of the Right yearn for a return to the "good old days," but such yearning is not likely to accomplish much against economic growth, scientific advance, and technological change. As Norman Macrae so aptly noted in *America's Third Century*, "It is pointless to say . . . that society must therefore return to being ruled by the old conventions, religious restrictions, craven obedience to the convenience of the boss at work. Individuals will not accept these restrictions now that they see that wealth and the birth control pill and transport technology make them no longer necessary" (1976). If we value the contribution that the family can make to individuals and society, we have no choice but to try to reconstitute it on a more democratic, egalitarian basis while enhancing its role as a vital, viable institution for socialization. Maintenance of an adequate level of investment in children by both the private and public sectors will play a central role in meeting that challenge.

Demography and Destiny

As we have seen, demographic factors such as fertility, mortality, and migration play an important role in determining how we live. When fertility is unusually high, family and social resources must be spread more thinly over a larger number of children. Also, a smaller fraction of them enjoy the advantages of the first-born. High fertility creates a large cohort that puts pressure on the schools, and then on the labor market for entry-level jobs. An unusually low birth rate, on the other hand, initially eases society's dependency burden, but creates problems decades later when the small cohort struggles to provide retirement benefits for the larger cohorts that preceded it.

The long-term trend toward lower fertility has radically altered the age distribution of the population — a change that has important social and economic implications, especially for the elderly. Mortality trends have also affected the age distribution and have had other significant impacts on American society. For instance, the more rapid decline in female death rates than in male death rates contributes to a markedly unbalanced sex ratio toward the end of life.

Internal migration is another demographic phenomenon that has played a major role in shaping the development of this country. The massive movement of poor, undereducated black families from the rural South to the large cities of the North created social problems for these families and contributed to the fiscal difficulties of the cities. Large-scale migration of young and old to the sun belt has also had considerable political and economic significance. Regional differences in income have been sharply reduced and political dominance by the Northeast and North Central regions has ended. The last four elected presidents of the United States — Johnson, Nixon, Carter, and Reagan — all built their political careers in the South or the West.

The age structure of the population often provides a good basis for anticipating future economic and social change. For instance, between 1980 and 1990 the population at ages 15–24 will *decline* by approximately 15 percent. The decrease in the number of college-age youth will put higher education in financial jeopardy and will drastically reduce new hirings of young faculty. If no offsetting action is taken, the nation may lose a generation of scholars — a loss that would have serious long-run consequences. During this same decade of the 1980s, the number of men and women 25–44 will increase by 26 percent, the number 65 and over by 19 percent, but the number 45–64 by only 4 percent. These uneven changes will affect birth and death rates, the crime rate, the demand for housing and medical care, and the supply of labor in ways that are partially predictable because of what is known about the different stages of the life cycle. Interstate migration is another phenomenon that can be predicted with some success. Most of the major migratory trends in the United States are consistent with an economic view of behavior based on the costs and benefits of moving.

Unfortunately, public officials tend to ignore predictable change until a crisis develops. When the birth rate fell in the 1960s, it was obvious that school enrollments would be down in the 1970s and 1980s. Remarkably few school districts, however, acted on this information until it was too late for a smooth adjustment. Similarly, given the baby boom of the 1950s, it is not difficult to predict that there will be a large increase in the number of elderly beginning around 2015, but Congress has so far failed to come to grips with the problem and take anticipatory action.

Predictability aside, there is considerable controversy as to whether government officials should deliberately intervene to affect demographic behavior. This controversy is beside the point. The choice is not between intervention or nonintervention, but between giving thoughtful attention to the demographic consequences of government policy or suffering the unintended results of policies pursued for other reasons. At a minimum, government should keep in mind the wise physician's maxim, "Do no harm." More positively, public policy should address situations where the exercise of free choice by individuals imposes costs or confers benefits on others, and these costs and benefits are not considered by the person making the choice. In such cases the government, through taxes or subsidies, should change the relative prices facing individuals so that when they choose what is best for themselves, they will also be making the choice that is best for society as a whole.

Wanting and Waiting

Many choices in life — those concerning fertility, schooling, occupation, migration, health — must explicitly or implicitly balance the satisfaction of current wants against benefits that may be realized in the future. The way an individual strikes this balance, along with natural and acquired abilities, influences success in life as measured by customary indicators such as income, occupation, and health. Other things equal, individuals with low rates of time discount — greater willingness and ability to wait — will stay in school longer, will undertake more post-school investment, will be less likely to smoke, and will in many other ways improve their future prospects.

Although we know that there is large variation among individuals in their rate of time discount, we know less about what determines those rates. Education is inversely correlated with time discount. As William Hazlitt noted, "Persons without education . . . see their objects always near, and never in the horizon" (1817). It is difficult, however, to determine whether additional schooling lowers the rate of time discount or whether those with low rates obtain additional schooling. Both effects are probably present. There is considerable evidence that the rate falls as children mature. Infants and young children tend to live very much for the present; the prospect of something only a week in the future usually has little influence over their behavior. As children get older their time horizons lengthen, but once adult status is reached there seems to be little correlation between time discount and age.

Although a greater willingness to invest in the future will, other things equal, raise lifetime income, there is nothing in economic theory to support the view that having a low rate of time discount is preferable to having a high rate. Preferences between the present and the future are, when viewed theoretically, like preferences between oranges and apples: it's all a matter of tastes or values. From a practical point of view, of course, differences in time discount at the individual and national levels are of great importance. A family, or a nation, that lives only for the present will not undertake the investments in physical and human capital that are essential ingredients for growth and development.

What role should public policy play in all this? As in the case of demographic factors, the first consideration should be to avoid policies that bias the choices individuals make with respect to investing in the future. If two individuals are equally situated, and one decides to save and invest in the future and the other does not, taxation and redistribution of the return on that investment seem inappropriate on the grounds of both efficiency and justice, except when the improvident person's income falls below a socially defined minimum. On the other hand, to the extent that differences in investment arise because of unequal opportunities (for instance, the child from a poor family who cannot raise the funds to invest in a college education), justice and efficiency considerations both suggest that public policy can play a positive role in improving access to capital.

POLICY CONFLICTS

The need to choose, to sacrifice some ultimate values to others, turns out to be a permanent characteristic of the human predicament.
— Isaiah Berlin

What constitutes a good society? What should public policy aim for? Unless there is reasonable consensus regarding objectives, public policy debate becomes an exercise in futility. As the historian R. H. Tawney wrote, "The condition of effective action in a complex civilization is cooperation. And the condition of cooperation is agreement, both as to ends to which efforts should be applied and the criteria by which its success is to be judged" (1926, p. 232). When objectives are considered one at a time, agreement is relatively easy to obtain. The difficult issues of public policy arise because no society can fully attain all its goals or fully satisfy the wants of all its members. The real problem is not one of choosing between good and evil or between the deserving and the undeserving, but between such highly valued goals as efficiency and justice or between satisfying the needs of children and those of the elderly. This section considers some of these conflicts and discusses how institutions such as the market, the government, and the family can be most fruitfully used in the pursuit of varied social objectives.

Conflicts among Goals

The good society requires both *efficiency* and *justice, freedom* and *security,* but unfortunately the pursuit of one must often be at the expense of another. Efficiency is maximized when resources are allocated so that their marginal benefit to society is the same in all uses — that is, when the last dollar spent for education yields the same benefit as the last dollar spent for health or transportation or housing or any other service. If benefits are not equal at the margin, reallocation could, in principle, make everyone better off because those who benefit from the change could compensate those who are hurt and there would still be a net benefit for society as a whole. This principle is often difficult to implement for two reasons: the facts needed to give flesh and blood to the theoretical skeleton are often unavailable; and it may not be feasible for those who benefit from the change to compensate those who lose from it. If these so-called side payments are not made, the proposed policy will be judged by *who* benefits and *who* loses (in other words, its distributive justice), as well as by its implications for allocative efficiency.

What institution is most appropriate for achieving efficiency? Both theory and experience suggest that the allocation of scarce resources through decentralized, competitive *markets* is usually preferable to centralized controls because there is more scope for individual initiative, more incentive for taking appropriate action, more information relevant to the interests and preferences of the individual decision maker, and more adaptability to changes in technology and tastes. However, private decision making through markets will not necessarily be more efficient if there is insufficient competition, if there is an adverse selection problem such as that involved in retirement annuities, or if there are negative or positive external effects such as those arising from pollution or vaccination.

Although a perfectly competitive market system is highly efficient, it may result in an *unjust* distribution of income. Even if each individual's income is strictly proportional to his or her contribution to production, some individuals will receive very high income while others will not earn enough for survival. It is difficult to reconcile such great inequality with elementary notions of justice, although some libertarians attempt to do so by focusing on the fairness of the process rather than the outcome (Nozick 1974). Their attempt fails, however, because it is impossible to establish a *moral* basis for inequality of opportunity, even though some income inequality can be justified to preserve efficiency and freedom. We are born unequal in abilities and advantages; justice, therefore, requires some redistribution of income. As Alexis de Tocqueville, a French aristocrat who was thoroughly aware of the conflict between equality and freedom, wrote in *Democracy in America,* "Equality may be less elevated, but it is more just, and in its justice lies its greatness and beauty."

If Justice requires redistribution, who should assume responsibility for this? *Government* will usually be the most effective institution to undertake this task, for at least two reasons. First, although much redistribution can be, and has been, accomplished within families, ethnic associations, and religious communities, only government can ensure redistribution from members of one group to members of another. Second, because of external effects, private philanthropy may not result in as much redistribution as society really wants. Suppose that many members of a community want to see financial aid provided to the poorest among them, and that each is willing to contribute a fair share, provided others will too. Under voluntary philanthropy each person has an incentive to hold back and let the others give as much as possible. Through government, however, which has the power to establish binding rules, the problem can be solved by legislating a redistributive tax.

Efficiency and justice conflict when the latter requires taxes and subsidies that alter incentives and distort the choices that individuals make with respect to work, saving, living arrangements, and so on. Sometimes, however, redistribution may increase efficiency through programs that provide greater equality of opportunity for investment in human capital. For instance, able youngsters from poor families might benefit greatly from additional schooling, but may lack the access to capital to make this possible.

In other instances, when some inefficiency is inevitable, redistributive programs can be designed to minimize the loss. Consider the case of a subsidized day care center that costs the taxpayers one hundred dollars per week per child, but provides a service worth only fifty dollars per week to an eligible family. If, instead of offering the family a choice between the center or nothing, an alternative program were to provide seventy-five dollars per week to be used by the family as it wished for child care, both the family and the taxpayers would be better off.

As with efficiency and justice, *freedom* and *security* are highly valued but often conflicting goals of our society. Freedom has many virtues. If you are free to choose, you can follow your own interests and preferences; if someone else restricts your choice or chooses for you, that person's interests and preferences may prevail. Moreover, even if that someone else tries to maximize *your* welfare, it is unlikely that he or she will know your circumstances, tastes, strengths, and weaknesses as well as you do. Finally, if you have an opportunity to choose, you can learn from the experience. You are the one who must live with the consequences of your choices, and therefore even inappropriate choices can often help you make better ones in the future.

Although the case for freedom is strong, this goal cannot be pursued without limit. Almost everyone concedes that some restrictions are warranted when the exercise of individual freedom endangers others or imposes large external costs. A more subtle but more pervasive limit to freedom arises when it conflicts with the individual's desire for security. In the face of the complexities and uncertainties of modern life, many people willingly vote for programs that restrict freedom — their own and that of others — in exchange for the promise of greater security. For instance, numerous laws deny consumers the freedom to buy products that have been judged to be dangerous. But not everyone makes the same evaluation of the tradeoff. Rational individuals will seek an optimal balance between freedom and security, but this balance varies among individuals, depending upon their ability to benefit from freedom and to bear the cost of insecurity. This variation is the major reason why it is so difficult to reach consensus on this issue.

Another problem for public policy arises when the principle of individual freedom is defended unevenly in different areas of life. Many who vigorously defend it in the social and cultural spheres, for example, just as vigorously advocate detailed government restrictions on freedom in the areas of consumption, investment, and work. But the general arguments they advance to justify government regulation of market transactions — imperfect information, external effects — could as easily be invoked to regulate sexual behavior, marriage, or living arrangements. Indeed, some social critics who deplore interference with economic freedom are quite ready to use the power of government to regulate these aspects of life. Such partial approaches will not serve the cause of freedom well. If freedom is a valuable goal, and I believe it is, it must be pursued in all aspects of behavior.

Conflicts Among Groups

Conflicts among goals such as freedom and security create problems for public policy, but conflicts among *groups,* defined by characteristics such as age, sex, or marital status, have even greater potential for social disruption. "Senior Citizens March on Capitol" and "Working Women Demand a Larger Share of the Pie" are the kind of headlines that are seen with increasing frequency as more of the nation's goods and services are directly allocated or indirectly regulated by government.

The cleavage between the elderly and other groups is one of the sharpest to emerge in recent years, as the population 65 and over grows in numbers and political power. The interests of younger adults frequently range across a wide number of issues that affect them differently as consumers, investors, taxpayers, and parents, but the elderly have a more clearly defined set of interests. Although they constitute only 16 percent of the voting-age population, their political influence is great because they can focus single-mindedly on a few issues of special relevance to them. Children, by contrast, have no political power themselves, and other age groups are not likely to devote political efforts exclusively to benefiting children.

Age is not the only basis for intergroup conflict. As we saw in Chapter 5, the interests of women and those of men are far from identical, primarily because women have a stronger desire for children and care more about their welfare. Thus, there are many public policies such as those subsidizing child care or promoting part-time employment that could favor women at the expense of men. If our society is to achieve "liberty and justice for all," traditional male *dominance* must end. Great care is needed, however, to distinguish this objective from the elimination of male *presence* within the family. The challenge to individuals and to public policy is to promote equality between men and women without "throwing out the father with the bath water."

Not only do the interests of women and men sometimes diverge, but so do the interests of some women compared with others. Those who wish to follow a traditional pattern of concentration on family with only secondary commitment to paid employment will be best off when the laws and social institutions are framed with them in mind. Women who put primary emphasis on a career in the market will benefit from laws and social institutions that assume *their* behavior as the norm. During the next decade there are likely to be tens of millions of women of each type, and it will be extremely difficult for public policy to serve fully the interests of both groups. For example, so long as many women have only a secondary interest in employment, employers will have trouble identifying those who are career-minded, at least initially. Thus, the problem of statistical discrimination is likely to continue, as employers form expectations partially based on the average behavior of all women. On the other hand, to the extent that many women are employed full time and earn a reasonable income, the laws and the courts are likely to be less than fully protective of those women who have made a complete commitment to their families.

Some diversity of interests among age, sex, and marital status groups is inevitable, but the growing tendency to try to resolve differences through government poses a great danger to our nation. A society that tries to settle all the detailed questions of life through the ballot box and the courts should not be surprised to find itself fragmented, polarized, and unstable. When large principles are at stake, there is no alternative to the political process; but for day-to-day adjustments regarding who does what and who gets what, both market processes and intrafamily decision making are usually smoother and less divisive. Markets are more impersonal than government; thus, although every group wants a larger share of the national output, the struggle within markets is not so explicitly focused. When income distribution problems are resolved within families, the divergence of interests does not disappear, but there is more possibility for softening the conflict over money by incorporating it within a larger framework of relationships, rights, and obligations. Also, it is easier to adjust intrafamily allocations to the changing needs and circumstances of individual family members.

SUMMARY OF POLICY RECOMMENDATIONS

It is not wisdom to be only wise,
And on the inward vision close the eyes. —George Santayana

In this book I have described major trends and important inter-group differences in a wide range of social phenomena, have analyzed these trends and differences in order to illuminate their causes and consequences, and have discussed related public policy issues that are of great concern to Americans at different stages of life. My primary objectives have been met. Some readers, how-ever, may want to see these analyses and discussions translated into policy recommendations. This concluding section, therefore, offers specific suggestions in five areas and also presents two general principles that could revitalize public policy by building on the strongest features of both liberal and conservative tradi-tions.

Specific Recommendations

As the preceding chapters make clear, there are many areas of American life that would benefit from changes in public policy. Based on the criteria of number of people affected, economic impact, and availability of workable solutions, highest priority should be given to *reform of the Social Security retirement system.* This system affects nearly every American; over $100 billion in retirement benefits are paid annually. It is basically a good program and should be continued, but several changes are cur-rently needed in order to correct injustices, increase economic efficiency, and restore the system's financial integrity. In the fall of 1982 a Presidential Commission investigated the problems of Social Security, and many remedies were proposed. In my judg-ment, the following modifications would provide the greatest improvement with the least disruption.

First, slowly and gradually raise the age of eligibility. Second, make the program universal so that it covers every man and woman. Third, make the individual's benefit (above a minimum level) proportional to the taxes paid. Fourth, define a minimum benefit available to all elderly as a matter of right; if the earned benefit does not at least equal the minimum benefit, the difference should be made up from general revenue.

These changes would improve the balance between revenues and expenditures without raising taxes or reducing benefits to current retirees. It would result in fairer treatment of women, and it would lead to a larger work force and a bigger gross national product. Most important, if these moderate changes are not made now, we will face a crisis that may destroy the system as the baby boom cohorts of the 1950s approach retirement age.

A second area requiring priority attention is health. *Reform of health insurance,* and concomitant changes in the organization of medical care, are needed because the cost of health care is increasing at a more rapid rate than the nation can sustain in the long run. Expenditures by private and public health insurance plans now exceed spending for national defense, and the present system of paying for care is incapable of stemming further increases. Most hospitals are reimbursed according to their costs and physicians according to their fees; thus, expenditures soar because neither the insured patient nor the hospital nor the physician has any incentive to hold them in check. The best solution to this problem would be to develop comprehensive health plans that deliver care for a fixed amount per person or per family per year — that is, "capitation" reimbursement. In each area of the country there should be several such plans competing on the basis of quality and cost, and the government should subsidize participation in these plans by the poor and the near-poor.

Short of this comprehensive approach, and as a partial solution to our present difficulties, several steps should be taken. First, Medicare and Medicaid beneficiaries should be offered a voucher option that would enable them to join existing comprehensive capitation plans as an alternative to the fee-for-service, cost-reimbursement system. Second, a ceiling should be established on the amount of employer-paid health insurance that employees can receive *tax-free;* this ceiling should be generous enough to include all present plans, but should help deter future increases. Third, all employees should be given a choice of health insurance plans, with the same contribution by the employer regardless of the plan selected, provided it meets federally established minimum standards. Fourth, if an employee chooses a plan that costs less than the employer's contribution, the employee should receive from the employer a tax-free rebate equal to the amount saved.

The objective of these reforms is not necessarily to keep health care expenditures from increasing in the future, but to ensure that these expenditures are the result of rational choices by physicians and patients who have considered the costs as well as the benefits of alternative courses of action.

For both Social Security and health insurance, the problems are fairly obvious and the possible solutions are relatively simple. The third area that I propose for priority attention, *increased investment in children,* involves more complex issues and solutions are less certain. Nevertheless, I favor expansion of subsidies for children, subsidies that would be available to all families regardless of marital status, work status of the mother, or income. Subsidies to low-income families, however, should be proportionately greater than to high-income ones. These subsidies would help reduce the widespread inequality of opportunity that still stands as a formidable barrier to efficiency and justice in our society. Efficiency suffers because many infants, children, and adolescents do not receive enough investment in human capital to realize their full potential as workers and citizens. Justice suffers because inequality of opportunity contributes to inequality of achievement.

Subsidies for child care provided at home or in the market would alleviate some of these problems. These subsidies would also help women in their efforts to achieve equality with men, for reasons explained in Chapters 3 and 5. Depending upon how they are structured, child subsidies could also contribute to a pronatalist policy, if further declines in fertility make such a policy necessary. There are many different ways to provide subsidies for children, and considerable study is desirable before launching any major programs. The needs of children, however, must be kept in the forefront of public discussion because the political power of other groups, such as the elderly, is so much greater than that of children.

If more attention were paid to children, there would be fewer crises in adolescence, but the problems of this stage — unwed motherhood, poor work skills and attitudes, crime, suicide — will not disappear. We should, therefore, *experiment with alternatives to conventional schools* for men and women ages 16-24. Many young people might benefit from an opportunity to leave their homes and schools to participate in residential programs that encompass work, training, and counseling. These experimental programs should appeal to advantaged as well as disadvantaged youth by providing an opportunity to perform a significant non-military service for the nation through the conservation and enhancement of natural and human resources. Youth who successfully complete such a program should be entitled to scholarships and other benefits similar to those given the veterans of World War II. These benefits would serve as an inducement to join the program and as a subsidy for further investment in human capital.

The best way to reduce unwed motherhood and unemployment among teenagers is to increase their skills and earning power, but *elimination of the minimum wage* would also improve their opportunities to work and make progress in life. At present we make it illegal for many young people to obtain valuable work experience by setting a minimum wage that is higher than their net value to employers. This policy bears particularly heavily on young black teenagers who, in many cases, must overcome other disadvantages such as growing up in low-income one-parent homes, attendance at trouble-ridden schools, and racial prejudice. The full benefits from the elimination of the minimum wage would take time to accrue, and many other policies are needed to improve the prospects for black youth. The minimum wage, however, needlessly makes their lives more difficult by imposing an artificial barrier to employment.

General Recommendations

In addition to the above specific recommendations, I have two general recommendations for public policy. First, in the future the government should pay more attention to preserving *efficiency* when designing redistributive programs. In general, a negative income tax or cash grants should be used rather than grants that are tied to the purchase of particular goods or services. Even when some tying is desired, such as in medical care or higher education, it will usually be preferable to give a voucher that can be used as the beneficiary deems best rather than restricting the aid to some particular institution or service.

The worst policies of all are those that attempt income redistribution by regulating particular markets through wage controls, rent controls, energy subsidies, and the like. This kind of interference introduces needless injustices and inefficiencies. Injustices arise because some of the people who benefit from the regulations are not the ones whom the policy is supposed to help — wealthy tenants in rent-controlled housing, for example. Inefficiencies arise because regulations are expensive to administer and because people change their behavior in order to take advantage of controlled prices, rents, and so forth. For instance, when the government holds the price of gasoline below its true cost, consumers use too much of it and producers supply too little.

Most important of all, we must recognize the need for *balance,* both in the goals that we set and in the institutions that we nourish in order to pursue these goals (Fuchs 1979). If we value efficiency *and* justice, freedom *and* security, the economic perspective tells us that we will often have to give up some of one goal in order to ensure the partial achievement of others. Both theory and history indicate that the best way to seek multiple goals is through a balance of institutions — market, government, family, and others. No single institution is superior for all goals; each functions best when complemented by the others. Moreover, diversification, be it of institutions, genes, or security holdings, is the wisest strategy for stability and survival in the face of an uncertain future.

Consider the market. It is a proven, efficient institution for the allocation of resources for production and the distribution of goods and services to consumers. We have only to look at the countries of Eastern Europe to see that centralized controls are much less efficient and that they carry unacceptable costs in loss of political, social, and religious freedom. At the same time, we need to recognize that the market alone cannot provide the basis for a good society. Its success over the last two hundred years is attributable in large part to the existence of strong *nonmarket* institutions such as the family, which has been the primary agent of socialization and, in conjunction with religion, the primary source of values.

The fruits of the market system — science, technology, urbanization, affluence — are undermining the institutions that are the foundations of the social order. Human beings need more than an abundance of material goods. They need a sense of purpose in life — secure relationships with other human beings — something or someone to believe in. With the decline of the family and religion, the inability of the market system to meet such needs becomes obvious, and government rushes in to fill the vacuum, but does so imperfectly and at great cost.

A substantial role for government in modern society is inevitable. Government is needed to help people cope with forces that would otherwise overwhelm them, to deal with external effects, and to redistribute income. We can no longer say with Jefferson, "That government is best which governs least," but it would be the height of folly to think that the more government we have the better off we are. Indeed, even though any particular government intervention may seem reasonable, we need to be aware that the cumulative impact of the growth of government is to weaken — and ultimately destroy — other useful institutions such as the market, the family, and private associations.

We must recognize the potential conflict between the family and the expansion of redistributive government. Despite its fading importance, the family is still the biggest barrier to equality in postindustrial society. Inheritances can be taxed, but as long as mothers and fathers pass on to their offspring their genetic endowment, their knowledge, and their special heritage and values, attempts to achieve complete equality will be frustrated. At some point in the future we will have to ask whether the last increment of equality is worth the loss of so valuable an institution as the family — one that can stand as a refuge from impersonal markets and authoritarian government.

The message for public policy is clear. Let the market do what only it can do well: allocate human, natural, and man-made resources to producers, and distribute goods and services to consumers. Let government do what only it can do well: maintain a legal and financial framework conducive to the smooth functioning of competitive markets, redistribute income to ensure a more just society, and use taxes and subsidies to eliminate differences between private and social costs and benefits. Let families and religious, philanthropic, and cultural institutions do what only they can do well: socialize the young, honor the old, transmit values, give texture and meaning to life, teach love, and inculcate faith in the possibility of human improvement.

The message for individuals is also clear. There is no magic path that can carry us to every goal. If we are wise, we will determine what we most deeply value and will realistically balance aspirations against resources. In short, we must choose, and the choices we make will help determine how we live. The wisdom of those choices will determine how well we live.

Tables
References
Index

Tables

Table 2.1.   Distribution of children by education of mother and educational distribution of all women, ages 35 – 44.

Education	Percent of Children		Percent of All Women Ages 35–44	
	1950	1979	1950	1979
No high school	49.2	10.7	39.1	8.1
Some high school	20.7	18.4	20.8	14.8
High school graduate	19.6	46.2	24.9	46.8
Beyond high school	10.6	24.6	15.2	30.3
Total	100.0	100.0	100.0	100.0
Average (mean) number of years of schooling[a]	9.4	11.9	10.1	12.3
Standard deviation[a] (years)	3.0	2.6	3.1	2.6
Relative inequality[b]	.32	.22	.31	.21

a. Summary statistics calculated from more detailed frequency distributions of years of schooling.

b. The coefficient of variation — that is, mean ÷ standard deviation.

Sources: U.S. Bureau of the Census, *Statistical Abstract of the United States, 1977;* idem, "Fertility of American Women, June 1979," *Current Population Reports,* series P-20, no. 358, table 8; idem, *Census of Population, 1960,* vol. 1, Characteristics of the Population, pt. 1, United States Summary, table 173.

Table 2.2. Percent of live births under 2,501 grams, 1974.[a]

	White	Black	All Races[b]
Education of mother			
Less than 12 years	7.8	13.7	9.4
12 years	5.0	11.0	5.9
13–15 years	4.3	10.1	5.0
16 years or more	3.8	8.7	4.2
Marital status of mother			
Married	5.2	10.4	5.8
Not married	9.1	13.9	11.9
Prenatal care			
First trimester	4.9	11.0	5.7
Second trimester	6.2	12.1	7.7
Third trimester	6.4	11.5	7.8
No prenatal care	15.3	25.7	18.9
Age of mother			
Under 20	7.5	14.0	9.4
20–29	4.9	10.9	5.7
30–39	5.5	10.9	6.1
40 or over	7.6	12.1	8.5
All births	5.4	12.0	6.5

a. Excludes plural births.
b. Includes other nonwhite.
Source: Adapted from Eisner et al. (1979).

Table 2.3. Low birth weight and socioeconomic characteristics by race and ethnicity, 1970.

	Mexican Origin	Puerto Rican Origin	Black	White
Low birth weight (1976)				
Percent under 2,500 grams	5.4	9.0	13.1	6.2
Income				
Dollars per capita	1,716	1,794	1,800	3,304
Dollars per adult equivalent[a]	2,247	2,340	2,283	3,962
Education (median years completed)				
Women 25–34	10.1	9.8	12.1	12.6
Women 35–44	8.4	8.6	11.0	12.4
Family				
Percent of families headed by women ages 25–34	10.9	25.9	29.6	7.2
Percent of families headed by women ages 35–44	12.9	23.3	29.2	8.5
Percent of children under 18 not living with both parents	19.8	34.9	42.7	12.8

a. Persons under 18 years of age = .5 adult equivalent.

Sources: National Center for Health Statistics, *Vital and Health Statistics,* series 21, no. 37, table D; U.S. Bureau of the Census, *Census of Population, 1970,* Detailed Characteristics, United States Summary; idem, *Census of Population, 1970,* subject report PC(2)-1B, "Negro Population"; idem, *Census of Population, 1970,* subject report PC(2)-1C, "Persons of Spanish Origin."

Table 3.1. Market-produced services for children, 1965 and 1978.[a]

	1965	1978	Average Annual Rate of Change, 1965 to 1978 (Percent)
Expenditures per pupil in public elementary and secondary schools (1978 constant dollars)[b]	1,030	1,823	4.8
Personal health care expenditures for each child under 18 (1978 constant dollars)			
Private	142	204	2.8
Public	26	82	8.8
Total	168	286	4.1
Gross national product per capita (1978 constant dollars)	7,210	9,858	2.4
Percent of three- and four-year-olds enrolled in school			
White	10.3	32.7	8.9
Nonwhite	11.8	41.4	9.7
Total	10.6	34.2	9.0

a. Adjusted for inflation by GNP deflator.

b. Current expenditures per average daily attendance: 1965 = 1965–66; 1978 = 1977–78.

Sources: U.S. Bureau of the Census, "School Enrollment — Social and Economic Characteristics of Students, October 1978," *Current Population Reports,* series P-20, no. 346, table 1; idem, "School Enrollment — Social and Economic Characteristics of Students, October 1975," *Current Population Reports,* series P-20, no. 303; National Center for Education Statistics, *Digest of Education Statistics, 1980,* table 71; Council of Economic Advisers, *Economic Report of the President, 1982,* tables B-1, B-28; Fisher (1980), table A.

Table 3.2. Preprimary enrollment of three- and four-year-old children by education of mother and family income, 1975.

	Percent Enrolled	
	3-Year-Olds	4-Year-Olds
Education of mother (*years*)		
Less than 8	8.0	37.1
8	11.5	22.4
9–11	11.2	25.3
12	17.3	35.9
13–15	34.3	53.2
16	47.2	72.6
17 or more	46.7	75.3
Family income (*dollars per year*)		
Less than 3,000	20.5	34.4
3,000–4,999	11.5	36.0
5,000–7,499	15.7	33.5
7,500–9,999	10.5	29.4
10,000 or more	26.8	45.8

Sources: U.S. Bureau of the Census, "Nursery School and Kindergarten Enrollment of Children and Labor Force Status of Their Mothers, October 1967 to October 1976," *Current Population Reports,* series P-20, no. 318, pp. 16–17; National Center for Education Statistics, *Preprimary Enrollment, October 1975,* p. 12.

Table 3.3. Living arrangements of children under 18 (percent of all children).

	All Races		1980	
Living Arrangement	1970	1980	White	Black
With divorced mother	3.3	7.5	7.0	10.9
With never-married mother	0.8	2.8	1.0	12.8
With mother, spouse absent	4.7	5.7	3.8	16.1
With father	1.1	1.7	1.6	2.0
Other	5.0	5.7	3.9	16.0
Total not with two parents	14.9	23.4	17.3	57.8

Source: U.S. Bureau of the Census, *Statistical Abstract of the United States, 1981,* table 73.

Table 3.4.   Arrangements for care of children (ages 3 – 6) of employed mothers, February 1975.

Child Care Arrangement	Employment of Mother, White		Employment of Mother, Black	
	Full Time (percent)	Part Time (percent)	Full Time (percent)	Part Time (percent)
In own home				
By parent	40	77	45	63
By other	13	5	13	13
In other home				
By relative	14	6	20	15
By nonrelative	23	10	15	6
In day care center	7	1	3	3
Other and not reported	3	1	4	—
Total	100	100	100	100

Source: U.S. Bureau of the Census, *Statistical Abstract of the United States, 1979,* table 579.

Table 4.1. **Changes in employment and school enrollment rates, by race and sex, 1960–1979 (percentage points).**

	White Men	Nonwhite Men	White Women	Nonwhite Women
Ages 16–19				
Employment rate	6.3	−15.1	14.1	−2.9
School enrollment rate	−1.3	13.6	7.7	12.1
In school, employed	3.0	−4.7	13.5	3.1
In school, not employed	−4.3	18.3	−5.8	9.0
Out of school, employed	3.3	−10.4	0.6	−6.0
Out of school, not employed	−2.0	−3.2	−8.2	−6.1
Ages 20–24				
Employment rate	0.6	−9.3	22.8	7.1
School enrollment rate	2.0	12.3	12.9	12.5
In school, employed	0.7	4.2	7.9	5.5
In school, not employed	1.3	8.1	5.0	7.0
Out of school, employed	−0.1	−13.5	14.9	1.6
Out of school, not employed	−1.8	1.5	−27.8	−14.0

Sources: U.S. Bureau of the Census, *Census of Population, 1960,* vol. 1, Characteristics of the Population, pt. 1, United States Summary, tables 194 and 197 (adjusted); U.S. Bureau of Labor Statistics, *Special Labor Force Report 241,* tables A and B.

Note: The figures for 1979 come from the Current Population Survey (CPS). The figures for 1960 are based on *Census of Population* data that I have adjusted to reconcile the employment rates by color and sex with those available from the CPS for 1960. In order to ensure that the 1960–1979 comparison was not biased by the use of data from two different sources, another comparison was made as follows. Changes from *1960* to *1970* in enrollment-employment status for each race-sex group were calculated using the *Census of Population* for those years. Changes in the same variables from *1970* to *1979* were calculated using CPS data. The sum of the two sets of changes yielded results that were very similar to those shown. For the category of major interest, out-of-school not-employed nonwhite males, the change as calculated by the alternative method is −5.3 percentage points at ages 16–19, and +3.6 percentage points at ages 20–24.

In all cases, the data are for civilian employment; fluctuations in the size of the armed forces may affect youth employment and unemployment. Military employment was relatively low and approximately equal in 1960 and 1975, but the proportion of military personnel who were nonwhite did rise appreciably between those years. I concentrate on the *employment* rate rather than the *unemployment* rate (the number not employed but seeking work, divided by the number in the labor force) because the latter is affected by persons dropping out of or entering the labor force, whereas the actual possession of a job is probably what is most relevant.

Table 4.2. Percent employed by enrollment status, by race and sex, ages 16 – 19 and 20 – 24, 1960 and 1979.

		White Men	Nonwhite Men	White Women	Nonwhite Women
Ages 16 – 19					
In school	1960	37.1	27.2	23.6	14.4
	1979	42.2	15.7	41.7	16.4
Not in school	1960	69.7	63.7	49.1	35.8
	1979	77.3	57.2	61.4	30.9
Ages 20 – 24					
In school	1960	55.1	54.7	43.4	33.9
	1979	53.4	43.1	54.6	40.8
Not in school	1960	86.7	80.0	42.1	41.5
	1979	88.8	75.0	67.7	49.8

Sources: U.S. Bureau of the Census, *Census of Population, 1960,* vol. 1, Characteristics of the Population, pt. 1, United States Summary, tables 194 and 197 (adjusted); U.S. Bureau of Labor Statistics, *Special Labor Force Report 241,* tables A and B.

Table 4.3. Ratio of nonwhite to white employment rate, by region, by enrollment status and age, 1960 and 1970.

	In School		Out of School	
	1960	1970	1960	1970
Ages 16 – 19				
Men, non-South	.55	.56	.66	.61
Men, South	.75	.56	.95	.78
Women, non-South	.54	.61	.63	.66
Women, South	.66	.56	.78	.72
Ages 20 – 24				
Men, non-South	.99	.96	.81	.80
Men, South	.84	.78	.91	.85
Women, non-South	.91	1.03	.94	.92
Women, South	.71	.85	1.01	.97

Sources: U.S. Bureau of the Census, *Census of Population, 1960,* vol. 1, Characteristics of the Population, pt. 1, United States Summary, tables 253 and 197; idem, *Census of Population, 1970,* Detailed Characteristics, United States Summary, tables 217 and 289.

Note: In 1970 the racial ratio is blacks/nonblacks; this ratio is slightly lower than nonwhite/white.

Table 4.4. Marital and fertility behavior at ages 15–19 and 20–24, selected years.

	White			Nonwhite	
	1950	1960	1978	1960	1978
Ages 15–19					
Births per 1,000 women	82	89	52	158	99
Percent of births to unmarried women	13	15	44	42	80
Abortions per 1,000 women	—	—	40	—	69
Percent of women not currently married	83	84	91	84	94
Ages 20–24					
Births per 1,000 women	197	258	112	294	146
Percent of births to unmarried women	4	5	16	20	49
Abortions per 1,000 women	—	—	48	—	102
Percent of women not currently married	34	31	52	38	69

Sources: U.S. Bureau of the Census, *Statistical Abstract of the United States, 1980*, tables 87, 95, and 102; idem, *Census of Population, 1960*, vol. 1, Characteristics of the Population, pt. 1, United States Summary, table 177; idem, "Marital Status and Living Arrangements, 1978," *Current Population Reports*, series P-20, no. 338, table 1; Centers for Disease Control, *Abortion Surveillance, 1978*, table 17; National Center for Health Statistics, *Vital and Health Statistics*, series 21, no. 23, p. 23; idem, *Vital Statistics of the United States, 1960*, vol. 1, table 1-W; idem, *Monthly Vital Statistics Report* 29 (April 28, 1980), tables 3 and 13.

Note: A dash indicates that data are unavailable.

Table 4.5. **Percent change in age-specific death rates from 1960 to 1977, selected causes.**

	Men			Women		
	15–19	20–24	25 and over[a]	15–19	20–24	25 and over[a]
All causes	12	12	−12	4	−7	−23
Suicide	154	160	1	113	152	11
Motor vehicle accidents	21	−2	−17	46	34	−12
Homicide	118	101	88	142	92	78
All other causes	−16	−10	−16	−27	−35	−26

a. Average of age-specific changes.

Source: National Center for Health Statistics, *Vital Statistics of the United States*, vol. 2, pt. A, 1960 and 1977 editions.

Table 5.1. **Work status, ages 25–44, by race and sex, 1979 (percent).**

Work Status	White Men	White Women	Black Men	Black Women
Worked for pay full time, year round	75.1	34.6	62.5	41.5
Worked for pay part time and/or part year	21.9	36.7	27.9	31.3
Did not work for pay	3.0	28.7	9.6	27.2
Total	100.0	100.0	100.0	100.0

Source: U.S. Bureau of the Census, "Money Income of Families and Persons in the United States, 1979," *Current Population Reports,* series P-60, no. 129, tables 51 and 53.

Table 5.2.   Annual earnings by age, sex, and years of schooling, full-time year-round white workers, 1979 (in dollars).

Years of Schooling	Ages 25–29		Ages 40–44	
	Men	Women	Men	Women
9–11	13,868	8,174	16,279	8,956
12	15,685	10,143	19,934	10,685
13–15	16,104	11,857	21,032	11,680
16	17,289	12,542	29,171	13,326
17 or more	19,398	14,581	33,718	18,076

Source: U.S. Bureau of the Census, "Money Income of Families and Persons in the United States, 1979," *Current Population Reports,* series P-60, no. 129, table 53.

Table 5.3.   Percent of the population in 1980 living in a state different from the one they lived in in 1975, by age and years of school completed.

Years of School Completed	Age			
	18–24	25–29	30–34	35–44
0–8	6.6	9.1	6.9	4.9
9–11	9.8	13.5	10.1	6.4
12	10.5	13.2	10.4	7.1
13–15	12.1	16.9	15.0	12.5
16	21.5	23.6	18.3	12.6
17 or more	27.0	30.7	23.7	16.4
All levels	11.4	16.8	13.8	9.2

Source: U.S. Bureau of the Census, "Geographical Mobility, March 1975 to March 1980," *Current Population Reports,* series P-20, no. 368, table 24.

Table 5.4. Net migration (inmigrants minus outmigrants) by region and race (in thousands).

Region	Birth to 1965[a]		1965–1970[b]		1975–1980[b]	
	Whites	Blacks	Whites	Blacks	Whites	Blacks
Northeast	−2,595	898	−771	50	−1,275	−175
North Central	−3,313	1,122	−719	108	−1,107	−51
South	−1,095	−2,624	890	−250	1,571	195
West	7,002	604	600	92	842	30

a. Compares region of residence in 1965 with region of birth.
b. Compares region of residence in 1970 (or 1980) with region of residence in 1965 (or 1975).
Sources: U.S. Bureau of the Census, *Census of Population, 1970,* subject report PC(2)-2D, "Lifetime and Recent Migration," table 9; idem, "Geographical Mobility: March 1975 to March 1980," *Current Population Reports,* series P-20, no. 368, table 40.

Table 5.5. Marital status of women 25–44, selected years, 1920–1980.

Year	Percent of Women Married			Percent of Women Never Married		
	25–29	30–34	35–44	25–29	30–34	35–44
1920	73.4	80.2	80.3	23.1	14.9	11.4
1930	74.4	81.6	81.6	21.7	13.2	10.0
1940	74.1	80.4	81.0	22.8	14.7	10.4
1950	83.3	86.2	84.3	13.3	9.3	8.3
1960	86.2	88.7	87.1	10.5	6.9	6.1
1970	82.5	86.1	85.9	12.2	7.4	5.7
1980	70.4	78.2	81.4	20.8	9.5	5.6

Sources: U.S. Bureau of the Census, *Historical Statistics of the United States, Colonial Times to 1970,* series A160-171; idem, *Statistical Abstract of the United States, 1981,* table 49.

Table 5.6. Changes in fertility of women ages 30–34 and 35–39, by birth order, 1970–1979.

	Ages 30–34		Percent Change	Ages 35–39		Percent Change
	1970	1979	1970–1979	1970	1979	1970–1979
First births						
Number (in thousands)	42	100	137	12	16	41
Per thousand women	7.3	12.1	66	2.1	2.4	14
Per thousand childless women	61.3	64.0	4	22.9	20.7	-10
Births of second order or higher						
Number (in thousands)	385	417	8	169	119	-30
Per thousand women	66.0	49.7	-25	29.6	17.0	-43
Per thousand women with at least one child	74.9	61.3	-18	32.6	19.2	-41
Total births						
Number (in thousands)	428	517	21	180	135	-25
Per thousand women	73.3	61.8	-16	31.7	19.4	-39

Source: National Center for Health Statistics, *Monthly Vital Statistics Report*, vol. 31, no. 2, supplement 2, May 27, 1982

Table 6.1. Self-assessed health status by age and income, 1976 – 1977.[a]

	Number of People (in thousands)		
	17 – 44	45 – 64	65 and Older
Excellent health			
High	20,381	8,320	1,058
Low	3,878	836	1,873
High/low ratio	5.26	9.95	0.56
Poor health			
High	200	367	154
Low	344	900	924
High/low ratio	0.58	0.41	0.17
Excellent high/low ratio relative to *poor* high/low ratio	9.07	24.27	3.29

a. High income = $15,000 and above; low income = under $5,000.
Source: U.S. Bureau of the Census, *Social Indicators III,* adapted from table 2/1.

Table 6.2. Household and per capita income, by sex and marital status of householder, in households with no related children under 18 in 1979.

Marital Status	Income Per Household (in dollars)		Persons per Household		Income Per Capita (in dollars)	
	Male Householder	Female Householder	Male Householder	Female Householder	Male Householder	Female Householder
Married, spouse present	23,196		2.32		9,998	
Married, spouse separated	16,514	8,784	1.29	1.45	12,802	6,058
Widowed	11,875	8,458	1.35	1.32	8,796	6,408
Divorced	17,420	12,288	1.37	1.41	12,715	8,715
Never married	15,907	13,300	1.49	1.39	10,676	9,568

Source: U.S. Bureau of the Census, "Money Income of Households in the United States, 1979," Current Population Reports, series P-60, no. 126, table 18.

Table 7.1. U.S. population ages 65 and over, selected years, 1900 – 2000.

	1900	1920	1940	1960	1980	2000[a]
(1) Millions of persons	3.1	4.9	9.0	16.7	25.5	31.8
(2) As percentage of total population	4.1	4.6	6.8	9.2	11.3	12.2
(3) As percentage of population 21 and older	7.6	8.0	10.7	15.3	17.2	17.7
(4) Percentage of elderly who are 75 or older	29.0	29.8	29.3	33.6	39.0	45.2
(5) Female/male ratio, 65 and over	.98	.99	1.04	1.21	1.48	1.50

a. Projected by the U.S. Bureau of the Census.

Sources: (1), (2), and (3) from U.S. Bureau of the Census, *Historical Statistics of the United States, Colonial Times to 1970,* series A29 – 42, except 1980. (4) and (5) from idem, *Census of Population, 1970,* Detailed Characteristics, U.S. Summary, table 53, except 1980. Statistics for 1980 from idem, "Population Profile of the United States, 1980," *Current Population Reports,* series P-20, no. 363, table 4.

Table 7.2. Gross domestic product per capita, labor force participation rates of men 65 and over, and percent of male population 65 and over for the United States 1890–1979, and OECD countries 1970.

United States	Gross Domestic Product Per Capita (1970 dollars)	Labor Force Participation Rate of Men 65 and Over	Percent of Male Population 65 and Over
1890	1,214[a]	73.9	3.85
1900	1,365[b]	68.3	4.01
1910	1,661[c]	58.1	4.20
1920	1,907	60.1	4.61
1930	2,137	58.3	5.35
1940	2,546	41.8	6.67
1950	3,439	41.4	7.75
1960	3,938	30.5	8.49
1970[d]	4,798	24.8	8.51
1979	5,768	20.0	9.36

OECD, 1970	Gross Domestic Product Per Capita (1970 U.S. dollars)	Labor Force Activity Rate of Men 65 and Over	Percent of Male Population 65 and Over
Turkey	881	73.8	4.04
Portugal	1,298	53.2	8.09
Greece	1,854	34.0	10.00
Spain	1,902	23.1	8.29
Ireland	2,041	44.5	10.24
Italy	2,357	15.3	9.04
Austria	2,496	8.6	11.39
Japan	2,836	54.4	6.32
Finland	3,022	15.1	7.06
United Kingdom	3,042	19.8	10.18
New Zealand	3,094	21.6	7.24
Iceland	3,219	42.8	7.80
Norway	3,276	26.1	11.30
Netherlands	3,291	14.4	8.95
Australia	3,334	22.8	6.89

Belgium	3,449	7.0	11.24
Switzerland	3,468	32.6	9.28
France	3,506	13.6	10.05
Denmark	3,516	23.9	10.87
West Germany	3,746	16.0	10.71
Luxembourg	3,846	10.7	10.80
Canada	3,923	20.9	7.10
Sweden	4,148	18.3	12.20
United States[d]	4,790	25.8	8.43
Median	3,248	22.2	9.12

a. 1889–1893 average.
b. 1897–1901 average.
c. 1907–1911 average.
d. Slight differences are due to differences in sources.

Sources for U.S. gross domestic product: 1890–1960: U.S. Bureau of the Census, Historical Statistics of the United States, Colonial Times to 1970, series F125 (1929 dollars). 1970, 1979: Council of Economic Advisers, Economic Report of the President, 1980, table B-9. All were converted to 1970 dollars using implicit GDP price deflator from Economic Report of the President, 1980, table B-4. I divided by Census Bureau population estimates (except 1979 estimate) to get per capita.

Sources for U.S. labor force participation rate: 1979: Employment and Training Administration, Employment and Training Report of the President, 1980, table A-2. 1940–1970: U.S. Bureau of the Census, Historical Statistics of the United States, Colonial Times to 1970, series D35. 1890–1930: Long (1958), table A-2 (based on census results, adjusted).

Sources for U.S. population: 1890–1970: U.S. Bureau of the Census, Historical Statistics of the United States, Colonial Times to 1970, series A119–A134. 1979: idem, Current Population Reports, series P-25, no. 870.

Sources for OECD countries: Gross domestic product: Kravis, Heston, and Summers (1978), tables 1 and 4. Labor force and population: International Labour Office (1977), table 2 (uses United Nations population estimates and own participation rates).

Table 7.3. Average Social Security retirement benefits and average hourly earnings, selected years, 1950–1980.

Benefits and Earnings	1950	1970	1980	Average Annual Rate of Change (percent per annum)	
				1950–1970	1970–1980
Average monthly benefit (1980 dollars)					
Per retired worker	151	250	341	2.5	3.1
Per widow[a]	127	216	308	2.7	3.5
Average hourly earnings (1980 dollars)[b]	4.59	6.85	6.66	2.0	-0.3

a. Includes some widowers.
b. Private nonagricultural sector, adjusted for overtime (in manufacturing) and for interindustry shifts in employment.
Sources: U.S. Bureau of the Census, *Historical Statistics of the United States, Colonial Times to 1970*, series H225 and H229; idem, *Statistical Abstract of the United States, 1981*, table 535; Council of Economic Advisers, *Economic Report of the President, 1982*, table B-38.

Table 7.4.   **Rate of change in mortality, ages 65 and over, 1950–1965 and 1965–1977.**[a]

	White Men	White Women	Nonwhite Men	Nonwhite Women
All causes				
1950–1965	−0.1	−1.5	0.1	−0.7
1965–1977	−1.1	−1.9	−1.0	−1.5
Heart disease				
1950–1965	−0.2	−1.3	−0.1	−0.7
1965–1977	−1.7	−2.6	−1.5	−1.8
Malignant neoplasms				
1950–1965	0.9	−0.8	2.8	0
1965–1977	1.1	0.4	2.2	2.4

a. Age-adjusted by the direct method: 1965 U.S. population for 1950–1965; 1977 U.S. population for 1965–1977.

Source: National Center for Health Statistics, *Health, United States, 1980,* tables 8, 15, and 17.

Table 7.5.   **Ratio of women to men ages 65 and over, by marital status, 1900–1980.**

Category	1900	1920	1940	1960	1980
Married	0.50	0.52	0.56	0.64	0.73
Widowed	2.21	2.14	2.33	3.31	5.34
Single	1.02	0.95	0.99	1.34	1.65
Divorced	0.57	0.53	0.58	1.06	1.30
All unmarried	1.97	1.86	1.90	2.61	3.84
All marital statuses	0.98	0.99	1.05	1.22	1.43

Sources: U.S. Bureau of the Census, *Historical Statistics of the United States, Colonial Times to 1970,* series A160–A171; idem, *Statistical Abstract of the United States, 1981,* table 49.

Table 7.6. Living arrangements of the elderly, by age and sex, 1980 (percent).

	65–74		75 and Over	
Category	Men	Women	Men	Women
Married, living together	79.4	48.1	67.7	22.1
Widowed, alone	5.4	28.6	15.6	43.4
Widowed, not alone	3.1	11.7	8.3	24.6
Other	12.1	11.6	8.4	9.9
Total	100.0	100.0	100.0	100.0

Source: U.S. Bureau of the Census, "Marital Status and Living Arrangements, March 1980," *Current Population Reports,* series P-20, no. 365, table 6.

References

Adams, Henry. 1918. *The education of Henry Adams.* Boston: Houghton Mifflin.

Administration for Children, Youth, and Families. 1978. *The status of children, 1977.* By Kurt J. Snapper and JoAnne S. Ohms. Washington, D.C.: U.S. Government Printing Office.

American Humane Association. 1979. *Annual statistical report: National analysis of official child neglect and abuse reporting, 1978.* Englewood, Colo.: Denver Research Institute.

Antonovsky, Aaron. 1967. Social class life expectancy and overall mortality. *Milbank Memorial Fund Quarterly* 45 (April): 31–73.

Ariès, Philippe. 1980. Two successive motivations for the declining birth rate in the West. *Population and Development Review* 6 (December): 645–650.

Aron, Raymond. 1968. *Progress and disillusion.* New York: Praeger.

Auster, Richard; Irving Leveson; and Deborah Sarachek. 1972. The production of health: An exploratory study. In *Essays in the economics of health and medical care,* ed. Victor R. Fuchs. New York: Columbia University Press.

Bane, Mary Jo. 1976. *Here to stay: American families in the twentieth century.* New York: Basic Books.

Banfield, Edward C. 1968. *The unheavenly city.* Boston: Little, Brown.

Banta, H. David, and Stephen B. Thacker. 1979. Assessing the costs and benefits of electronic fetal monitoring. *Obstetrical and Gynecological Survey* 34 (August): 627–642.

Barro, Robert J. 1978. *The impact of Social Security on private saving: Evidence from the U.S. time series.* Washington, D.C.: American Enterprise Institute for Public Policy Research.

Becker, Gary S. 1964. *Human capital.* 2nd ed. 1975. New York: Columbia University Press.

———— 1965. A theory of the allocation of time. *Economic Journal* 75 (September): 493–517.

———— 1976. *The economic approach to human behavior.* Chicago: University of Chicago Press.

———— 1981. *A treatise on the family.* Cambridge, Mass.: Harvard University Press.

Becker, Gary S.; Elisabeth M. Landes; and Robert T. Michael. 1977. An economic analysis of marital instability. *Journal of Political Economy* 85 (December): 1141–87.

Becker, Gary S., and Gregg Lewis. 1973. On the interaction between the quantity and quality of children. *Journal of Political Economy* 81 (March/April, pt. 2): S279–S288.

Becker, Gary S., and Nigel Tomes. 1976. Child endowments and the quantity and quality of children. *Journal of Political Economy* 84 (August): S143–S162.

Belmont, Lillian, and Francis A. Marolla. 1973. Birth order, family size, and intelligence. *Science* 182 (December 14): 1096–1101.

Belsky, Jay, and Laurence D. Steinberg. 1978. The effects of day care: A critical review. *Child development* 49 (December): 929–949.

Bergmann, Barbara R.; Judith Radlinski Devine; Patrice Gordon; Diane Reedy; Lewis Sage; and Christina Wise. 1980. The effect of wives' labor force participation on inequality in the distribution of family income. *Journal of Human Resources* 15 (Summer): 452–455.

Berlin, Isaiah. 1970. *Four essays on liberty.* New York: Oxford University Press.

Bloustein, Edward J. 1982. The school and the society. Speech to New Jersey Association of School Administrators, May 3.

Bombardier, Claire; Victor R. Fuchs; Lee A. Lillard; and Kenneth E. Warner. 1977. Socioeconomic factors affecting the utilization of surgical operations. *New England Journal of Medicine* 297 (September 29): 699–705.

Bowen, William G., and T. Aldrich Finegan. 1969. *The economics of labor force participation.* Princeton: Princeton University Press.

Bowers, Norman. 1979. Young and marginal: An overview of youth employment. *Monthly Labor Review* 102 (October): 4–16.

Bronfenbrenner, Urie. 1970. *Two worlds of childhood: U.S. and U.S.S.R.* New York: Russell Sage Foundation.

——— 1976. Research on the effects of day care on child development. In *Toward a national policy for children and families,* appendix. Washington, D.C.: National Academy of Sciences.

Burkhauser, Richard V., and John A. Turner. 1980. The effects of pension policy through life. In *Retirement policy in an aging society,* ed. Robert L. Clark. Durham, N.C.: Duke University Press.

Butler, Robert N. 1975. *Why survive? Being old in America.* New York: Harper and Row.

Butz, William P., and Michael P. Ward. 1979. Will U.S. fertility remain low? A new economic interpretation. *Population and Development Review* 5 (December): 663–688.

Cain, Glenn G. 1966. *Married women in the labor force: An economic analysis.* Chicago: University of Chicago Press.

California Assessment Program. 1982. *Survey of sixth grade school achievement and television viewing habits.* Sacramento: California State Department of Education.

Caplow, Theodore; Howard M. Bahr; Bruce A. Chadwick; Reuben Hill; and Margaret Holmes Williamson. 1982. *Middletown families.* Minneapolis: University of Minnesota Press.

Centers for Disease Control. 1980. *Abortion surveillance, 1978.* Issued November 1980, Atlanta, Georgia.

Chhabra, Rami. 1980. Some are (still) more equal than others. *Sweden Now* 6.

Chernichovsky, Dov, and Douglas Coate. 1980. The choice of diet for young children and its relation to children's growth. *Journal of Human Resources* 15 (Spring): 255–263.

Cogan, John. 1981. Black teenage employment and the minimum wage: A time series analysis. Hoover Institution working paper, September.

——— 1982. The decline in black teenage employment: 1950–1970. *American Economic Review* 72 (September): 621–638.

Cohen, Ronald S.; David K. Stevenson; Natalie Malachowski; Ronald L. Ariagno; Keith J. Kimble; Andrew O. Hopper; John D. Johnson; Kent Ueland; and Philip Sunshine. 1982. Favorable results of neonatal intensive care for very low-birth-weight infants. *Pediatrics* 69: 621–625.

Colle, Ann Dukes, and Michael Grossman. 1978. Determinants of pediatric care utilization. In *The economics of physician and patient behavior.* Supplement issue, *Journal of Human Resources* 13: 115–158.

College Entrance Examination Board. 1977. *On further examination.* Report of the Advisory Panel on the Scholastic Aptitude Test Score Decline. New York: College Entrance Examination Board.

Community Service Society of New York. 1982. *Day care and the working poor: The struggle for self-sufficiency.* New York: Community Service Society.

Council of Economic Advisers. 1980, 1982. *Economic report of the President.* Washington, D.C.: U.S. Government Printing Office.

Danziger, Sheldon. 1980. Do working wives increase family income inequality? *Journal of Human Resources* 15 (Summer): 444–451.

Degler, Carl. 1980. *At odds.* New York: Oxford University Press.

de Lone, Richard H. 1979. *Small futures.* New York: Harcourt Brace Jovanovich, for the Carnegie Council on Children.

de Tocqueville, Alexis. 1966. *Democracy in America.* Trans. George Lawrence, 1966. New York: Harper and Row.

De Tray, Dennis. 1978. Child schooling and family size: An economic analysis. Paper no. R-2301-NICHD. Santa Monica, Calif.: Rand Corporation.

Easterlin, Richard. 1968. *Population, labor force, and long swings in economic growth: The American experience.* New York: Columbia University Press, for the National Bureau of Economic Research.

——— 1980. *Birth and fortune: The impact of numbers on personal welfare.* New York: Basic Books.

Economist, The. 1982. Money and divorce. Vol. 283 (April 24–30): 75–84.

Eisner, Victor; Joseph V. Brazie; Margaret W. Pratt; and Alfred C. Hextor. 1979. The risk of low birth weight. *American Journal of Public Health* 69 (September): 887–893.

Elder, Glen H., Jr. 1975. Adolescence in the life cycle: An introduction. In *Adolescence in the life cycle: Psychological change and social context,* ed. Sigmund E. Dragastin and Glen H. Elder, Jr. New York: Halsted-Wiley.

Employment and Training Administration. 1977. *Dictionary of occupational titles.* 4th ed., U.S. Department of Labor. Washington, D.C.: U.S. Government Printing Office.

Employment and Training Administration. 1980, 1981. *Employment and training report of the President.* Washington, D.C.: U.S. Government Printing Office.

Enthoven, Alain C. 1980. *Health plan.* Menlo Park, Calif.: Addison-Wesley.

Eron, Leonard D. 1982. Parent-child interaction, television violence, and aggression of children. *American Psychologist* 37 (February): 197–211.

Farel, Anita M. 1980. Effects of preferred maternal roles, maternal employment, and socio-demographic status on school adjustment and competence. *Child Development* 51 (December): 1179–86.

Farrell, Phillip, and Victor R. Fuchs. 1982. Schooling and health: The cigarette connection. *Journal of Health Economics* 1 (December): 217–230.

Feinberg, Lawrence. 1981. Asian students excelling in area, U.S. schools. *Washington Post,* July 21.

Feldstein, Martin. 1974. Social security, induced retirement, and aggregate capital accumulation. *Journal of Political Economy* 82 (September/October): 905–926.

——— 1982. Social security and private saving: Reply. *Journal of Political Economy* 90 (June): 630–642.

Fisher, Charles R. 1980. Differences by age groups in health care spending. *Health Care Financing Review* 1 (Spring): 65–90.

Freeman, Richard. 1976. *The over-educated American.* New York: Academic Press.

——— 1980. The facts about the declining economic value of college. *Journal of Human Resources* 15 (Winter): 124–142.

Friedan, Betty. 1963. *The feminine mystique.* New York: Norton.

——— 1981. The myth of super mom. *Family Weekly,* November 8, 1981.

——— 1981. *The second stage.* New York: Summit Books.

Fuchs, Victor R. 1956. Population growth concepts and the economy of tomorrow. *Commercial and Financial Chronicle,* December 13.

——— 1968. *The service economy.* New York: National Bureau of Economic Research.

——— 1971. Differences in hourly earnings between men and women. *Monthly Labor Review* 94 (May): 9–15.

——— 1974a. *Who shall live? Health, economics, and social choice.* New York: Basic Books.

——— 1974b. Recent trends and long-run prospects for female earnings. *American Economic Review Proceedings* 64 (May): 236–242.

——— 1974c. Some economic aspects of mortality in developed countries. In *The economics of health and medical care,* ed. Mark Perlman. London: Macmillan.

——— 1976. From Bismarck to Woodcock: The "irrational" pursuit of national health insurance. *Journal of Law and Economics* 19 (August): 347–359.

——— 1979. Economics, health, and post-industrial society. The E. S. Woodward Lectures in Economics delivered at the University of British Columbia, Vancouver, November 1–2, 1978. Copyright 1978, held by the University of British Columbia. *Milbank Memorial Fund Quarterly/Health and Society* 57 (Spring): 153–182.

——— 1981a. Economic growth and the rise of service employment. In *Towards an explanation of economic growth,* ed. Herbert Giersch. Tübingen, West Germany: J. C. B. Mohr (Paul Siebeck).

——— 1981b. Low-level radiation and infant mortality. *Health Physics* 40 (June): 847–854.

——— 1982a. Self-employment and labor force participation of older males. *Journal of Human Resources* 17 (Summer): 339–357.

——— 1982b. Time preference and health: An exploratory study. In *Economic aspects of health,* ed. Victor R. Fuchs. Chicago: University of Chicago Press.

——— and Richard Perlman. 1960. Recent trends in southern wage differentials. *Review of Economics and Statistics* 62, pt. 1 (August): 292–300.

Gil, D. G. 1970. *Violence against children: Physical child abuse in the United States.* Cambridge, Mass.: Harvard University Press.

Glendon, Mary Ann. 1981. *The new family and the new property.* Toronto: Butterworths.

Goode, William J. 1964. *The family.* Englewood Cliffs, N.J.: Prentice-Hall.

Griner, Eve Powell; W. Parker Frisbie; and Lauren J. Krivo. 1982. Infant mortality and mother's marital status: A comparative analysis of the Spanish surname population with blacks and anglos. Mimeo, Texas Population Research Center, series 4, no. 4.005. Presented at 1982 Population Association of America meetings in San Diego.

Grossman, Michael. 1972. *The demand for health: A theoretical and empirical investigation.* New York: Columbia University Press, for the National Bureau of Economic Research.

——— 1976. The correlation between health and schooling. In *Household production and consumption,* ed. Nestor E. Terleckyj. *Studies in Income and Wealth,* vol. 40. New York: Columbia University Press, for the National Bureau of Economic Research.

Grossman, Michael, and Steven Jacobowitz. 1981. Variations in infant mortality rates among counties of the United States: The roles of public policies and programs. *Demography* 18 (November): 695–713.

Grubb, W. Norton, and Marvin Lazerson. 1982. *Broken promises.* New York: Basic Books.

Guttmacher Institute, The Alan. 1981. *Teenage pregnancy: The problem that hasn't gone away.* New York: Alan Guttmacher Institute.

Hack, Maureen; Avroy A. Fanaroff; and Irwin R. Merkatz. 1979. Current concepts: The low birth-weight infant—evolution of a changing outlook. *New England Journal of Medicine* 301 (November 22): 1162–65.

Harris, Jeffrey E. 1981. Ten expressions for the mortality risk of cigarette smoking. Mimeo, Massachusetts Institute of Technology, Department of Economics. Paper presented at the International Workshop on the Analysis of Actual versus Perceived Risks, National Academy of Sciences, June 1–3, Washington, D.C.

———— 1982. Prenatal medical care and infant mortality. In *Economic aspects of health,* ed. Victor R. Fuchs. Chicago: University of Chicago Press.

Hartunian, Nelson S.; Charles N. Smart; and Mark S. Thompson. 1980. The incidence and economic costs of cancer, motor vehicle injuries, coronary heart disease, and stroke: A comparative analysis. *American Journal of Public Health* 70 (December): 1249–60.

Hazlitt, William. 1817. *The round table.* Edinburgh: A. Constable.

Heaton, Tim B.; Daniel T. Lichter; and Glen V. Fuguitt. 1982. The geographic redistribution of blacks and nonblacks: Thirty years in perspective. Mimeo, Pennsylvania State University, Department of Sociology. Paper presented at Population Association of America meetings in San Diego, April 30.

Hill, C. Russell, and Frank P. Stafford. 1980. Parental care of children: Time diary estimates of quantity, predictability, and variety. *Journal of Human Resources* 15 (Spring): 219–239.

Hobbs, Nicholas, and Sally Robinson. 1982. Adolescent development and public policy. *American Psychologist* 37 (February): 212–223.

Hofferth, Sandra L. 1982. Children's family experience to age 18: A cohort life table analysis. Mimeo of paper presented at Population Association of America meetings in San Diego, May. Washington, D.C.: Urban Institute.

Hurd, Michael D., and Michael J. Boskin. 1981. The effect of social security on retirement in the early 1970s. National Bureau of Economic Research, working paper 659.

Hurd, Michael D., and John B. Shoven. 1983. The economic status of the elderly. In *Financial aspects of the U.S. pension system,* ed. John B. Shoven and Zvi Bodie. Chicago: University of Chicago Press.

Hutchens, Robert M. 1979. Welfare, remarriage, and marital search. *American Economic Review* 69 (June): 369–379.

Iden, George. 1980. The labor force experience of black youth: A review. *Monthly Labor Review* 103 (August): 10–16.

Inkeles, Alex. 1980. Modernization and family patterns: A test of convergence theory. *Conspectus of History* 1: 59–60.

Institute of Medicine. 1978. *Adolescent behavior and health.* Washington, D.C.: National Academy of Sciences.

International Labour Office. 1977. *Labor force estimates and projections, 1950–2000.* 2nd ed. Geneva: International Labour Office.

Jacobson, Howard N. 1980. Commentary on "A randomized controlled trial of prenatal nutritional supplementation." *Pediatrics* 65 (April): 835–836.

Kamerman, Sheila, and Alfred Kahn. 1979. The day-care debate: A wider view. *The Public Interest* 54 (Winter): 76–93.

Kaplan, Helen Singer. 1981. When you earn more than he does: The sexual and psychological implications. *Savvy* 2 (November): 82–87.

Keniston, Kenneth, and the Carnegie Council on Children. 1977. *All our children.* New York: Harcourt Brace Jovanovich.

Keyfitz, Nathan. 1980. Population appearances and demographic realities. *Population and Development Review* 6 (March): 47–64.

King, Allan G. 1978. Industrial structure, the flexibility of working hours, and women's labor force participation. *Review of Economics and Statistics* 60 (August): 399–407.

Kittner, Dorothy R. 1977. Forced retirement: How common is it? *Monthly Labor Review* 100 (December): 60–61.

Kotlikoff, Laurence J., and Lawrence H. Summers. 1981. The role of intergenerational transfers in aggregate capital accumulation. *Journal of Political Economy* 89 (August): 706–732.

Kravis, Irving B.; Alan W. Heston; and Robert Summers. 1978. Real GDP per capita for more than one hundred countries. *Economic Journal* 88 (June): 215–242.

Kumar, S. P.; E. K. Anday; L. M. Sacks; R. Y. Ting; and M. Deliyoria-Papadopoulos. 1980. Follow-up studies of very low birth weight infants (1,250 grams or less) born and treated within a perinatal center. *Pediatrics* 66 (September): 438–444.

Lasch, Christopher. 1977. *Haven in a heartless world.* New York: Basic Books.

Lazear, Edward, 1979. Why is there mandatory retirement? *Journal of Political Economy* 87 (December): 1261–84.

Leibowitz, Arleen. 1977. Parental input and children's achievement. *Journal of Human Resources* 12 (Spring): 242–251.

Leibowitz, Arleen; Marvin Eisen; and Winston Chow. 1980. Decision-making in teenage pregnancy: An analysis of choice. Working draft WD-421-3-HEW. Santa Monica, Calif.: Rand Corporation.

Leonard, Jonathan S. 1979. The social security disability program and labor force participation. National Bureau of Economic Research, working paper 392, August.

Levinger, George, and Oliver C. Moles, eds. 1979. *Divorce and separation.* New York: Basic Books.

Lillard, Lee A. 1977. Inequality: Earnings vs. human wealth. *American Economic Review* 67 (March): 42–53.

Linder, Staffan Burenstam. 1970. *The harried leisure class.* Trans. from Swedish by the author and Keith Bradfield. New York: Columbia University Press.

Lindert, Peter H. 1977. Sibling position and achievement. *Journal of Human Resources* 12 (Spring): 198–219.

Long, Clarence. 1958. *The labor force under changing income and employment.* National Bureau of Economic Research, general series no. 65. Princeton: Princeton University Press.

Lubitz, James; Marian Gornick; and Ron Prihoda. 1981. Use and costs of medicare services in the last year of life. Internal working paper, September 21. Office of Research, Demonstrations, and Statistics; Health Care Financing Administration. Washington, D.C.: Department of Health and Human Services.

Luft, Harold S. 1981. *Health maintenance organizations: Dimensions of performance.* New York: John Wiley.

Macrae, Norman. 1976. *America's third century.* New York: Harcourt Brace Jovanovich.

Mare, R. D. 1980. Social background and school continuation decisions. *Journal of the American Statistical Association* 75 (June): 295–305.

Marshall, Alfred. 1920. *Industry and trade.* 3rd ed. London: Macmillan.
——— 1961. *Principles of economics.* 9th ed. Originally published 1890. London: Macmillan, for the Royal Economic Society.

Maslow, Abraham H. 1959. *New knowledge in human values.* New York: Harper and Brothers.

Mason, Karen. 1976. Comment: The social institutions of occupational segregations. In *Women and the work place.* Chicago: University of Chicago Press.

Masur, Gerhard. 1961. *Prophets of yesterday.* New York: Macmillan.

McIntosh, C. Alison. 1981. Low fertility and liberal democracy in Western Europe. *Population and Development Review* 7 (June): 181–207.

Menchik, Paul L. 1980. Primogeniture, equal sharing, and the U.S. distribution of wealth. *Quarterly Journal of Economics* 94 (March): 299–316.

Michael, Robert T. 1972. *The effect of education on efficiency in consumption.* National Bureau of Economic Research, occasional paper no. 116. New York: Columbia University Press.

—————— 1982. Why did the U.S. divorce rate double within a decade? Forthcoming.

Michael, Robert T.; Victor R. Fuchs; and Sharon R. Scott. 1980. Changes in the propensity to live alone: 1950–1976. *Demography* 17 (February): 39–56.

Mincer, Jacob. 1962. Labor force participation of married women: A study of labor supply. In *Aspects of labor economics,* Conference of the Universities–National Bureau Committee for Economic Research. Princeton: Princeton University Press.

—————— 1974. *Schooling, experience and earnings.* New York: Columbia University Press.

Mincer, Jacob, and Haim Ofek. 1982. Interrupted work careers: Depreciation and restoration of human capital. *Journal of Human Resources* 17 (Winter): 3–24.

Minkler, Meredith. 1981. Research on the health effects of retirement: An uncertain legacy. *Journal of Health and Social Behavior* 22 (June): 117–130.

Mischel, Walter. 1974. Processes in delay of gratification. In *Advances in experimental social psychology,* vol. 7. New York: Academic Press.

Modigliani, Franco. 1966. The life cycle hypothesis of saving, the demand for wealth and the supply of capital. *Social Research* 33 (Summer): 160–217.

Montaigne, Michel de. 1948. *The complete works of Montaigne.* Trans. Donald M. Frame. Stanford: Stanford University Press.

Munnell, Alicia H. 1974. *The effect of social security on personal savings.* Cambridge, Mass.: Ballinger.

National Center for Education Statistics. 1977. *Preprimary enrollment, October 1975.* Washington, D.C.: U.S. Government Printing Office.

—————— 1980. *Digest of education statistics, 1980.* Washington, D.C.: U.S. Government Printing Office.

National Center for Health Statistics. 1940–1977. *Vital statistics of the United States.* Published annually. Washington, D.C.: U.S. Government Printing Office.

—————— 1973a. *Vital and health statistics,* series 21, no. 23. Teenagers: Marriages, divorces, parenthood, and mortality. By Alice M. Hetzel and Marlene Cappetta. Washington, D.C.: U.S. Government Printing Office.

—————— 1973b. *Vital and health statistics,* series 21, no. 25. Remarriages: United States. By Kristen M. Williams and Russell P. Kuhn. Washington, D.C.: U.S. Government Printing Office.

——— 1980a. *Vital and health statistics,* series 21, no. 37. Factors associated with low birth weight, United States, 1976. By Selma Taffel. Washington, D.C.: U.S. Government Printing Office.

——— 1980b. *Health, United States, 1980.* Washington, D.C.: U.S. Government Printing Office.

——— 1980–1982. *Monthly vital statistics report.* Public Health Service, Hyattsville, Maryland.

——— 1981. *Vital and health statistics,* series 11, no. 221, Hypertension in adults 25–74 years of age, United States, 1971–1975. By Jean Roberts and Michael Rowland. Washington, D.C.: U.S. Government Printing Office.

National Clearinghouse on Aging. 1980. *The older worker.* Statistical report on older Americans, no. 6. By Teresita Chan and Donald G. Fowles. Washington, D.C.: U.S. Government Printing Office.

National Institute of Mental Health. 1982. *Television and behavior: Ten years of scientific progress and implications for the eighties,* vol. 1, summary report. Washington, D.C.: U.S. Government Printing Office.

Newhouse, Joseph P.; Willard G. Manning; Carl N. Morris; Larry L. Orr; Naihua Duan; Emmett B. Keeler; Arleen Leibowitz; Kent H. Marquis; M. Susan Marquis; Charles E. Phelps; and Robert H. Brook. 1981. Some interim results from a controlled trial of cost sharing in health insurance. *New England Journal of Medicine* 305 (December 17): 1501–7.

Newman, Morris J. 1979. The labor market experience of black youth, 1954–78. *Monthly Labor Review* 102 (October): 17–27.

Newsweek. 1978. Teen-age suicide. Vol. 92 (August 28): 74–77.

Nielsen Company, A. C. 1981. *Nielsen report on television.* Northbrook, Ill.: A. C. Nielsen Company.

Nozick, Robert. 1974. *Anarchy, state and utopia.* New York: Basic Books.

Okun, Arthur M. 1975. *Equality and efficiency: The big tradeoff.* Washington, D.C.: Brookings Institution.

Paffenbarger, Ralph S. Jr.; Stanley H. King; and Alvin L. Wing. 1969. Characteristics in youth that predispose to suicide and accidental death in later life. *American Journal of Public Health* 59 (June): 900–908.

Parsons, Donald O. 1980. Racial trends in male labor force participation. *American Economic Review* 70 (December): 911–920.

Polachek, Solomon. 1981. Occupational self-selection: A human capital approach to sex differences in occupational structure. *Review of Economics and Statistics* 63 (February): 60–69.

Pomerance, Jeffery J.; Christinia T. Ukrainski; Tara Ukra; Diane H.

Henderson; Andrea H. Nash; and Janet L. Meredith. 1978. Cost of living for infants weighing 1,000 grams or less at birth. *Pediatrics* 61 (June): 908–910.

Potomac Institute. 1979. *Youth and the needs of the nation.* Washington, D.C.: Potomac Institute.

President's Research Committee on Social Trends. 1933. *Recent social trends in the United States.* New York: McGraw-Hill.

Principal. 1980. One-parent families and their children: The schools' most significant minority. Vol. 60 (September): 31–37.

Robbins, Lionel Charles. 1932. *An essay on the nature and significance of economic science.* London: Macmillan.

Rosenzweig, Mark R., and T. Paul Schultz. 1982. The behavior of mothers as inputs to child health: The determinants of birth weight, gestation, and rate of fetal growth. In *Economic aspects of health,* ed. Victor R. Fuchs. Chicago: University of Chicago Press.

Ross, Heather L., and Isabel V. Sawhill. 1975. *Time of transition: The growth of families headed by women.* Washington, D.C.: Urban Institute.

Rumberger, Russell W. Forthcoming. Dropping out of high school: The influence of race, sex, and family background. *American Educational Research Journal.*

Rush, David; Zena Stein; and Mervyn Susser. 1980. A randomized controlled trial of prenatal nutritional supplementation in New York City. *Pediatrics* 65 (April): 683–697.

Salkever, David. 1982. Children's health problems: Implications for parental labor supply and earnings. In *Economic aspects of health,* ed. Victor R. Fuchs. Chicago: University of Chicago Press.

Sanderson, Warren, and Robert J. Willis. 1971. Economic models of fertility: Some examples and implications. In *New directions in economic research,* 51st Annual Report of the National Bureau of Economic Research.

Schelling, T. C. 1968. The life you save may be your own. In *Problems in public expenditure analysis,* ed. S. B. Chase. Washington, D.C.: Brookings Institution.

Schultz, Theodore W. 1963. *The economic value of education.* New York: Columbia University Press.

Schulz, James H. 1976. *The economics of aging.* Belmont, Calif.: Wadsworth.

Schumpeter, Joseph A. 1942. *Capitalism, socialism and democracy.* 2nd ed. New York: Harvard Brothers.

Sinclair, John C.; George W. Torrance; Michael H. Boyle; Sargent P. Horwood; Saroj Saigal; and David L. Sackett. Evaluation of neonatal-intensive-care programs. *New England Journal of Medicine* 305 (August 27): 489–494.

Smith, James P., ed. 1980. *Female labor supply: Theory and estimation.* Princeton: Princeton University Press.

Smith, James, and Finis Welch. 1981. No time to be young: The economic prospects for large cohorts in the United States. *Population and Development Review* 7 (March): 71–83.

Sowell, Thomas. 1981. *Ethnic America.* New York: Basic Books.

Spence, A. Michael. 1973. Job market signaling. *Quarterly Journal of Economics* 87 (August): 355–374.

Steiner, Gilbert Y. 1981. *The futility of family policy.* Washington, D.C.: Brookings Institution.

Sternglass, Ernest J. 1969. Infant mortality and nuclear tests. *Bulletin of Atomic Scientists* 25, no. 4: 18–20.

Surgeon General. 1964. *Smoking and health.* Report of the Advisory Committee to the Surgeon General of the Public Health Service. Washington, D.C.: U.S. Government Printing Office.

——— 1979. *Smoking and health.* A Report of the Surgeon General, Public Health Service. Washington, D.C.: U.S. Government Printing Office.

Taubman, Paul, and Sherwin Rosen. 1982. Healthiness, education, and marital status. In *Economic aspects of health,* ed. Victor R. Fuchs. Chicago: University of Chicago Press.

Tawney, R. H. 1926. *Religion and the rise of capitalism.* New York: Harcourt Brace.

Tomes, Nigel. 1981. The family, inheritance, and the intergenerational transmission of inequality. *Journal of Political Economy* 89 (October): 928–958.

U.S. Bureau of the Census. 1950–1981. *Statistical abstract of the United States.* Published annually. Washington, D.C.: U.S. Government Printing Office.

——— 1964. *Census of population, 1960.* Vol. 1, Characteristics of the population, pt. 1, United States summary. Washington D.C.: U.S. Government Printing Office.

——— 1965–1982. *Current population reports.* Series P-20, P-23, P-25, and P-60. Washington, D.C.: U.S. Government Printing Office.

——— 1973a. *Census of population, 1970.* Detailed characteristics, final report PC(1)-D1, United States summary. Washington, D.C.: U.S. Government Printing Office.

——— 1973b. *Census of population, 1970.* Subject reports, final report PC(2)-1B, Negro Population. Washington, D.C.: U.S. Government Printing Office.

—— 1973c. *Census of population, 1970.* Subject reports, final report PC(2)-1C, Persons of Spanish Origin. Washington, D.C.: U.S. Government Printing Office.

—— 1973d. *Census of population, 1970.* Subject reports, final report PC(2)-2D, Lifetime and Recent Migration. Washington, D.C.: U.S. Government Printing Office.

—— 1973e. *Census of population, 1970.* Subject reports, final report PC(2)-8B, Earnings by Occupation and Education. Washington, D.C.: U.S. Government Printing Office.

—— 1975. *Historical statistics of the United States, colonial times to 1970,* Bicentennial edition. Washington, D.C.: U.S. Government Printing Office.

—— 1980. *Social indicators III.* December. Washington, D.C.: U.S. Government Printing Office.

U.S. Bureau of Labor Statistics. 1975. *Special labor force report 172.* Job tenure of workers, January 1973. Reprinted from Howard Hayghe, *Monthly Labor Review* 97 (December 1974): 53–57, with supplementary tables.

—— 1981. *Special labor force report 241.* School and work among youth during the 1970s. By Anne McDougall Young. Washington, D.C.: U.S. Government Printing Office.

Wallerstein, Judith S., and Joan Berlin Kelly. 1980. *Surviving the breakup: How children and parents cope with divorce.* New York: Basic Books.

Wells, H. G. 1934. *Experiment in autobiography.* Vol. 2. New York: Macmillan.

Williams, Ronald L., and Peter M. Chen. 1982. Identifying the sources in the recent decline in perinatal mortality rates in California. *New England Journal of Medicine* 306 (January 28): 207–214.

Willis, Robert J. 1973. A new approach to the economic theory of fertility behavior. *Journal of Political Economy* 81 (March/April, pt. 2): S14–S64.

—— 1980. The old age security hypothesis and population growth. In *Demographic behavior: Interdisciplinary perspectives on decision-making,* ed. T. Burch. Boulder, Colo.: Westview Press.

Wood, C.; P. Renou; J. Oats; E. Farrell; N. Beischer; and I. Anderson. 1981. A controlled trial of fetal heart rate monitoring in a low-risk obstetric population. *American Journal of Obstetrics and Gynecology* 141 (November 1): 527–534.

Zajonc, R. B., and Gregory B. Markus. 1975. Birth order and intellectual development. *Psychological Review* 82 (January): 74–88.

Zelnik, Melvin, and John F. Kantner. 1977. Sexual and contraceptive experience of young unmarried women in the United States, 1976 and 1971. *Family Planning Perspectives* 9 (March/April): 55–71.

Zimmerman, Carle C., and Merle E. Frampton. 1935. *Family and society.* New York: Van Nostrand.

Index